THE FIGHTING PARSON

GREAT WEST AND INDIAN SERIES XVII

THE FIGHTING PARSON

the biography of

COLONEL JOHN M. CHIVINGTON

by

REGINALD S. CRAIG

WESTERNLORE PRESS . . . 1959 . . . LOS ANGELES 41

COPYRIGHT 1959 BY
WESTERNLORE PRESS

Library of Congress Catalog No. 59-14854

PRINTED IN THE UNITED STATES OF AMERICA BY WESTERNLORE PRESS

TO MY WIFE GRACE

Preface

IN THIS book an attempt will be made to tell the story of a frontier preacher, turned soldier, who played an important part in the civilization and settlement of the turbulent frontier which was opened with the discovery of gold along the base of the Rocky Mountains in 1858. This event was one of the factors which upset the plans of the national government for a permanent Indian country west of the Missouri River. Thus, it was inevitable that the rush of gold seekers would result in friction with the Indians and the horrors of savage warfare. In dealing with the red men the settlers were handicapped by the vacillating policy of the Washington authorities, who never had any conception of the magnitude nor nature of the problems they were endeavoring to solve.

Colonel John M. Chivington made a name for himself in the New Mexico campaign against the Confederates, but his reputation was badly damaged by the stories concerning his conduct of the Sand Creek campaign against the savages of the plains.

The controversy over this incident has continued over the period of nearly a century following the affair. Most of the people of Colorado have been convinced of the fact that Colonel Chivington was fully justified in his attack on the Cheyennes at Sand Creek, and that the affair was a hard fought battle greatly to the credit of the colonel and his Colorado volunteers. However, the Indian Bureau and many of the colonel's personal enemies succeeded in arranging three hearings with indecisive results, which tended to cast reflections on the honor of the colonel and his men. Based on these rather one-sided congressional and military investigations, some historians have labeled the affair a brutal "massacre" of friendly Indians.

The author's decision to enter this long standing controversy arose, to some extent, from a recent tendency to revive the matter after a number of years during which it had remained relatively dormant. In their search for material, some television producers have turned to Sand Creek, and have presented programs which are all grossly unfair to Colonel Chivington, and which range from an emphasis on the adverse parts of the evidence produced at the hearings to a complete fabrication entirely at variance with any of the facts, or asserted facts, relative to the campaign.

It is felt that the younger generation, particularly in Colorado and the Rocky Mountain region, should have access to the full story of Colonel Chivington, covering his life as a circuit rider carrying the Gospel to the frontier and his service as a soldier fighting against the Confederates and savage Indians. Some of the material forming the basis of the account in this book is set forth in the appendices. Appendix A gives a complete list of all authorities consulted. Appendix B, which is a legal analysis of the Sand Creek hearings and the evidence produced therein, provides some of the basis for the version of the affair adopted in this work. For the benefit of readers who may wish to follow this matter further, Appendices C and D have been included to present some examples showing the nature of the evidence produced at the hearings.

I wish to acknowledge assistance I have received from many people and organizations in gathering material for this story. These include the State Historical Society of Colorado, the Denver Public Library, the Bancroft Library of Berkeley, California, Clarence A. Lyman of Mill Valley, California, Dr. Martin H. Hall of the Arkansas State College and Dr. Martin Rist of the Iliff School of Theology in Denver. Last, and most important, invaluable aid was furnished by Mr. John T. Dormois of Kansas City, Kansas, who turned over to the writer a very large collection of research data which he had accumulated on the life of Colonel Chivington and the Chivington family history.

REGINALD S. CRAIG.

Los Angeles, California
June 22, 1959

Table of Contents

Table of Illustrations

COL. JOHN MILTON CHIVINGTON

Prologue

IT WAS LATE in the afternoon of March 28, 1862. Near Glorieta, New Mexico, a little Union force of eight hundred men had been fighting stubbornly all day under continuous attack by wave after wave of numerically superior Texan forces. From time to time they had been forced to fall back and regroup to avoid encirclement, but their lines had been maintained intact. At this point in the battle, conscious of his inferior numbers and heavy losses in this unequal strife, the colonel commanding ordered a general retreat. Just as this movement commenced, and before the last of the Northern batteries was ready to be taken from the field, three Confederate officers appeared under a flag of truce and asked for a conference. They were passed through the Union lines, and, after hard riding, overtook the Federal commander in his newly established camp beyond the Pecos River. They then made the strange request of the foe they had driven from the field for an armistice to care for their dead and wounded, which was readily granted. It was several hours later before the Union leader learned the reason for this unexpected action. The major of his regiment, who had been sent with a provisional battalion early in the day to harass the enemy's rear, had been successful beyond anticipation. He had, in fact, destroyed the Confederate trains, with all of the necessary supplies for continuance of the campaign.

General Sibley and his invading Texans must have been as surprised at the outcome of the battle as the Union commander. Prior to this engagement their campaign to overrun New Mexico and Colorado had met with considerable success. Colonel Edward R. S. Canby of the Regular Army, with a force consisting largely of untrained New Mexico volunteers, had been unable to halt the Confederates, who had advanced to a point beyond Santa Fe. True, two days before, they had received a setback at the fight in Apache Canyon. There they had been driven back by a contingent of newly arrived Colorado volunteers commanded by a giant major with a voice like the roar of a bull. Nevertheless, the Texans had a large preponderance of trained manpower. Further, the campaign was well planned and organized by an experienced general officer, a former logistics expert of the United States Army. However, the tide was turned by this same "Yankee" major. With his battalion, he suddenly descended what appeared to be the almost vertical side of a mountain, overran the rear guard, spiked its cannon, and destroyed the supply train. Then and there the South lost its chance to finance its war effort by gaining control of the western gold fields, and was forced to abandon its grand plan for western empire under the Confederacy.

Who was the Union officer responsible for stopping the Confederate advance at Glorieta, with the loss of their supplies and consequent abandonment of their carefully planned invasion?

The importance of this campaign has been overlooked by most historians. Accordingly, Colonel John M. Chivington is now primarily known for his part in the Sand Creek Indian engagement and the resulting controversy, which has continued over the years. This account will attempt to set the record straight. After nearly a century of inaccurate and unfounded tradition, the facts will be brought forth, and the reader left to assign to him a proper place in the history of the Rocky Mountain region.

John Milton Chivington was a remarkable personality. To the Texas veterans, who had been routed when he appeared on the battlefield, he appeared to be of unbelievable stature, with a scowl that would have scared the devil himself. When he was enrolled in the military service in August 1861, at the age of forty, he was in his prime—six feet four and one half inches tall, weighing two hundred and sixty pounds without any fat, with piercing black eyes and coarse reddish-brown hair. In spite of his size he was very agile, and his strength and endurance seemed without limit.

Frank Hall has described him in the following terms:[1] "Though wholly unskilled in the science of war, with but little knowledge of drill and discipline, Major Chivington, of herculean frame and gigantic stature, possessed the courage and exhibited the discreet boldness, dash and brilliancy in action which distinguished the more illustrious of our volunteer officers during the war. His first encounter with the Texans at Apache Canyon was sudden, and more or less of a surprise. The occasion demanded not only instantaneous action, but such disposition of his force as to render it most effective against superior numbers and the highly advantageous position of the enemy. He seemed to comprehend at a glance the necessities of the situa-

---

[1]Hall, Frank, *History of the State of Colorado*. Chicago: The Blakely Printing Co., 1889, Vol. I, pp. 286-287.

tion, and handled his troops like a veteran. His daring and rapid movement across the mountains, and the total destruction of the enemy's trains simultaneously with the battle of Pigeon's Ranch again attested his excellent generalship. . . . He hesitated at nothing. Sure of the devotion and gallantry of his men, he was always ready for any adventure however desperate, which promised the discomfiture of his adversaries. . . . That he was endowed with the capabilities of a superior commander none who saw him in action will deny."

A Boy Grows To Manhood

JOHN CHIVINGTON'S fighting qualities were inherited from his father, Isaac, a pioneer of Irish descent, who was born in 1790. Isaac settled in Warren County, Ohio, where, on April 18, 1810, he married Jane Runyon, a comely girl of Scotch ancestry.[1] They purchased two sections of land for sixty-four cents an acre, and began the task of carving a home out of the wilderness in a location near Lebanon, about twenty miles northeast of Cincinnati.

Using a brush lean-to for temporary shelter, Isaac proceeded with the construction of a one room and loft log cabin, which was soon completed with the help of his pioneer neighbors. Within a few short weeks of their marriage, Isaac and Jane moved into their home which stood in a clearing near the banks of a small stream. Most of their land was covered with a heavy

---

[1]*Probate Records Warren County, Ohio.* License No. 451, Book 1, p. 57.

stand of virgin timber, which was of little value, since it was merely an obstacle to placing the land under cultivation.

Isaac was of huge proportions, six feet six inches tall, and with tremendous strength and endurance. He attacked the clearing of the land with all of his vigor and enthusiasm and soon became an expert with the woodsman's axe. Within two years he had between fifteen and twenty acres cleared when his work was delayed by war.

From the beginning of the Northwest Territory there had been trouble with the Indians. For many years settlement of the area had been delayed by the fierce opposition of the Shawnee, Delaware, Wyandot and other tribes, who fought under the slogan, "White men shall not plant corn north of the Ohio River." In this attitude they were encouraged by British agents, who were anxious to recover a portion of their former western lands. Finally, General "Mad" Anthony Wayne defeated the red men at the Battle of Fallen Timbers. Thereafter, on August 3, 1795, he negotiated the Treaty of Greenville, which provided for the cession of certain Indian occupied areas and insured the settlers of peace lasting over fifteen years.[2]

When the War of 1812 started, the tribes of the Northwest were nearly all allied with the British in an effort to drive the "Long Knives" out of the Indians' former hunting grounds. Actually, an alliance of several western tribes against the settlers had been formed by the Shawnee Chief Tecumseh a few years before the war. General Harrison had moved into the Shawnee country in an effort to deal with this threat, when he was attacked on November 6, 1811, in his camp on the Wabash near the mouth of Tippecanoe Creek. Although the resulting battle was not decisive, the Shawnee warriors were driven off

---

[2]Hafen. LeRoy R. and Rister, Carl Coke, *Western America*. (Second Edition) New York: Prentice-Hall, Inc., 1953, pp. 138-139.

with heavy losses. This action, in effect, opened the War of 1812 in the west.

Faced with the British and their allies of the Indian Confederation, the settlers north of the Ohio River were in a very dangerous situation. Accordingly, they volunteered for service in amazing numbers. Probably there has never been a higher percentage of the population placed under arms in any section of the country, either before or since. Although many of the men were not seasoned frontiersmen, they quickly learned the lessons of survival in wilderness warfare. Isaac Chivington was one of these recruits. He took part in General Harrison's invasion of Canada and the Battle of the Thames,[3] where the British and Indians were defeated. In this engagement Tecumseh was killed and the red men's confederation was dissolved for lack of a leader.

With the return of peace, Isaac resumed the clearing of his land. Actually, he became more of a woodsman than a farmer, although he put the land under cultivation as soon as it was cleared. As the population of the area increased, a market developed for the products of the forest, and he began to sell some of the harvested timber. After a time he began to specialize in hardwoods, searching the woods for the best specimens of white oak and hickory, which were abundant in the valley of the Little Miami, where Isaac's land was located. Here, in an early day, there was a luxuriant stand of hardwood of many species, which grew to magnificent size and was of good texture. The white oak, in particular, was found in specimens three to four hundred years old and three to four feet in diameter.

After cutting, Isaac would saw the wood into eight foot lengths, which were fashioned into balks eight inches square

<hr>

[3]*The Square and Compass* (Denver), Oct., 1894. "Death of Brother J. M. Chivington, First M. W. Grand Master of Masons in Colorado."

and well hewn to true dimensions with an adze. These were stored until high water in the spring, when the year's accumulation was formed into a raft and floated down the Little Miami and Ohio Rivers to Cincinnati. Here the timber sold for a good price, since select hardwood was in considerable demand for the manufacture of wagons, coaches and farm implements.

Isaac and Jane Chivington spent their entire married life in the small cabin on their homestead in Warren County. Here were born their six children, four of whom survived the perils of infancy. The eldest son Lewis learned to wield an axe at an early age, and by 1824, when he was thirteen, he was helping his father in the woods. Their only daughter Sarah was about five years younger than Lewis. John Milton Chivington was born on January 27, 1821,[4] and his younger brother Isaac in August 1822. All of the Chivington boys grew to great size, considerably over six feet in height.

By 1825 over a quarter of a section of land in the Chivington holding had been cleared of timber. In order to realize a profit on the increased value of this acreage, Isaac and Jane decided to dispose of the major portion. Accordingly, one hundred and forty-six acres were sold[5] at the market value and a small area of the cleared land retained for their own cultivation.

Within another year disaster fell on the family. At this point in time it is impossible to say what happened with any degree of certainty. Although Isaac senior was a man of great strength and vitality, he may have overestimated his capacity to take hardship. Perhaps he contracted pneumonia as a a result of overwork and exposure, or he may have been a victim of an acci-

---

[4]Chivington, J. M., *The First Colorado Regiment*. Manuscript on file in Bancroft Library, Univ. of Calif., Berkeley, Calif., p. 1.

[5]*Probate Records of Warren County, Ohio.* Deed, Isaac and Jane Chivington to Benjamin Whitacre, Vol. 12 of Deed Books, p. 109.

dent in the woods. In any event, in August 1826, the father of the family was dead,[6] and the support and raising of the four children devolved on Jane. Lewis carried on the business of clearing the land and cutting and marketing hardwood in Cincinnati, while Jane cultivated the cleared land with the help of the smaller children.

There was no regular school in the vicinity, although the settlers had constructed a log school house, and secured a small stock of readers, spellers and arithmetic books. School was held whenever an itinerant teacher would arrive in the community looking for an opportunity to open a subscription school, with his salary based on a monthly fee for each pupil. Usually such teachers would stay only long enough to accumulate a small sum of money before moving on to more lucrative locations. During the rare interludes when school was held, John, Isaac and Sarah were in regular attendance. Most of their primary education, however, was received from their mother and the few books in the family library. John studied industriously and learned rapidly. A dictionary was secured on one of the trips to Cincinnati. With its aid the boy acquired a wide vocabulary by reading Milton's *Paradise Lost,* the *Bible* and a badly used Episcopalian prayer book.[7]

When John and Isaac reached the age of thirteen they went to work in the timber with their older brother, who taught them the rudiments of the woodsman's art. In his work in the woods John soon showed evidence of a passion for perfection which followed him all his life. His balks were all exactly eight feet long and hewed to a surface almost as smooth as though it had

---

[6]*Probate Records of Warren County, Ohio.* Docket of Estates—No. o—pp. 308, 316 (administration of estate of Isaac Chivington).

[7]Lyman, Clarence A., *The Truth About Colonel John M. Chivington.* Unpublished manuscript (written in 1956), p. 8.

been planed. Each was branded at the end with his initials, and his work usually sold for a higher price than the relatively rough specimens prepared by his brothers. When the balks were ready for delivery in the spring, at least two of the brothers usually rode the raft to Cincinnati. After sale of their produce, they would buy such scarce items in the stores as they could conveniently carry, and walk the twenty miles back home.

When John was eighteen he took over the business of marketing the timber. By 1840 he was beginning to spend considerable time in Cincinnati, where he became acquainted with a number of local people. In this way he met Martha Rollason, the daughter of a Virginia family, who was employed as a servant girl in the home of some of his friends. She had been reared on a large plantation, where her father owned many slaves. After her mother's death and her father's remarriage, things became so unpleasant that she left home with a small inheritance she had received from her mother's estate. She journeyed by stage and river boat to Cincinnati, where she had heard that there was a demand for teachers. It soon became evident that her Southern education, which was largely of a cultural nature, did not provide sufficient background in the practical subjects in demand on the Ohio frontier. Therefore she accepted employment as a domestic, the only other honorable field open to a young woman.

Although not beautiful, Martha Rollason was an attractive girl, short in stature but with a good figure. She could read and write in both English and French, was an expert seamstress, and could milk a cow and make good butter. With these qualifications, John did not hesitate, although she was about two years his senior. He decided that Martha was the wife for him, and they were married before the year was out. To facilitate the support of his family, young Chivington apprenticed himself to a carpenter, and, within a short time, thoroughly mastered the trade.[8]

In 1842 he attended a series of revival meetings held by a noted evangelist, who became the Methodist Bishop of Southern Ohio a short time later. Chivington was so impressed with the revivalist's plea for fighters in the battle for righteousness that he became a member of the church. A short time later he decided to enter the ministry, where he could take a more personal part in the war against evil. John went to see the bishop, who was greatly pleased. He had many places for such a man in the wild, lawless country in his diocese. He suggested entry into the ministry after minimum preparation, which included reading the *Bible,* studying certain books on doctrine, and a little experience preaching as a deacon. With his ideal of perfection, Chivington refused to consider such a program. "I do not propose to preach the word of God in ignorance," he said. "Until I can give a reason for every particle of faith that is in me, I shall not enter the pulpit."[9]

John could not afford to leave home to attend a Methodist seminary. Accordingly, the bishop ordered textbooks which he loaned to the young student. In conformity with Chivington's request for subjects of basic general knowledge, these books included, in addition to theological works, volumes on world history, current science and economics. Continuing to work at his trade, John studied for two years, reading at nights and during all free periods. Finally, having finished his course of study, he was duly ordained, and in September 1844 he took his first

---

[8]Dunn, J. P., Jr., *Massacres of the Mountains.* New York: Harper & Bros., 1886, p. 402.

[9]Lyman, *The Truth About Col. John M. Chivington,* pp. 31-32.

charge at Zoar Church in the Goshen Circuit of the Ohio Conference.[10]

---

[10]Mumey, Nolie, "John Milton Chivington—The Misunderstood Man," *Roundup,* November, 1956.

II

The Parson Begins His Fight

AT THIS TIME Ohio was settling rapidly, and the frontier character of the area was disappearing as the more adventurous among the population moved westward to the new lands beyond the Mississippi. Nevertheless, many of the towns along the river were badly in need of action by the law-abiding element to reduce the prevalence of vice and crime. There was plenty of room for the influence of a hard working pastor with a fighting spirit. In this work Chivington soon gained a reputation as a fighter, which stood him in good stead. Early in his career the new parson was impressed with the fact that, in many communities, the members of the Masonic Order were the largest group which was working to establish and maintain law, order and morality. These were his kind of people, and in 1846 he became a member of the order, joining the newly organized lodge in Butlerville, Ohio.[1]

---

[1]Dormois, John T., Coleman, F. M. and Farley, A. W., *Centennial Wyandotte Lodge No. 3 A.F. & A.M.* Pamphlet published in Kansas City, Kansas, 1954, p. 13.

As John and Martha moved to new locations, they left a series of revitalized parishes behind them. They never stayed over two years in any community. New assignments were always in locations where congregations were weak and the lawless element was in charge. Whatever the condition of the church on his arrival, Reverend Chivington always left it solvent and with a loyal congregation. The community could usually also count on the benefits of an energetic Masonic lodge, improved schools, and a good library, largely due to his efforts. He was a leader in the fight for right and decency.

When the Chivingtons had been married for a year, their son Thomas was born. He was followed by their daughters, Elizabeth Jane in 1842 and Sarah in 1844.[2] Although John loved the girls, he often failed to openly demonstrate his affection. On the other hand, it was apparent that Tom was his favorite and the idol of his father's eyes. As the children grew older this caused some discord in the home, especially when the boy tried to take advantage of his father's esteem.

Feeling his services were needed farther west, John left Ohio in June 1848, and moved to Quincy, Illinois, where he entered the Illinois Conference of the Methodist Episcopal Church.[3] In his new assignments Chivington continued as the protector of his people. To the fullest of his ability he devoted himself to their welfare. He advised them in their troubles, settled their disputes, and intervened on their behalf to secure the leniency of the court under all proper conditions. Many first offenders were released by the judge to the custody of their pastor, who vouched for their good behavior in the future. In many cases he was respected, and even supported in his efforts to provide good

[2]Chlanda, Winifred O., *Notes on Ottaway Family History* (undated); and Kaufman, Patricia K., *Chivington Family History* (letter April 23, 1958).

[3]Chivington, *The First Colorado Regiment,* p. 1.

schools and otherwise improve the community, by the saloon-keepers and the gambling element. When he sent out word that a member of his congregation should not have alcoholic beverages, these friends of his often saw to it that the man was without supplies. The work with the women of the flock, which was one of the principal supports of the church, was left to Martha, since Chivington lived primarily in a man's world.

At this period in history it was the policy of the leaders of the Methodist Church to avoid a stand on the slavery issue, in the hope of preventing a split in the church. Although John disliked slavery, he considered it a political matter that the South should decide for itself. Martha, on the other hand, felt that slavery, as it was conducted on her father's plantation, was a benefit to both the blacks and the whites. Thus, during their first years in the work of the church, both were well satisfied with the official policy of neutrality. The pastor's attitude on this issue, however, was changed soon after their arrival in Illinois.

Chivington's congregation included a mulatto nursemaid who attended church regularly and was considered to be one of the small number of free negroes living in the north. This idea was changed suddenly with the arrival of a deputy United States marshal from southern Tennessee with a warrant for her arrest as a runaway slave. When Chivington heard of this man and his errand he quickly spirited the fugitive to the parsonage, where Martha took charge and questioned her. In reply the girl told the following story: "I lived in a big house on a Tennessee plantation, where I worked as a ladies' maid and was treated as a member of the family until my mistress died. Then they sold me to a man who ran a resort in Natchez. I was a Christian, so I ran away. When I got to Illinois I told people I was a 'free nigger,' and now God will punish me for that lie."

Having received information as to the location of his intended prisoner, the officer approached the parsonage. It was a warm summer evening and John stood on the porch awaiting his arrival, bare armed and without his outer shirt. Placing his foot on the lower step in token of entry, the deputy marshal produced his warrant and prepared to read from it. "Take your foot off that step," rumbled Chivington. "I am an officer of the law," the deputy replied, "armed and with authority to use force, if necessary." The parson raised his clenched fists and flexed his muscles. "I too carry arms," he announced. "Take your foot off that step." For a few moments the two stood silent, but Chivington's baleful glare and imposing figure were too much for him. After a short hesitation he left without further ceremony, mumbling about legal action.[4]

From that moment on John's whole attitude was changed on the primary issue of the day. The fighting spirit which he had inherited from his Irish ancestors was aroused, and he became an implacable foe of slavery and all that it stood for. This was the beginnning of his fight on the whole institution.

After less than a year in Quincy, Chivington was transferred to the Missouri Conference of the Methodist Church. In the fall of 1846 he arrived at Pleasant Green in that state, where he served for several years as a "circuit rider." In this capacity he carried the gospel to various outlying small communities by riding from one to the other in a series of tours to complete his entire circuit. He remained in this conference for eight years, during which, in addition to the circuit at Pleasant Green, he served the churches at Hannibal, La Grange and Shelbyville in eastern Missouri, St. Joseph in western Missouri and Wyandotte in Kansas.

---

[4]Lyman, *The Truth About Col. John M. Chivington*, pp. 43-44 (where this incident is described).

VIEW OF A PORTION OF DENVER IN 1859

—*Courtesy, State Historical Society of Colorado.*

LARIMER STREET, DENVER, IN 1865

—*Courtesy, State Historical Society of Colorado.*

Chivington never protested when he was assigned to new tasks in out of the way places. He had enlisted as a fighter for the Lord, and was willing to serve where needed. Martha too, as a loyal wife, carried her share of the load at each new parish. However, after a number of years of this kind of service, among the poor and lowly, and often uncouth, she felt that they were entitled to a change. On several occasions the bishop made promises that a charge in a larger town would be made available for them, but at each annual conference her hopes were deferred by a new emergency.

While in the Missouri Conference, Chivington was sent out to the Indian country west of the Missouri River to serve as a missionary to the Wyandot Indians,[5] arriving in 1853 at the Indian settlement of Wyandotte, later known as Kansas City, Kansas. Although they had a long record of war with the American whites, the Wyandots were pacified, and at least partly civilized, at that time. However, a number of them still clung to the old tribal religion, and many were still illiterate, and ignorant of the English language.

These Indians were found by the early French explorers along the St. Lawrence River in the middle of the sixteenth century, and were called Hurons by the French. In the middle of the seventeenth century they were attacked and nearly destroyed by the Iroquois. Some of the remnants of the tribe placed themselves under protection of the French at Quebec and others fled west. Eventually the fugitives reached the land included in the present State of Ohio, where they ultimately claimed most of the area.

Later it was by permission of the Wyandots that the Shawnees from the south and the Delawares from the east settled north

---

[5]Chivington, *The First Colorado Regiment,* p. 1. Spelling of the tribal name is changed to "Wyandotte" when used as a place name.

of the Ohio River. With the help of these tribes they bitterly contested the advance of the white settlers in the Northwest Territory, and during the War of 1812 allied themselves with the British. At the close of the war large tracts of land were confirmed to them in Ohio and Michigan. In 1842 the last of this land was sold, and the tribe removed to a reservation in what later became the State of Kansas.[6]

The Wyandots were not very well satisfied with their new home at first. Although they had agreed to the sale of their eastern land, the new location seemed bleak and forbidding. The government had persuaded them to accept this reservation as a part of the plan of Monroe and Calhoun, which called for the movement of all Eastern tribes behind a permanent Indian frontier west of the Mississippi. The relocation of the red men had barely been completed, however, when the rush of migration to the west forced the abandonment of the "permanent Indian country" idea. The passage of the Kansas-Nebraska Act in 1854 established the territories of Kansas and Nebraska and threw both of them open for settlement. Thus the Wyandots were being crowded once more, and there was ill feeling between them and the settlers.

With the help of the more educated members of the tribe, Chivington did not encounter much difficulty in getting the Wyandots to listen to his message. Under his direction, they built a log church near their village. Here he preached to them through an interpreter,[7] and converted many of them to Christianity. When the white settlers arrived, the Methodist missionary was instrumental in promoting good relations between the two races. Like all eastern tribes, the Wyandots had always

[6]Swanton, John R.. *Indian Tribes of North America*. Washington: U. S. Govt. Printing Office, 1953, p. 235.

[7]Dormois, Coleman and Farley, *Centennial Wyandotte Lodge*, p. 10.

cultivated the land, raising corn and certain vegetables to supplement their supply of game. Here in the heart of the best farming land in the continent, they were developing into full time tillers of the soil. With the assurance that the whites would not encroach on their lands, and the opportunity to trade their produce at the white settlements, they accepted the newcomers as farming neighbors. The parson also convinced the white settlers that these Indians were not predatory savages who were merely waiting an opportunity for loot and murder.

Acting under a "dispensation" issued by the Masonic Grand Lodge of Missouri, the Reverend Chivington, in August 1854, met with several of the leading citizens of the town and organized the first Masonic lodge in the Territory of Kansas.[8] Chivington served as the first Master of the lodge, which was an active organization from the beginning. It was truly representative of the community, since its original membership was composed of a few whites, with a majority of Wyandots. This lodge, which is still an important factor in the life of the community, is now known as Wyandotte Lodge No. 3 A. F. and A. M. of Kansas City, Kansas. In his work with the white population he served as the pastor of what is now known as the Washington Avenue Methodist Church in that city.

Late in 1854, with his work of organizing the mission to the Wyandots completed, Chivington finally received recognition for his ten years of labor in small communities. He was transferred to an important parish in St. Joseph, Missouri. Martha was pleased with this development, since, although primitive by Eastern standards, St. Joseph was by far the largest community in which they had been stationed, and there were improved opportunities for the education of the children.

---

[8]Dormois, Coleman and Farley, *Centennial Wyandotte Lodge*, p. 8.

A large number of the west bound traders, miners and settlers left the Missouri River at the mouth of the Kaw, where
the course of the stream turns to the northwest, and where
Kansas City now stands. Nevertheless, a large portion of this
traffic left the river at all of the settlements and steamboat land-
ings from Independence to Omaha and beyond, using a net-
work of trails which led to the west. One of the larger and more
important of these river ports was "St. Joe," which at that time
had the reputation of being one of the toughest cities in the
country. All along the river front were lines of saloons, gambling houses and dives catering to the lowest forms of vice and
sin. Travelers on their way west with expense money on their
persons here often became the victims of murder and robbery.

Chivington's first task was the organization of his congregation, followed by efforts to improve the quality of the local
schools. With this work well under way, he began action to
clean up the river front. Dressed in his usual neat black suit
and white shirt he formed a one man patrol of the area. He
kept himself physically fit at all times by chopping wood, and
was ready for any emergency. With his commanding presence,
his gigantic physique, his reputation as a fighter and his power-
ful bass voice, he was soon known and respected along the
river bank. He never condemned the gamblers and saloon-
keepers directly, but tried to arouse the self-respect of the less
vicious element among them. From such he asked for cooperation for better schools, public improvements and less of the
lower types of vice dens. They gave their cooperation. The
worst of the dives were closed up and some of the more undesirable individuals invited to take the next steamboat down the
river. Further, support from the river front was always forthcom-
ing in any effort for the betterment of the community.

In his sermons Chivington did not stress the fine points of religious doctrine. Contrary to the viewpoint of most ministers of his time, he considered such matters unimportant. He was endeavoring to bring the benefits of religion to the people, and, if they sincerely accepted the Divine Will, no more was needed. In connection with his mission to the Wyandots, he once wrote to a friend that he "found that the savages seemed eagerly seeking some word of God, some light in the darkness of failure to understand the Almighty." Continuing in a vein of religious tolerance which would probably have shocked the bishop, he added, "Manitou is merely the Indian conception of the Supreme Being, and I find that conception is not unlike our idea of God."[9]

When the Spaniards took over Louisiana from France, they began to offer free land to American settlers to provide a population which would resist penetration of the area by the English from Canada. Among the early arrivals in that part of the territory now included in the state of Missouri were Daniel Boone and his sons, who had come to take advantage of this offer. They found a deposit of salt, which was then an expensive luxury, and the whole country around the location became known as Boone's Lick. A route was established to the area called the Boone's Lick Trail, over which the backwoodsmen from Virginia, Kentucky and Tennessee swarmed in, to provide the nucleus of population for the new region.[10]

These people knew little of the refinements of civilization, and lived much like the Indians. They were experts with their long rifles, and could not afford to waste powder and lead. When

---

[9]Casey, Lee Taqyor, "Col. John M. Chivington—Soldier," *Rocky Mountain News*, March 3, 1929.

[10]Vestal, Stanley, *The Missouri*. New York: Farrar and Rinehart, Inc., 1945, pp. 76-77.

they "drew a bead on a critter," usually its time had come, whether it was a "b'ar" or a "cussed Injun." At first they could not afford much in the way of "foofuraw," as they called civilized luxuries, and the taverns and stores were modest in proportion. Although their ancestral roots were in the South, they had no interest in slavery.

Nevertheless, slavery became the issue which so tragically divided the people of Missouri. From the beginning of the French occupation there had been slaves in the area, and later settlers from the old South brought their slaves with them. Accordingly, in 1821, Missouri was admitted into the Union as a slave state. As the sentiment for and against slavery developed in the country, the slave owners in Missouri became acutely aware of the disadvantages of the adjacent free areas. Since Illinois and Iowa joined Missouri on two sides, opportunity was offered for the escape of slaves to free area on the east and north. This opportunity was increased by the activities of many antislavery people in the North who were helping slaves to escape by the "underground railroad" in violation of federal law.

With the forces for and against slavery violently contending on the question of expansion of slave territory, Congress avoided the issue in 1854 when it passed the Kansas-Nebraska Act. This legislation established the territories of Kansas and Nebraska, and provided that the settlers should decide for themselves whether the areas would be slave or free. This was an open invitation for the free-soil and proslavery men to enter the two territories and contend with each other for the decision. In Kansas, lying immediately west of Missouri, the situation was particularly acute, since the proslavery men were determined that Missouri would not be enclosed by free territory on a third side.

This was the beginning of border warfare which the people of Kansas and Missouri continued to wage until long after the formal end of the war at Appomattox. Before the official start of the Civil War this strife consisted of guerilla operations in which the most inhuman acts were perpetrated on both sides. After the war many of the guerillas continued as bandits. In the early border raids it was first the Missourians, known as "Border Ruffians," who attacked free-soil settlements in Kansas. Finally, under the supervision of federal troops, a fair election was held in Kansas, and the free-soilers carried the day. Thereafter most of the raids were in the other direction, as the Kansans, known as "Jayhawkers," rode against Missouri by night, carried off negroes and stock and killed settlers.

With the beginning of the struggle for Kansas, Chivington came out at once for the free-soilers, following his belief that slavery was an evil to be fought at every opportunity. Although there was in Missouri a deep feeling of attachment for the Union which ultimately defeated secession, there was no substantial sentiment against slavery. Therefore, and since the pro-slavery forces were very active and vindictive, the parson's position placed him in great personal danger. He preached against slavery and took an active part in the campaign to free the negroes as well as in efforts for their escape. On several occasions mobs gathered to prevent him from preaching. However, with his obvious possession of an ample supply of "muscular Christianity," he always avoided serious trouble, and many who came to heckle stayed to listen.[11]

Undoubtedly Chivington's activities as a free-soil supporter in the relentless border warfare, which was waged without mercy on both sides, had much to do with the hardening of his

[11]Dunn, *Massacres of the Mountains*, p. 402.

position on slavery. This included the adoption of an intolerant attitude toward those who supported the South in the great struggle. Like other Kansas free-soilers, he became an uncompromising Union man, and his dislike for anything savoring of treason got him into trouble on numerous occasions.[12] In this feeling he apparently made no exceptions, even in favor of close relatives. His brother Lewis espoused the cause of the South, and became a colonel in the Confederate forces. He was killed leading his regiment at the bloody Battle of Wilson's Creek, which took place in southeastern Missouri on August 10, 1861. In later years John was never known to mention his Confederate brother's name.

At the time of the early border struggle there was a split in the Methodist Church, which divided it into Northern and Southern branches in Platte County, Missouri, just north of St. Joseph. In that county there was also formed a society whose members wore a wisp of hemp on the lapels of their coats. It was their aim to drive all free-soil men from the country, and particularly Reverend Chivington. They sent him a notice not to preach any more in that county, under penalty of being tarred and feathered. He sent word back that he would preach the next Sunday, and on that day the members of the society attended the church in a body with a supply of tar and feathers. Soon Chivington appeared in the pulpit. Placing the *Bible* in position, he laid down two pistols, one on each side of the *Bible,* and announced, "By the grace of God and these two revolvers, I am going to preach here today."[13] No one questioned his right to continue uninterrupted. From then on he was gen-

---

[12]Dunn, *Massacres of the Mountains*, p. 403.

[13]Speer, John, *Report to Fred Martin of Interview with Mrs. John M. Chivington,* dated March 11, 1902. Manuscript on file in Library of Kansas State Historical Society, Topeka, Kansas.

erally known along the border as the "Fighting Parson," and this name followed him in later years.

Being entirely a stranger to the emotion of fear, incidents of this nature had very little effect on Chivington. However, it was obvious that his life was in real danger, and his friends finally persuaded him to accept a transfer. He was sent to Omaha, Nebraska, where he arrived in the fall of 1856,[14] and, within a short time he was appointed Presiding Elder of the Omaha District, Kansas-Nebraska Conference of the Methodist Church.

---

[14]Chivington, *The First Colorado Regiment*, p. 1.

III

The Overland Trail

IN JULY 1858 gold was discovered at the base of the Rocky Mountains in an area which was then included in the western part of the Territory of Kansas. Eastbound travelers carried the news to the Missouri River, and exaggerated accounts were published in Missouri and Kansas newspapers. Excitement ran high as the westbound gold seekers began to gather at each of the river towns. It was a vast repetition of the California gold rush of ten years earlier. By spring most of the towns presented the appearance of army camps, with tents all around the outskirts, and covered wagons in all directions. There was great rivalry between the various river ports to secure the business generated by this great throng. Each town advanced a claim that it was the starting point of the shortest, safest or quickest route, or the route with the best roads and water. In some cases, however, the business men themselves became imbued with the gold fever, and left the advantage of increased trade to join the westbound argosy.

There were three general routes to the new gold fields in the Pike's Peak area. One was in the north, which followed the old California Overland Trail along the Platte River for most of the way. The others were the Arkansas River route in the south and the Smoky Hill Trail in the center. The Smoky Hill route was the shortest, but it had the disadvantages of poor water supplies and greater danger from Indian attacks. Accordingly, after the first few years, the Platte River Trail, which was shorter than the Arkansas road, was used by most travelers headed for the Pike's Peak region.

It has been estimated that one hundred thousand gold seekers left the Missouri River for the Rocky Mountain fields in the spring of 1859, and that fifty thousand actually reached their destination. Their principal gathering point was at the mouth of Cherry Creek, where the town of Denver had been started the previous year, as had Pueblo, Boulder and a few other communities. It soon developed that the discovery had been of very low grade, and that available placer claims would not even pay fair wages. Immediately there was a great movement out of the area which took approximately one-half of the new arrivals back to the Missouri. These conditions caused a great economic slump in the area. Town lots in Denver, with log houses, were sold for from ten to twenty dollars, and miner's picks at from ten to fifteen cents each. The few men who were engaged in gold mining washed about a dollar a day from the low grade gravel.

As the throng of disappointed gold seekers started east they began to meet the westbound travelers, and great debates took place as to whether to go on or to return. Outbound travelers, in many cases, had writing on the sides of their wagons stating where they were from and that they were bound for Pike's Peak, some stating "Pike's Peak or bust." On the way back many added "busted." At about this time new gold discoveries were made in the high mountains, which halted the stampede back to the Missouri, and the settlements along the base of the Rockies continued to develop.

The new gold discoveries were reported, and the assets of the country emphasized by the first newspaper in the area, *The Rocky Mountain News,* which appeared in Denver on April 23, 1859.[1] With the exploitation of the new mines the fame of the district spread. The rush of gold seekers to the foot of the Rockies continued for many years, and as late as 1866 great numbers were still crossing the plains to the rich mining territories.

In 1858 the Chivingtons were well established and satisfied in Omaha, where they had been for two years. John had his district well organized, with the best available pastors in each town, and a supply for the Omaha pulpit to take over when he was visiting outlying areas. With his assistance the schools had been improved, and vice and crime were at a minimum. The elder continued active in fraternal work. On September 20, 1857, he took part in the formation of the Masonic Grand Lodge of Nebraska, and was appointed Grand Chaplain.[2] Martha was pleased with Omaha as a place to complete the education of her children, although only two of them were still living at home. On April 8, 1858, at the age of sixteen, Elizabeth Jane had married Charles Ottaway, a capable young man who was engaged in the freighting business.[3]

However, the Fighting Parson was not destined for the enjoyment of a quiet and well ordered manner of life for any considerable period of time. An experienced church administrator with a fighting spirit was needed in Nebraska City to organize the local district of the church and to combat the forces of evil,

---

[1]Hafen and Rister, *Western America,* p. 407.
[2]Dormois, Coleman and Farley, *Centennial Wyandotte Lodge,* p. 13.
[3]*Ottaway Family Bible.*

which were largely in control. The new presiding elder went to work upon his arrival, after driving alone from Omaha with a span of fast mules and a light wagon. His first task was the re-opening of the local church. Driving down the main street, which was lined with saloons, gambling halls and vice dens, he stopped at each corner. Here he announced in a stentorian voice, "I am your new Methodist pastor. Services will be held in the Methodist church at eight tonight."

Arriving at the church late in the afternoon, Chivington entered and discovered that a long bar had been installed in the building and that it was being used as a rum shop. "Who dares to profane the house of God?" he cried in a wrathful voice. Thereupon the customers scattered before his forbidding presence, but the rum seller stood his ground. In an effort to justify his operations, the dealer produced a deed signed by the former pastor of the church, who had left his post to join the gold rush. The Fighting Parson tore the deed into little pieces, and, without another word, rolled out the barrels of liquor from behind the bar, broke them open and spilled their contents in the street. One of the bolder of the bystanders asked by what right he had seized and destroyed another man's property. "The authority of Almighty God!" the elder roared in reply. There were no more objections, and he proceeded with the restoration of the church to a condition suitable for service as a place of worship.[4]

As the presiding elder of the surrounding district, Chivington soon had Nebraska City and the other local churches reorganized to a position of strength. In this work he was aided by his younger brother Isaac who had become a Methodist minister some years before and had recently been assigned to Nebraska City. The cleanup of vice and crime was the next item on the

---

[4]This incident described by Lyman in *Truth About Col. Chivington.*

program of the Fighting Parson. With the help of the better element in the community, the worst dives were closed, and the
undesirable residents "invited" to take a long trip down the
river.

The Chivingtons spent nearly two years in Nebraska City,
during which the religious and civic life of the town was greatly
improved. Early in 1860 the Bishop asked John to accept an assignment as Presiding Elder of the Rocky Mountain District of
the Methodist Church, which had recently been created and
added to his diocese. This district, which embraced the new gold
fields and other settlements in the Pike's Peak region, was urgently in need of religious establishments to serve the twenty-
five thousand people who had settled there. It offered a chal-
lenge and special opportunity for saving souls, which could
not be ignored by a fighter for the Lord, the Bishop said. Martha
was against this program. She wanted a place with more civilization, not less. However, John was soon convinced that his
destiny lay in the west, and he persuaded her to agree to share
the great adventure with him.

It was March 1860 when the Fighting Parson was formally
appointed Elder of the Rocky Mountain District. On April 9,
with his family and two wagons loaded with household goods,
he set out on the Overland Trail from Nebraska City. The spring
rains had been very heavy and the prairie was green with new
grass. The trail along the Platte River was at that time literally
lined with almost every conceivable type of vehicle, all en route
to Pike's Peak and the Colorado gold fields. After a few days on
the trail it became apparent that all traffic was not headed west,
since they began to meet discouraged adventurers who had
turned back, both those who had left the Missouri too early in
the spring and others who had come all the way from the mountains. The first had been so intent on leading the overland migra-

tion that they did not wait for the grass to grow in sufficient amounts to provide feed for their stock. The second group, whose search for gold had been unsuccessful, was shouting for vengeance against two of the publishers of the 1858 guide books to the gold fields. "Hang Byers and D. C. Oaks for starting this damned Pike's Peak hoax," they cried.

Although the Overland Trail followed the Platte River for a considerable portion of its length, it had many branches at its eastern end connecting to the various Missouri River ports of departure. Only one of its tributaries, the Mormon Trail along the north bank, started at the mouth of the Platte. The roads from southern Nebraska and all Kansas and Missouri points converged until they met in one broad highway, which carried a continuous stream of vehicles. Staring in amazement at this never ending flow of traffic, the Indians named it the "Great Medicine Road of the Whites."

Since the roads were in relatively good condition, the Chivingtons averaged twenty miles a day, reaching Fort Kearney in eight days. This post stood on the south bank of the Platte River in a semiarid locality with very few trees. In the absence of any troubles with the Indians in the area, it had never been enclosed with a stockade. It consisted of an open, cantonment type facility, with a parade ground in the center surrounded by the various military buildings interspersed with a few cottonwood trees. The branches of the road all joined into one highway east of the fort, and there was a ford close by which provided a connection with the trail on the north bank of the river.

Chivington stopped only long enough to replenish his supply of drinking water. He had no other particular needs, and civilians were not allowed to camp on the military reservation. There was a camping area and general supply point for travelers at Kearney City two miles to the west. However, this place found no favor in the parson's eyes. Primarily it was a center of liquor, vice and iniquity, normally referred to as Dobytown—a snare for the soldiers from the fort, as well as unwary travelers. The place was a source of ceaseless concern and annoyance to the officers at Fort Kearney. Not only were the soldiers continually found there drunk, but teamsters and travelers, who had been drugged, robbed, or fleeced at gambling, often applied at the post for help. Passing Dobytown by, the Chivingtons found themselves a good, private camp ground on the bank of the river several miles to the west.

Beyond Fort Kearney they followed an easy road up the Platte through an arid and treeless land, until they reached the forks of the river one hundred miles to the west. Continuing along the south fork for another sixty-five miles they came to the first ford, known as the Lower California Crossing. In the earlier days most of the emigrants crossed the South Platte at this point and passed over a narrow strip of land to the North Platte.[5] However, since quicksand made this ford extremely hazardous, it was not generally used in later years. The Chivingtons continued past the first crossing for an additional thirty-five miles to the Upper California Crossing, where the town of Julesburg had been established two years before at the mouth of Lodgepole Creek. Here the road divided. One branch took the ford over the river and continued along the course of Lodgepole Creek to reach Laramie, and, ultimately, California or Oregon. The other branch, which was taken by the Chivingtons, continued along the South Platte to Denver.

At a point about fifteen miles from Denver, Chivington met an old friend on his way back to the Missouri, who advised

---

[5]Gardiner, Dorothy, *West of the River*. New York: Thomas Y. Crowell Co., 1941, p. 76.

turning back. He said he had been in Denver ten days and had not seen a piece of gold bigger than the end of his thumb. However, the Fighting Parson was not searching for gold, and they went on. Reaching their destination on the fourth of May, they went into camp on the east bank of Cherry Creek near the present location of Broadway.[6]

On the following day, which was Saturday, Chivington purchased lumber to be used in building a home for his family. On Sunday he held services in a grove of cottonwood trees at the present location of the Union Depot. A large crowd turned out to hear the new elder's first sermon, and the Lord's work was under way in Denver. On Monday he bought brick, and commenced the erection of the first brick house in Denver on what was then known as Ferry Street and later as Eleventh Street. Construction proceeded as fast as the elder's scanty means would permit, and within a few weeks it was ready for occupancy.

Chivington began at once the task of organizing his district in the service of the Lord. His first concern was the firm establishment of the Denver congregation and the erection of a suitable church to shelter its activities. While Martha began work with the women, Chivington made contact with the business men, including the owners of the saloons and gambling halls. Many of them agreed to help with the building project. *The Rocky Mountain News* gave him publicity, and the First Methodist Church was soon housed in a small but adequate edifice. A few years later this structure was replaced with the famous Lawrence Street brick church, which formed a landmark for many years at the corner of Fourteenth and Lawrence Streets. The First Methodist Church of Denver developed from a mis-

---

[6]Chivington, J. M., *The Prospective (Retrospective)*. Manuscript on file in Bancroft Library, Berkeley, Calif., p. 6.

sion established in 1859, which was the first religious establishment in the city. As rapidly as the Bishop could send out ministers they were assigned to the various other settlements and mining camps in the area to establish churches or missions.

At this time Denver was a raw new community with few women other than dance-hall girls and prostitutes. In the absence of the usual restraints of a settled community, there was considerable wildness among the young men. Duels and gun fights were common. At one time several hundred people formed a crowd that witnessed a duel in which the acting governor, S. W. Bliss, killed Dr. S. Stone, a member of the legislature and judge of the miners' court. The prospects of profit from the gold strikes attracted a large number of the criminal element, and the fighting and killing became more vicious and widespread. Finally, a vigilance committee was formed and, within a few months, a considerable degree of order was restored.

In the absence of an organized government with regular courts, certain extra-legal judicial bodies were organized for the trial of persons accused of crime. These were known as miners' courts in the camps and people's courts in the towns. A president was elected by the persons present, and he, in turn, appointed a judge and in some cases associate judges, a clerk and a sheriff who appointed his deputies. A jury of twelve men was selected or the crowd acted as the jury, voting for acquittal or conviction.[7] Chivington witnessed several of such trials, and, on one occasion, assisted the Reverend Keeler, pastor of the first Episcopal church established in Denver, in giving spiritual comfort to a man who had been sentenced to be hanged by one of these courts.

---

[7]Dick, Everett, *The Story of the Frontier*. New York: Tudor Publishing Co., 1941, p. 282.

The Denver House was a typical example of the gambling establishments where Elder Chivington received assistance in raising his church construction fund. It was thirty by one hundred feet in size, with log walls and a frame roof covered with canvas. Cotton cloth was used to cover the window openings, since there was at that time no glass in the area. The front part of the building housed a big bar and a number of gambling tables, while the back was divided into sleeping compartments by low partitions of frame and canvas. The gambling games continued night and day, and the noise of dice, oaths of the players, and the cries of the dealers created such a din that sleep was next to impossible in the guest rooms. To add to the confusion, drunken and dissatisfied customers often punctuated their remarks by firing their revolvers.

As soon as he had the organization of the Denver congregation well under way, the new presiding elder made his first tour of the mining camps and other settlements in his districts. At Central City, the center of mining interest at that time, he held services in the open air, preaching to a vast throng which almost entirely filled the gulch where the placer workings were located. Following the sermon, nine hundred and eighty from the crowd took communion. From Central City Chivington proceeded to camps at Hamilton, Buckskin Joe, Georgia Gulch, French Gulch, Breakenridge, and down through South Park and Ute Pass to Colorado City, where he arrived on the Fourth of July.

At Idaho Springs he could locate no suitable place to hold services, either indoors or out. He was about to give up, and was returning to his lodgings, when he was approached by a saloon and gambling hall operator, who came out of his place of business as the elder was passing by. "Parson," said he, "I would like to offer my place of business to you for your services, if you will not be offended." "Of course not," said Chivington. "The

Lord will be with those who gather together in His name, no matter what the surroundings." "I only make one condition," said the proprietor. "Nights and Sundays are my best times for business, but I will divide the time with you, if the sermon is not too extended." "Your condition and offer are accepted with my heartfelt thanks," replied the elder. The bar and gambling tables were covered with awnings, and Chivington conducted what he had reason to believe was a "profitable season of worship."[8]

With all his driving energy the Fighting Parson entered into all the activities for the improvement of the community, and, wthin less than a year, he became very well known throughout the territory. He helped in organizing local schools and was active in fraternal work. He was one of the leaders in the formation of the Masonic Grand Lodge of Colorado, and was chosen as the first Grand Master of Masons in Colorado on August 2, 1861.[9]

Soon after the arrival of the Chivingtons in Denver, their daughter Sarah married Thomas Pollock, who was in command of a wagon train bound for southwestern Colorado. Immediately after the wedding the bride left with her husband on a trip of exploration and settlement in the San Juan Basin. Their son Thomas also left home at about this time and went to work on his own, ultimately establishing himself in the freighting business. Although their children were all gone, John and Martha were so busy in their work for the church and community that they had little time left for loneliness. Also their eldest daughter was established in the vicinity, since her husband had moved his business from Omaha to Denver.

---

[8]Chivington, *The Prospective (Retrospective)*, pp. 9-10.
[9]*Square and Compass*, Oct. 1894, "Death of Bro. J. M. Chivington."

IV

A Nation Divided

C HIVINGTON migrated to Denver with the expectation that, in that frontier outpost, there would be little possibility of involvement in the explosive issues of the day. However, the great Pike's Peak gold rush had brought settlers from all sections of the country. Although the Northerners were in a majority, there were a great many Southerners in the area, and it was apparent that sentiment for the cause of the South was running strong in Denver.

The presiding elder was extremely busy organizing his district, and thus managed to avoid the heated political arguments which took place from time to time. However, this attitude disappeared when the news of the secession of South Carolina reached Denver during the winter. A southern acquaintance, who met him on the street with this news, asked what the North would do when thirteen other states followed South Carolina's example. Chivington replied that such a situation would be grave indeed, and that "nothing would be left the government but to thrash them back into the Union." The man from the South then made the assertion that such action would be impossible, since, as the elder well knew, "one Southerner can whip five Yankees." The Fighting Parson replied that he was a Yankee, born and raised in the North, and suggested a test of the fighting ability of the two sections. "If you will go out in the town and find four others from the South," he said. "I will undertake to thrash the earth with all five, and settle the matter right here on Ferry Street." The elder's fighting reputation was formidable, and the Southerner declined with the remark that Chivington was Irish and not a "Yankee."[1]

The secession of South Carolina had pointed to the breach in the governmental organization of the nation. Although this political separation was terminated by the war, many of the underlying issues are unsettled after nearly a century of peace. From the founding of the republic, there had been a conflict in economic and political views arising from the fact that Negro slavery existed in the southern states, but not in the remainder of the country. With the passage of time, the development of the two sections diverged. Further, the moral issue of slavery versus freedom added its weight to the factors which were inexorably pushing the country along the inevitable road to civil conflict. One of the big points of contention was the issue of extension of slave territory. The people of the North, as their feelings were aroused, began to vigorously oppose this extension on moral grounds. The South, on the other hand, was faced with the necessity for expanding slavery to the new western states and territories. Otherwise, the rapid western advance of Northern population, with the creation of new free states, would disturb the voting balance in the Senate, with the danger of

---

[1]Chivington, *The Prospective (Retrospective)*, pp. 13-15.

legislation which would destroy their way of life. There was also an economic necessity for the creation of new slave territory. In the absence of an expanding market for slaves, there would be a surplus arising from the rapid increase in their numbers, which would decrease their market values to the detriment of the entire southern economy.

During the administration of President Pierce, Jefferson Davis served as Secretary of War. He made considerable progress in modernizing and reorganizing the army to better fit it for the task of guarding the frontier and assisting in the settlement of the newly acquired western lands. During this period Major Henry H. Sibley of Louisiana was given the mission of providing the service with new and improved equipment. Sibley, who was a West Point graduate with some frontier experience, became an expert on logistics and made valuable contributions to the improvement of this branch of the military art. The field heating stove and tent, which he devised, and which bore his name, became standard equipment of the United States Army, and were in use by that service for over fifty years.

During the succeeding administration of President Buchanan, John B. Floyd of Virginia became Secretary of War. One of the problems of that time was the provision of reliable communications with the new State of California and its rich gold fields. Since the northern route was subject to closure at certain seasons by heavy snow in the high mountains, the route through the southern deserts seemed preferable. In order to protect this road from marauding Indians, several strong forts were constructed in New Mexico, Arizona and Texas, which were designed as bases for a southwestern army. Although the decision to establish these bases was made ostensibly to guard communications with California, it later furnished the South with a remarkable opportunity to seize control of the best access to the Pacific gold fields.

The main supply base was established at Fort Union, near Las Vegas, New Mexico. Fort Defiance in eastern Arizona, Fort Craig in southern New Mexico and Fort Bliss in western Texas were the principal other southwestern outposts. All were difficult for a Northern army to reach and rescue, as was later proven. Whether by accident or design, most of the prewar conditions existing in the area were favorable to an invasion by the Confederates. The New Mexico territorial secretary, Alexander M. Jackson, was a very strong Southern sympathizer and a personal friend of Jefferson Davis. Colonel W. W. Loring of North Carolina was in command of the Department of New Mexico, and it has been charged that he intended to surrender posts in the territory to the Rebels. If this were the case, he was forced to resign and leave his command before such a plan could be carried out.

In addition, Secretary of War Floyd, for over a year preceding the secession of South Carolina, dispatched large quantities of military supplies and equipment to army installations in the south and southwest. There is some evidence that this was done with the expectation that this materiel would fall into Southern hands and facilitate the arming and equipping of their military forces when the need arose.[2] In the case of New Mexico it may well be that Colonel Loring was expected to convert these items to the use of the Confederacy. During this period New Mexico also received quite a number of troops of the Regular Army, largely under the command of officers from the southern states, who might be expected to persuade many of their men to desert

---

[2]Hafen and Rister, *Western America*, p. 379.

and join the Confederate forces.[3] These officers could also be expected to help in influencing civilians of the area to aid in the secession movement when the time arrived. All of these factors were considered when the South decided on its grand plan of strategy in the far west, the conquest of Colorado, New Mexico and California, with the rich western gold fields.

When Lincoln was elected, a majority of the leaders in the south took the position that the southern states would have to leave the Union to protect their way of life. Nor was this feeling confined to the leaders. The big majority of the people were determined on separation, although only a very small percentage of the population was involved in the ownership of slaves to any appreciable extent. The large slaveholders were confined to a comparatively few plantation owners, and the rest of the people either owned no slaves, or, at most, one or two. There were some southern leaders who knew that all this meant disaster. Conspicuous among them was old Sam Houston, Governor of Texas. He knew that secession would lead to war and the end of slavery. "Are the people mad?" he asked.[4]

Throughout the winter following the election of 1860 the tide of secession rolled over the south. The opposition of Sam Houston was not enough to stop it from engulfing Texas, and thus setting forces in motion which would vitally affect the career of the Fighting Parson. On January 28, 1861, a convention met in this state, adopted an ordinance of secession and passed a resolution submitting it to the voters, who ratified it by a vote of three to one. Thus Texas left the Union twenty-five years from the day its independence from Mexico was declared, and,

---

[3]Whitford, William C., *Colorado Volunteers in the Civil War*. Denver: The State Historical and Natural History Society, 1906, p. 26.

[4]Henry, Robert S., *The Story of the Confederacy*. New York: Grosset & Dunlap, 1936, p. 17.

incidentally on General Houston's birthday.[5] After the vote of the people, the convention took action requiring all officers of the state to appear before it and take an oath to support the Confederacy. Following the failure of Governor Houston and Secretary of State E. W. Cave to comply, the convention declared their offices vacant, and Texas entered the Confederacy under the leadership of its lieutenant governor.

Undoubtedly many southern leaders had given serious thought to the possibility of acquiring the output of the California gold mines by conquest. However, if the state could have been persuaded to desert the North, an attempt at conquest would not have been necessary. As a matter of fact, there was in California a large and influential body of citizens of southern birth and sympathies, who actively worked to bring about secession from the Union. They had no expectations that they could get the new state actually to join the Confederacy. They merely hoped that, by reviving the old plan for a Pacific Republic, they could weaken the North by the withdrawal of California.[6] The loyalty of Federal troops stationed in California was assured when President Lincoln appointed General Edwin V. Sumner to supersede General Albert Sydney Johnston in the command of the Pacific Division of the United States Army. This action, coupled with the strenuous efforts of the loyal elements in the citizenry, kept California in the Union. Nevertheless, many southerners, among whom the most conspicuous was General Johnston, made their way back to the theatre of war to join the armies of the Confederacy.

Between Texas, the southwestern anchor of the new Southern nation, and California stretched the Territory of New Mexico,

---

[5]Wharton, Clarence R., *History of Texas.* Dallas: Turner Co., 1935, p. 270.

[6]Cleland, Robert G., *A History of California, The American Period.* New York: The MacMillan Co., 1930, p. 356.

which in 1860 included all of the present states of New Mexico
and Arizona and the southern tip of Nevada. When the war
started in the spring of 1861, Colonel William W. Loring left
his command in New Mexico, and joined the Confederacy with
a number of other southern officers. Command of the department devolved on Colonel Edward R. S. Canby, the senior loyal
officer remaining on duty in the area. To protect this vast territory from invasion and block the routes from Texas to the Colorado and California gold fields, Canby had only a handful of
regular troops. These forces consisted of the Third Infantry,
parts of one or two other infantry regiments, most of the Third
Dragoons and a few batteries of artillery.[7] After the loss of
southern officers returning to the Confederacy and the desertion
of men who had no desire to serve in time of war, the roster of
all units was considerably below authorized strength. Further,
near Fort Defiance, the Apaches and Navajos were actively hostile, tying down a garrison of two hundred men.

Not only in New Mexico, but throughout the entire country,
the Regular Army was so located and in such reduced numbers
as to be of little effectiveness in the initial stages of the war.
The ten infantry regiments, four regiments of dragoons and
supporting artillery units, which constituted the combat forces,
were scattered over the west to protect the frontier against Indian depredations. During the first three months after the fall
of Fort Sumter, two hundred and sixty-nine out of a total of
nine hundred officers resigned their commissions to join the
South, and twenty-six were dismissed for the same reason. Although sixty-five West Point cadets from southern states resigned, a majority of the alumni from the South remained with

---

[7]Ganoe, William A. (Major Inf., U.S.A.), *History of the United States Army*. New York: D. Appleton Co., 1945, p. 245.

the Union. Thus the Regular Army was forced to close ranks and undertake the task of organizing and training the volunteer units being raised to form the new Union Army.

Following the secession of Texas, General David E. Twiggs treacherously surrendered all United States Army posts and property in the state. Thereafter, Lieutenant Colonel John R. Baylor occupied the forts west of San Antonio with Texas militia; and, during July, 1861, he took possession of Fort Bliss for the Confederacy. Forty miles to the north, the Union garrison at Fort Fillmore was a potential threat to his slender hold on the west Texas outpost. Accordingly, rather than wait for possible attack from that location, a quick campaign was launched in an effort to protect the forts already seized for the South.

Baylor marched up the river with several companies of mounted rifles, supported by artillery. Although he had received information of the approach of the Texans, Major Isaac Lynde, the commander at Fort Fillmore, who was a veteran of thirty-four years in the infantry, took no advance precautions. When the Confederates reached the town of Mesilla near the fort, Lynde ordered nearly all of his garrison of four hundred men out in a short-lived attack. This was followed by a retreat of two miles to the fort to the astonishment of most of his officers. The next day the major undertook another retreat to Fort Stanton, one hundred and fifty miles to the northeast, leaving Baylor and his tiny force of two hundred and fifty men in control of the river and the fort. After twenty-four hours on the trail, Baylor overtook the fleeing garrison. In spite of the pleas and protests of the Union officers, who condemned his action as suicidal and cowardly, Lynde unconditionally surrendered to the Texans seven companies of regular infantry and three companies of mounted rifles.

Federal forces in Fort Stanton withdrew to Albuquerque, and the troops at Fort Thorn felt obliged to abandon their post for the safety of nearby Fort Craig. By virtue of Major Lynde's surrender, Baylor had been placed in control of all southern New Mexico. In conformity with the desires of most of the white inhabitants, he formally took possession of this area for the Confederacy as the "Territory of Arizona," proclaiming himself its military governor.

These actions by Lieutenant Colonel Baylor were the initial moves by the South in a plan to seize vast areas and their resources to aid in the success of their military operations. The seizure of New Mexico would, of itself, have little value to the Confederacy, since it was sparsely populated, largely arid and had few natural advantages. However, it provided a highway to other lands and resources, which certain Southern leaders considered would throw the balance of power to them in their struggle with the North. These areas and their facilities included the gold fields of Colorado and California, and the vast mountain areas from Denver, through Salt Lake City, to the Pacific ports of California. The conquest of these territories would provide ample space for the extension of slavery, and serve as an outlet for surplus slaves, thus strengthening the Southern economy.[8] Also, by conquest or purchase, the Mexican states of Chihuahua, Sonora and Baja California were to be added to the Confederacy, greatly increasing its power and prestige. This was General Sibley's plan for Southern victory, which was accepted by President Jefferson Davis, although the latter attached primary concern to the occupation of New Mexico, Colorado

---

[8]*Battles and Leaders of the Civil War.* New York: Thomas Yoseloff, Inc., 1956 Edition, Vol. 2, p. 700 (Chapter entitled "Sibley's New Mexico Campaign—Its Objectives and the Causes of its Failure" by T. T. Teel, Major, C.S.A.).

and California, with the capture of supplies and seizure of the gold fields.[9]

An important factor considered by the Southern planners was the attitude of the population of the territories involved. Although most of the people of New Mexico were loyal to the Union, their attachment was apathetic. California had a strong element in favor of the South, while approximately one third of the settlers in Colorado were disloyal to the government. The Mormons of Utah were considered good prospects for Southern attachment, due to resentment generated by the actions of some Northern people in persecuting their sect. Many of the savage Indians of the west and southwest might be easily incited to attack when the troops of the North were occupied elsewhere. It seemed that all of these factors would operate in favor of the success of the plan and to the embarrassment of any Union forces which might be assigned to stop its consummation.

---

[9]Hafen and Rister, *Western America,* p. 378.

V

Muster of the Colorado Volunteers

SEVERAL efforts were made by the people of the Pike's Peak region to form a territorial government during 1860 and the first part of 1861. In one such venture, officials elected for the provisional Territory of Jefferson attempted to carry out some governmental functions for a time. Finally, the Territory of Colorado was created by a bill which passed the Congress and became a law on February 28, 1861. The territorial officers appointed under this act arrived in June 1861, and relieved the representatives of the provisional territory of the responsibility of governing the area and maintaining law and order.

William Gilpin, first Territorial Governor of Colorado, was born in Pennsylvania in 1822, and graduated from West Point in 1840. He was a learned, upright man with extended military experience, including service in the Seminole War and the Mexican War and command of an expedition against the plains Indians of Colorado in 1847. Although appointed by President Lincoln, he was without written instructions or funds. His verbal instructions, given hastily between more important decisions, conferred broad powers. His main task was to see that the new territory was kept in the Union. He was to protect and defend the area; and, if troops were needed, he was to raise and command them.[1]

In the territory there were many Southern sympathizers who might attempt to seize or loot the area for the Confederacy. There was also the likelihood that hostile Indians would take advantage of the outbreak of civil conflict to attack the settlements. Under these conditions, Governor Gilpin felt called upon to take counter measures in defense of the district. Accordingly, proceeding secretly to avoid a premature clash with the local Southerners, he raised two infantry companies of picked men, and armed them with weapons quietly purchased wherever they could be found. John P. Slough and Samuel F. Tappan, who had been active in recruiting these companies, were named as captains, one in command of each.[2]

In the meantime, Samuel H. Cook and his friend George Nelson had enlisted eighty men in the gold fields, with the understanding that they would proceed to the states and seek entrance into the service as a volunteer mounted company. About the middle of August, they all arrived in Denver on the first stage of their journey east. Governor Gilpin, having already decided to raise a full regiment of volunteers persuaded them to stay in Colorado and join the new unit.[3] They were promised that, as a company of the regiment, they would be mounted for scouting purposes, furnished with good arms

---

[1]Bancroft, Hubert Howe, *The Works of,* Vol. XXV, *History of Nevada, Colorado, and Wyoming.* San Francisco: The History Co., 1890, p. 415. (Hereafter cited as Bancroft, *Nevada, Colorado and Wyoming.*)

[2]Chivington, *First Colorado Regiment,* p. 2.

[3]Whitford, *Colorado Volunteers in the Civil War,* p. 45.

and equipment and have plenty of active service. Quarters were provided for them on Ferry Street in West Denver, and they immediately proceeded to elect officers. Cook was chosen as captain and George Nelson and B. F. Marshall lieutenants.

As the prevailing national feeling on slavery and the conflict in views became intensified, the people of Colorado were drawn into the controversy. The Fighting Parson immediately declared his position on this issue and on the threats of secession which were being voiced in the South. In one of his sermons he stated, in the words of Stephen Douglas, "Until the national unity is restored, let there be but two parties—patriots and traitors." This aroused the resentment of loyal Southern supporters, who formed a committee to protest the use of the church for the dissemination of such ideas, claiming them to be political. In a sermon, delivered a few weeks later at the funeral of a Union recruit, Chivington made the following reply to this charge: "I am a man of lawful age and full size, and was an American citizen before I became a minister. If the church had required me to renounce my rights of manhood or American citizenship before I became a minister, I should have respectfully declined."[4]

After the battle of Bull Run, the disaffected in Denver boldly avowed their principles. They raised a "Secesh" flag, which, however, did not fly long, secretly bought up arms and, in various ways, commenced marshaling their forces to seize the infant territory. These actions, together with the capture of Forts Bliss and Fillmore by Baylor with a small group of Confederates and his reported march on Santa Fe, decided the governor. On August 29th, he announced the formation of the First Colorado

---

[4]Beardsley, Isaac H., *Echoes From Peak and Plain*. Cincinnati:Curts & Jennings and New York: Eaton and Mains, 1898, p. 242 (quoting from article by Chivington).

Regiment of volunteers, appointed John P. Slough colonel and S. F. Tappan lieutenant colonel, and called for volunteers to fill the ranks of the organization.[5]

When this news reached Chivington he immediately called on the governor to offer his services. "I will be glad to appoint you as chaplain of the regiment," said Gilpin. "I appreciate your offer," the elder replied. "However, I feel compelled to strike a blow in person for the destruction of human slavery and to help in some measure to make this a truly free country. Therefore, I must respectfully decline an appointment as a non-combatant officer, and at the same time urgently request a fighting commission instead." "Very well," replied the governor. "We still have one vacancy for a field officer. I will appoint you major of the regiment." Chivington's reputation throughout the territory was of great assistance in securing enlistments. Recruiting offices were opened in Denver, Gregory, Idaho Springs and beyond the range; and within two months the required complement of men was obtained.

Included in the first list of officers were the following captains and company commanders, who later played important parts in the military history of the area: E. W. Wynkoop, Company A; Jacob Downing, Company D; Scott J. Anthony, Company E; and Sam F. Cook, Company F.[6] The staff also included an officer of future importance in the person of Lieutenant George L. Shoup.

Major Chivington's military knowledge was confined to information he had gained through a short term of service in an Ohio militia company and some reading in books on military history

---

[5]Chivington, *First Colorado Regiment*, p. 2.

[6]Hollister, Ovando J., *History of the First Regiment of Colorado Volunteers.* (Originally published in Denver in 1863.) Reprinted as *Boldly They Rode.* Lakewood: The Golden Press, 1949, pp. 5 & 6. (Hereafter cited as *History of the First.*)

and tactics. Nevertheless, since it was soon apparent that he had a grasp of military affairs far beyond that of any other officer in the regiment, Colonel Slough placed him in charge of the drill and training of the men.

A site was selected for a military post on the Platte, two miles from the center of Denver City, which was called Camp Weld in honor of the secretary of the territory. Comfortable and adequate barracks were constructed at a cost of forty thousand dollars; and, as fast as the companies were filled, they went into quarters there. Notices like the following were occasionally seen in the daily papers:

> "Yesterday Capt. S. M. Logan, with Company B,
> numbering 101 men, arrived from the mountains
> and went into quarters at Camp Weld. The men
> look hale and hearty, and are in excellent spirits."

Following their arrival during the latter part of August, the mounted men of Captain Cook's Company F remained in town for from two to three months. As their recruiting progressed, it became necessary to move them to the old Buffalo House, where there was sufficient room to accommodate their increasing numbers. A corral just below and across the street contained the company horses, and was used as the company guard house. There was no difficulty in escaping from the back of the enclosure, however, and the prisoners confined in the corral enjoyed the freedom of the town. Collisions between them and the local "secesh" occurred occasionally, but never with any serious results. Officially the men were obliged to remain in quarters, and a pass was required even to go to any other part of the city.

Acting under the verbal broad authority given him at the time of his appointment, Governor Gilpin financed the expenses of raising the regiment by the issuance of drafts on the federal treasury. The buildings at Camp Weld and the uniforms, arms, supplies and equipment for the troops were all procured in this manner. To handle the administration of affairs for the troops, he appointed a military staff which included Adjutant General R. E. Whitsett, Quartermaster Samuel Moer, Paymaster John S. Fillmore and Purchasing Agent Morton C. Fisher. In the course of his administration, drafts amounting to approximately three hundred and seventy-five thousand dollars were issued. At first they were readily accepted by the merchants and other suppliers, upon the undisputed assumption that, as the accredited officer of the government, he had the right to issue them. However, in the absence of written authority, the drafts were not honored when first received in Washington. Although they were ultimately audited and paid in full, many people were forced to sell their holdings at a loss; and the resulting dissatisfaction led to the removal of Governor Gilpin in April 1862 and his replacement with Governor John Evans.[7]

Governor Gilpin was not a man who believed in half measures. He decided to raise at least two regiments of volunteers, although he did not announce this fact at first. Late in August 1861, at about the same time that he formed the First Regiment, he appointed James H. Ford a captain and Theodore H. Dodd a first lieutenant, and authorized each of them to raise a company of infantry. Recruiting was carried on through the fall of 1861 in the vicinity of Canyon City. About the middle of December, when their ranks were full, both companies marched separately to Fort Garland where they were mustered into the United States service for three years, with both leaders as captains. Dodd's unit was provisionally designated as Company A and Ford's as Company B of the Second Colorado Infantry.

----

[7]Bancroft, *Nevada, Colorado and Wyoming,* p. 427.

Both companies were sent to New Mexico in response to Colonel Canby's urgent call to Governor Gilpin for assistance in repelling the imminent Texan invasion. Dodd left first and arrived at Fort Craig in time to take part in the Battle of Valverde on February 21, 1862, where his men performed gallantly to the credit of the Colorado volunteers. Captain Ford's company reached Santa Fe on March 4th, after a hard march through deep snow, and was sent to Fort Union to reinforce its weak garrison, arriving at that post on March 11th. When the Second Regiment was organized at a later date, the provisional designations were reversed, Ford's unit becoming Company A and Dodd's Company B. Still later, when the regiment was transferred to the cavalry arm, Ford became its colonel and Dodd its lieutenant colonel.

In October the First Colorado received its first active assignment. It was discovered that a group of Southern sympathizers was being organized under a certain Captain McKee, a former Texas ranger. It was their intention to plunder the banks and business houses of Denver and leave for Texas to join the Confederate Army. McKee and forty of his partisans were arrested and confined in the city jail. A detachment of the First Regiment was sent to the rendezvous of the Southerners near Russellville, about forty miles from Cherry Creek. Some of the members of the group were taken into custody at that place, but about one hundred escaped and captured a government train near Fort Wise (later renamed Fort Lyon) on the Arkansas River. This band was likewise overtaken and forty-one captured and brought back to Denver to join their companions in the city jail. Here they became a source of annoyance, since they had to be guarded and fed and no one knew what disposition to make of them.

Captain Cook had been sent to Fort Wise with a mounted detachment of one hundred men, largely from his own company, to escort the prisoners back to Denver. The eighteen day trip presented an opportunity for the captain to teach his men some of the principles of march discipline. One of the men of F Company later wrote that, at first, the boys were slow and heedless about falling in, feeding, saddling up and performing other essential functions. Accordingly, the captain issued standing orders that the guard was to be taken from the left end of the line where tardy arrivals were forced to fall in. In a few days there *was* no left. At the first note of assembly, the men seized their arms and crowded together like a flock of sheep worried by dogs, and one morning they formed in three circles. The captain looked at them an instant with a twinkle in his eye. Then, turning away, he said to the sergeant, "Detail the guard in the future." It is related that for the rest of the trip the men got up promptly at reveille, fell in rapidly and never required more than ten minutes to pack up and start.

As the fall progressed into winter, the lack of activity other than drill engendered a mutinous spirit in the troops at Camp Weld, who had been enlisted for active service at the front. The men were mainly of good quality, but the monotony of barracks life drove them into mischief. They were also made reckless by a belief that a lack of authority for Governor Gilpin to raise troops and issue warrants for their expenses might prevent them from entering the service under their present organization. They were publicly accused as being "chicken thieves, jayhawkers, turbulent and seditious, a disgrace to themselves and the country." Nevertheless, the enforced idleness and the prevalent though erroneous idea that they would never be recognized or paid gave some excuse for the peccadilloes of the volunteers at Camp Weld.

Late in the autumn, two companies of the regiment, under the command of Lieutenant Colonel Tappan, were sent to garrison Fort Wise, two hundred miles southeast of Denver. Company F was moved from its location in town to occupy the vacated quarters at Camp Weld where Major Chivington was in immediate charge. If the mounted company was moved to the barracks to relieve the town of its presence, the action failed of its object. As the major said, "They only came to camp to get their meals."[8]

The unrest in the unit was accentuated in November, when the regiment was mustered into the federal service for a term of three years. Captain Marion's Company K had been enlisted as mounted rifles, and when Colonel Slough attempted to muster them in as infantry, they refused to take the oath. The captain backed up their position and was arrested. The men left the barracks, announcing the intention of releasing their captain and leaving the country, either for the states or New Mexico. Effective precautions having been taken to prevent such action, most of the men returned to camp during the next few days and were quietly mustered in. Some difficulty occurred in Company G at the same time and for the same reason. The result was the cashiering of Captains Marion and Hambleton. S. M. Robbins became captain of Company K and W. F. Wilder captain of Company G. Later Captain Hambleton was given an honorable discharge and enlisted in the Third Colorado Regiment, in which he eventually became a second lieutenant.

The people of Denver became alarmed at the growing insolence of the soldiers, among whom no one seemed disposed or able to enforce much discipline. Accordingly, on December 1st, a special police force was organized to preserve the property of citizens from the nightly prowling squads of mischievous or drunken soldiers. From then on it became the object of many

---

[8]Hollister, *History of the First*, p. 35.

of the men to create and foment variance with these minions of the city. With the approach of the holidays the depredations of the soldiers increased, as the boys began to forage to secure materials for a celebration. On Christmas eve parties might have been seen making their way noiselessly through back alleys, whispering ominously on street corners, or carefully reconnoitering the rear areas of residential premises. It was rough on the town, but the men had been four months without pay, there was no money in the regiment, and Christmas on bread and beef did not appeal to their adventuresome spirits.

Major Chivington was a born leader of men and he understood the restless spirit of the pioneers who formed the body of the regiment. From his position as their immediate commander at Camp Weld, he knew that they wanted to go to the front, and that they were tired of lying in camp. On some occasions, as many as two or three companies at a time were stripped of their arms and, with their officers, put under arrest for mutiny. The major later wrote: "We knew that when the warm weather came on they would mutiny and go off. I wrote to Major General Hunter in command of the department at Fort Leavenworth, what the state of affairs was, and he sent my letter back to be sent through military headquarters, . . . I replied with a second letter as sharp as his rebuke was, that I knew what I was about and I repeated it, and that I would be very much pleased to be dismissed from the service for trying to get my regiment to the front, and thought I would be sustained when it got to higher authorities, when the facts were known."[9]

Ennui was becoming intolerable to the men of the First, who were accustomed to rough, stirring work, when news came from New Mexico of the Texan invasion. In the first days of the year,

---

[9]Chivington, *The First Colorado Regiment*, p. 4.

an express arrived from the south with the news of the advance of Brigadier General Sibley and three or four thousand Texans, and a call for assistance from Colonel Canby. Since the First had already been mustered into the federal service, the regiment could not be moved out of Colorado except by orders from Department Headquarters, which were requested by Acting Governor Weld.

Keeping their attention on this development as the beacon star of their existence, the men of the First Regiment endured the impositions put upon them without a murmur. During the last few weeks of their stay at Camp Weld they were issued worthless clothing, or none at all, and subsistence was practically nonexistent. The people had become tired of feeding and clothing the regiment on government credit without immediate prospect of receiving cash reimbursement. As a consequence, the quartermaster quit furnishing, and the men were thrown on their own resources. It must be stated that, in the matter of food at least, they supplied themselves very well. Hogs, sheep and other stock in the vicinity were roundly taxed, nor did good, fine beef within the area escape their toll.

On the 10th of January Captain Cook was ordered to report to Lieutenant Colonel Tappan at Fort Wise with the major portion of Company F, and, near the end of the month, the remainder of the company joined them there. One night there was a raid on the sutler's store at the post, apparently engineered by the men from F Company. These troopers were even less disciplined than the remainder of the regiment, due perhaps to their original maintenance of quarters in town apart from the other companies. Late in the evening a group of soldiers quietly approached the store and broke in the door with a large rock. While some acted as lookouts, the rest rifled the place and made off with the plunder which was safely hidden. Guards making

their regular rounds a short time later noted the broken door
and reported the incident to Post Headquarters. Patrols of regular troops were immediately dispatched to look for the stolen
goods and apprehend the thieves. They made a search of the
quarters occupied by the volunteers without success, and the
raiders felt secure in enjoying their loot. However, on a second
search after midnight, Lieutenant Warner, the post commander,
and a squad of regulars burst into the room occupied by some of
the men in F Company, and found the boys with the contents of
a stolen package of candy scattered over the table.

"Fall in!" shouted the lieutenant. As the men took their
places in formation, he walked along the line and solemnly
wrote down their names on a list of suspects. "Take your blankets and move to the long corral for the rest of the night,"
ordered the post commander. "Sergeant," he continued, "search
the room for stolen goods." The next day he called in Lieutenant Marshall, the acting company commander, and directed him
to place the men on the list under arrest. However, the board
appointed to investigate the affair was composed of volunteer
officers, who settled the matter by paying the sutler for his losses
out of their own pockets and reading a lecture to their men.

Lieutenant Warner was the first regular officer with whom
the soldiers of the First had come in contact, and the results
were not promising. The lieutenant viewed the volunteers with
great disfavor, and, on their part, they considered him an intolerable nuisance.[10]

------

[10]Hollister, *History of the First,* p. 39.

VI

The Rebel Invasion

AMONG the officers of the United States Army stationed in New Mexico at the outbreak of the war was Major Henry H. Sibley, who resigned his commission on May 13, 1861 and entered the service of the Confederacy. During his earlier career he had served with distinction in the Seminole War, the War with Mexico, expeditions against the Mormons and in Indian hostilities. He superintended the construction of Fort Union with its arsenals and storage buildings, the main army supply base in the territory. On the 8th of July, having been appointed brigadier general, Sibley reported to Richmond. Here he was assigned the mission of driving the Union troops from New Mexico and of securing all of the arms, supplies and materials of war located therein. He was instructed to proceed at once to Texas, to raise a brigade for these purposes and, if successful in his campaign, to organize a military government in northern New Mexico. It appears he was chosen for this command due to his service in the Rio Grande Valley and the area to the west, and his knowledge of the country and its people.

For several months Sibley was busy raising and equipping the units of his force which were marched to a concentration point at Fort Bliss as rapidly as they were organized and outfitted. Thus it was not until December 14 that he arrived at Fort Bliss and took personal command of his troops, which were then designated as the Army of New Mexico, but later usually called Sibley's Brigade. When the units were all concentrated, the brigade was composed of three regiments of mounted infantry, two batteries of artillery and three independent companies, a total of nearly three thousand, five hundred men.[1] One of the mounted regiments included a battalion of five companies under the command of Lieutenant Colonel Baylor, whose initial operations in southern New Mexico had opened the gate for Sibley's invasion. Baylor's men, and sometimes the whole brigade, were often referred to by the Union soldiers as "Baylor's Babes."

On December 20 General Sibley issued a proclamation to the people of New Mexico, declaring that the territory pertained to the South, due to its geographical position, similarity of institutions, commercial interests and future destiny. In this document he appealed to his "old comrades in arms" still in the Union ranks to give up allegiance to "the usurpers of their government and liberties," and to aid him in enforcing Confederate authority. The proclamation further stated: "I am empowered to receive you into the service of the Confederate states—the officers upon their commissions, the men upon their enlistments." The appeal for desertion received no response from the Federal troops in the area. The officers, with the exception of one who later deserted, had already made their choice between the North and the South, and, generally speaking, the enlisted men of the army remained loyal to the Union.

---

[1] Whitford, *Colorado Volunteers in the Civil War*, p. 33.

Soon after Canby assumed command of the Department of New Mexico, he was faced with the appalling news of Lynde's surrender to the Texans, with the resulting loss of trained troops. This was quickly followed by the receipt of intelligence that two expeditions were being formed to attack his territory. One was specified as under organization by Van Dorn in northern Texas, with the purpose of advancing up the valley of the Canadian River to attack Fort Union. The other was being assembled by Sibley at San Antonio, with the mission of joining Baylor in an invasion up the Rio Grande from Fort Bliss. Based on this information, Canby felt that he was required to keep strong forces at Fort Union and Fort Craig, with a reserve force at an intermediate point to reinforce either location.[2]

During the summer and fall of 1861 Canby made strenuous efforts to prepare for attack by the Confederates. Initially he had one thousand men of the New Mexico militia, poorly organized and untrained, to support the small group of regular troops remaining under his command after the cowardly surrender of Major Lynde. He proceeded to raise five regiments of volunteers which were distributed to strengthen the garrisons of the department.[3] The works at Fort Craig were enlarged and strengthened, and the post was heavily provisioned to serve as a main base of operations. Fort Union, his main supply depot, was well located for a northern base of operations. However, like most frontier posts, it was designed to resist attack by Indians, and was not well suited as a protection against assault by a trained army of white soldiers. To partially correct this defi-

---

[2]*Battles and Leaders of the Civil War,* Vol. 2, pp. 698-699. (Chapter entitled "Canby's Services in the New Mexico Campaign" by Latham Anderson, Brig. Gen., U.S.V.)

[3]Horgan, Paul, *The Great River, The Rio Grande in North American History.* New York and Toronto: Rinehart & Co., Inc., 1954, Vol. 2, p. 824.

ciency, Canby constructed extensive earthwork fortifications near the old post, with well protected storage facilities, into which he moved the more important classes of military supplies. With its great store of war materiel and its strategic locaton, Fort Union was considered by Colonel Canby as the key to the military situation, which had to be held at all cost.

In response to Canby's first request for assistance late in the year, Governor Gilpin dispatched the two independent companies of volunteers which had been raised for incorporation in the proposed Second Colorado Regiment. One of these companies, as has been previously mentioned, was sent to Fort Craig and the other to Fort Union. Canby then proceeded to concentrate four thousand men at Fort Craig for an attack on Fort Bliss. However, before he was able to launch his campaign, Sibley's invasion was in full swing.

From the spring of 1861, when Colonel Loring left his post without waiting for the acceptance of his resignation, Canby had been serving as department commander without any official confirmation from higher authority. However, by General Orders Number 97, of November 9, 1861, the Department of New Mexico was officially reestablished and placed under the command of Colonel E. R. S. Canby, 19th United States Infantry.[4]

Sibley lost two months at or near Fort Bliss waiting for delayed reinforcements from San Antonio. In the meantime he was endeavoring, with little success, to raise a regiment of natives by enlistment and conscription. He sent a detachment of troops to Tucson to secure the western part of New Mexico for the Confederacy. Also, in furtherance of the grand plan of strategy for winning a western empire, he sent one of his offi-

---

[4]*Battles and Leaders of the Civil War,* Vol. 2, p. 104. (Chapter entitled "The Confederate Invasion of New Mexico and Arizona" by George R. Pettis, Brevet Capt., U.S.V.)

cers, Colonel James Reily, with a communication to the head of
the Mexican State of Chihuahua, and received a satisfactory
reply. According to Sibley's report, the exchange of messages
amounted to a treaty between the two governments pledging
friendship and goodwill. A similar mission was sent to the State
of Sonora, but nothing was secured therefrom except the privi-
lege of purchasing supplies in the state for cash.

On the 7th of February, with all available men and supplies
finally in readiness, Sibley launched his advance up the valley
of the Rio Grande, with three thousand men, fifteen pieces of
artillery and a long and heavy supply train. On the 12th of the
month he was encamped on the west bank of the river seven
miles below Fort Craig. There was some fruitless maneuvering,
and, on the 19th, the Texans withdrew down the river and
crossed to the east bank. Late that day the main column of the
Confederates was seen proceeding north across the river from
Fort Craig. By nightfall the sentries at the fort could observe
their camp fires, and, when the wind was right, hear the voices
of the invaders.[5] Sibley was camped on the only open ground
between the lava beds and ravines to the south and the abrupt
Valverde mesa five miles farther north.

At Fort Craig, Canby waited for an attack, or perhaps a siege.
However, on the 20th when he saw the enemy supply train moving north across the river, he decided Sibley was trying to bypass
the fort beyond the range of its guns. In this manner the Rebels
would arrive at the upper ford beyond the mesa, where there
was an open plain with easy approaches on each side of the
river. The fields on the west bank in this location were called
the Hay Camp, due to the custom of the soldiers from the fort
of growing feed there for their animals. Canby tried to attack by

---

[5]Horgan, *The Great River,* Vol. 2. p. 824.

fording the river, but his men were unable to advance against the heavy fire of the enemy from protected positions, and, at dawn on the following day, the Union troops recrossed the river. Soon thereafter, it appeared that Sibley's troops were arriving in strength at the ford above the mesa, and Canby hastily made ready all the men he could spare from the garrison and dispatched them to the Hay Camp. On their arrival, these troops observed the Texans on the plain across the river, and opened fire on them at nine o'clock in the morning. Thus began the Battle of Valverde, a desperate day-long struggle, which nearly cost the Union the control of New Mexico.[6]

Early in the day the Union forces crossed the river in strength, in the face of a heavy fire that killed many in the water. Artillery played a prominent part in the battle. On the Federal side were two batteries. One was a regular artillery unit commanded by Lieutenant Robert Hall. The other was a provisional unit, manned by men from the Second and Third Regular Cavalry and commanded by Captain Alexander McRae of the last named unit. The Confederate artillery also included two batteries, one commanded by Major Trevanion T. Teel, and the other by Lieutenant John Riley. Artillery duels were conducted across the river until the Union forces dragged their pieces to the east bank. Here they were placed in strong positions outside the range of small arms, from which they forced the Confederates back into some sand hills on the edge of the old bed of the river. Most of the Federal troops were ordered to cross the river early in the afternoon, including the Second Regiment of New Mexico volunteers, five companies of which refused to advance in the face of their old enemies, the Texans.[7]

[6]Horgan, *The Great River*, Vol. 2, p. 825.

[7]Whitford, *Colorado Volunteers in the Civil War*, p. 64.

The command was changed once for each of the opposing forces. General Sibley was initially in immediate command of the Confederates, but, due to illness, he was forced to transfer his authority to Colonel Thomas Green in the early afternoon. The Union troops were first controlled by Lieutenant Colonel Benjamin S. Roberts of the Third United States Cavalry, a gallant and able leader who was then serving as colonel of the Fifth New Mexico Infantry. Shortly after noon Colonel Canby arrived on the field and relieved Colonel Roberts of command.

Hall's battery was emplaced near the southern end of the battle line, while McRae's positions were on the north flank, three-quarters of a mile away. Both units had adequate numbers of supporting troops assigned for their protection. Throughout most of the afternoon the two armies spent their time in maintaining a desultory fire. However, at one time, on the southern end of the field, a company of Texan lancers charged Captain Dodd's company of Colorado Volunteers, which formed a hollow square and quickly repulsed the attack. Throughout the day this company, though it had never before been under fire, fought like a unit of veterans, suffering the highest proportion of casualties of any Federal unit engaged.

Until late in the day it seemed that the battle would be a draw. At this time a cavalry charge was launched against McRae's strong battery of six guns. This was followed immediately by a furious assault by the main body of the Confederates, which had been pinned down in the sand hills. The smaller force attacking Hall's battery on the Union right was driven off with heavy losses by the gallant supporting action of Captain Wingate's battalion of regular infantry and Colonel "Kit" Carson's New Mexico volunteers.[8] The Texans attacking the Northern

---

[8]*Battles and Leaders of the Civil War,* Vol. 2, p. 107. (Chapter by Petis, "The Confederate Invasion of New Mexico and Arizona.")

left swept down the slopes of the sand hills into a storm of grape and canister, and for eight minutes the fighting was terrific beyond description. McRae's battery was inadequately supported, although troops were immediately available. Two companies of the Seventh Regular Infantry and a full regiment of New Mexico volunteers, which were within twenty yards of the battery, were ordered and implored by Colonel Canby in person to charge the enemy. Nevertheless, not one company advanced to the relief of the hard pressed battery, nor even fired upon the approaching enemy; and McRae and all his officers and men died in defense of their guns.[9]

The guns of the crack Union battery were thus lost to the Rebels. Canby saw that further resistance was useless with only Hall's battery, and ordered the troops remaining on the east bank to recross the stream. The captured guns and the Confederate batteries were brought to bear on the withdrawing Federals. The crossing was accomplished, but with heavy losses; and the troops, with their remaining battery, re-formed on the far bank. The cavalry covered the retreat to Fort Craig, which was conducted in fairly good order, and with small loss in men or munitions.

In his report to Washington,[10] Canby described Sibley's force as consisting of three regiments of mounted infantry, two batteries of artillery and three independent companies, having a nominal aggregate strength of nearly three thousand, but probably reduced by sickness and detachments to a force of twenty-six hundred. He gave his own strength as eleven companies of regular infantry, five companies of regular cavalry, McRae's

---

[9]Whitford, Colorado Volunteers in the Civil War, p. 66.

[10]*War of the Rebellion: Official Records of the Union and Confederate Armies* (hereafter cited as *Rebellion Records*), Series I, Vol. IX. Washington: U. S. Govt. Print. Off., 1893, pp. 487-493.

battery, various volunteer units and unorganized militia elements, with a total aggregate present of thirty-eight hundred and ten. The casualties were extremely heavy. Canby gave the Union losses as sixty-eight killed, one hundred and sixty wounded and thirty-five missing. General Sibley reported Confederate losses of forty dead and about one hundred wounded.[11]

Like many other important battles, there has been some controversy regarding the strategy of the losing commander. Many have felt that the result would have been different had Colonel Roberts remained in command throughout the day, apparently since all went well for the Union cause under his leadership. Others have taken the opposite viewpoint, stating that when Canby arrived on the field shortly after noon, he was faced with an impossible situation, his troops being one half on each side of the river. The clear facts seem to be, however, that the battle was lost by the cowardice of officers and men of the certain regular and volunteer units who refused to obey orders to support the artillery. The troops on the Union side outnumbered the Confederates, and, while not brilliantly commanded, were sufficiently well led to have won the day in the absence of mutiny.

On the morning following the battle, General Sibley sent Lieutenant Colonel William R. Scurry and two other officers to Fort Craig, under a flag of truce. They made a demand for the surrender of the fort, which was promptly rejected. It has been reported that these officers were misled by the apparent number and caliber of the guns mounted in the fort, since some that appeared to be of large size were actually wooden logs. In any event, the first phase of the invasion was accomplished with the defeat and immobilization of the main Union force in the ter-

---

[11]*Rebellion Records,* Series I, Vol. IX, pp. 505-506.

ritory. Sibley could now afford to leave Canby at Fort Craig, march north to the larger cities of the territory and prepare to take Fort Union with its vital supplies.

After remaining in camp near the field of Valverde for two days burying their dead and caring for their wounded, the Rebels pushed rapidly north along the river to the larger towns. It was hoped that, in these localities, provisions could be obtained to augment their rations in hand, which were barely sufficient for five days. On March 2, as the advance guard was approaching Albuquerque, Sibley saw three columns of smoke standing above the town, which rose from burning supply depots.[12] The Union garrison had withdrawn to Santa Fe, and the town was entered unopposed. The Federal troops at Santa Fe also burned their supplies and set out for Fort Union. These actions were a result of a "scorched earth" policy adopted by Canby. On the night following the battle of Valverde he had sent dispatches by courier, advising the commanders of all garrisons of Sibley's victory, and issuing orders to destroy all government property, and particularly provisions, where there was a danger that these supplies would be captured by the Rebels.

In their advance north the Confederates met a cool and sometimes hostile reception. In retaliation, they exacted money and confiscated property belonging to families favoring the Union cause. In addition, the Texans seized all available commissary, forage and clothing supplies in amounts sufficient to provide them for a period of three months. With his supply problem thus temporarily solved, Sibley formed the decision to advance on Fort Union with his entire force as soon as the troops could be prepared, and, if possible, to seize that post with its great

---

[12]Horgan, *The Great River,* Vol. 2, p. 826.

store of military supplies. Success in this action would remove the last menace to his full possession of the territory and complete the first step in his plan of conquest.

The advance guard of the Confederate force was to consist of five hundred mounted men under Major Charles L. Pyron, who was sent forward from Albuquerque to Santa Fe. Most of the remainder of the brigade was placed under the command of Lieutenant Colonel Scurry, who was ordered to proceed, with a column including the supply train, from Albuquerque to Galisteo, which is about fifteen miles from the western end of Glorieta Pass. It was planned that Major Pyron and the advance guard would join him there after securing possession of Santa Fe. Colonel Scurry had served with distinction in the Mexican War as a major in a Texas regiment under General Taylor. He was the conspicuous Confederate hero at the Battle of Valverde, where he organized and directed the ferocious charge which ended the fighting.

VII

The Advance South

IN RESPONSE to the request of acting Governor Weld, made in the early part of January 1862, the following order was finally received in Colorado Territory on February 14:

> Headquarters, Department of Kansas,
> Fort Leavenworth, Kan., February 10, 1862.

To His Excellency, Acting Governor of Colorado, Denver City, Colo.:

Send all available forces you can possibly spare to reinforce Colonel Canby, commanding Department of New Mexico, and to keep open his communication through Fort Wise. Act promptly and with all the discretion of your latest information as to what may be necessary and where the troops of Colorado can do most service.

> D. HUNTER,
> Major-General, Commanding.[1]

Several days were spent in assembling the meager stock of equipment and supplies to prepare as well as possible for the

---

[1]*Rebellion Records,* Series I, Vol. IX, p. 630.

long winter march ahead. At last, on the 22nd of February, the main body of the First Colorado Regiment set out from Camp Weld. Progress was slow, due to the intense cold and deep snow, and the first night was spent at Camp Chivington only six miles from Denver. The colonel, most of the other officers and some of the enlisted men returned to Denver for the night. Major Chivington, who had remained with the command, got the troops up, broke camp and had the column under way early the following morning. The regiment continued its marches from day to day. Progress improved as the men became used to the routine of the trail, and, by the evening of the 27th, they had reached a campsite within four miles of Colorado City.

Since regimental transportation was extremely limited, it was possible to provide only three wagons per company, and Company I was furnished only two. A big majority of the officers and men in this company were German immigrants, and they conceived the idea that they were being discriminated against in the matter of transportation due to their nationality. Accordingly, on the morning of the 28th, when the command was given to break camp and form in line for the day's march, Company I refused to obey. Their officers announced that the men would go no farther until they were furnished with the same number of wagons as the other companies.

This touched off a heated dispute between Colonel Slough and Lieutenant Kerber, the company commander. Slough then attempted to quell the mutiny by calling on Companies A and E to load with ball ammunition to force Company I into line, and, finally, the colonel drew his own pistol. Thereupon, sixty men of Company I leveled their Springfield rifled-muskets on Slough, and a voice announced, "You shoot Kerber, and we'll fill you full of holes." The regimental commander wheeled his horse, turned to Major Chivington and said, "Bring the regiment forward until you are from four to six miles below Colorado City, and make camp." He then touched spurs to his mount and rode off to the south.[2]

The major explained to the officers and men of Company I that no slight was intended, but that wagons were just not available. He assured them that as soon as another team could be secured they would be assigned transportation equal to the other companies. Satisfied with the major's explanation, the lieutenant ordered his men to face about. They then discharged their weapons into the air and fell into line. Scouts were sent out when the regiment reached its new camp in the afternoon, and an additional team and wagon were secured and assigned to Company I.

Proceeding down the Fontaine-qui-bouille to the Arkansas River, they crossed the stream and went into camp in a grove of cottonwood trees on the site later occupied by South Pueblo. In an effort to remedy the acute transportation shortage, four parties were sent out with orders to requisition all animals, wagons and harness that could be found. Although no wagons were secured, twenty-six head of horses and mules were brought back. A heavy snowstorm, followed by rain, created considerable inconvenience and some suffering in this camp due to a shortage of tents.

While they were encamped at this location a messenger arrived from Fort Union informing the colonel of the results of the conflict at Valverde and Sibley's rapid march up the Rio Grande. As a result, orders were issued to step up the rapidity of the advance in an effort to reach Fort Union and prevent it from falling into the hands of the Rebels.

---

[2]Chivington, John M., "The Pet Lambs" *Sunday Denver Republican*, Apr. 20, 1890, p. 24.

Meanwhile, Lieutenant Colonel Tappan and his three companies had been impatiently waiting at Fort Wise for authority to join the march south. Marching orders were finally received on March 1, and on the same day an express arrived from the south with news of the engagement at Valverde. After a day and a half of preparation, they left on March 3, and made camp in a heavy snowstorm on the first night out. On the next night they reached Bent's old fort, where they were met by Captain Garrison, Chief of Subsistence at Fort Union, who had come by special coach to urge their speedy advance. Tappan issued orders to leave all baggage behind, except a change of shirts and two blankets for each man, and the rate of march was accelerated. On March 5 they left the Arkansas and set out for the Purgatoire, seventy-five miles away. On this march they were met by Lieutenant Sanford of Company H, who had been sent as a messenger by Colonel Slough. He informed Tappan that the seven companies in the main body had crossed the Arkansas on the previous day, and that the two detachments were to meet at the crossing of the Purgatoire. Late in the afternoon of March 7 Tappan arrived at the rendezvous one hour after the main column, both groups having marched forty miles that day.

The camp of the full ten companies of the regiment, united for the first time in many months, had all the bustle of a small town. The men fell in and gave the colonel three cheers and a tiger, but he only raised his cap without speaking. One of the volunteers later wrote of this incident: "How little some men understood human nature. He had been our colonel for six months; had never spoken to us; and on the eve of an important expedition, after a long absence, could not see that a few words were indispensable to a good understanding."[3]

---

[3]Hollister, *History of the First*, p. 47.

The next night camp was made a short way up the mountain above Trinidad, and many of the men spent the night in carousal at the village. This was annoying to the Fighting Parson, who later wrote, "It seemed to me that his Satanic Majesty must have had a going up and down place somewhere on the banks of the Purgatoire, and from about the time we went into camp until we broke camp and left there next morning he held high carnival." Early the following morning the command started up the Raton Pass, reaching the summit about noon. Here they met a messenger with a dispatch from Colonel Paul, who was in command at Fort Union, advising that Sibley and his Texans were in close proximity, with attack expected hourly. Paul also stated that the fort was mined for destruction, and requested all possible speed in advance. The receipt of this news "added wings" to the speed of the regiment, and the Red River was reached in the late afternoon just as the mail coach arrived, making its regular stop at this point on its route to Fort Union and Santa Fe. Colonel Slough boarded the coach, leaving Major Chivington in command, with orders "to hasten forward at the greatest possible speed."

The men had not eaten since daylight, and the command halted and had both dinner and supper at once. Although the men had already made a long and difficult day's march over the mountains, the major formed them in line again. He explained the general military situation as shown by the latest dispatches and asked, "All who will make a forced march for the night to save Fort Union, step two paces to the front." Every man stepped out.[4] All baggage and equipment, excepting arms and two blankets per man, were left in the charge of a corporal's guard, and the regiment set out for its goal, eighty miles distant. With the

---

[4]Chivington, *The First Colorado Regiment*, p. 5.

wagons empty of their loads, many of the men were enabled to ride, but three to four hundred were forced to continue on foot. All stragglers were picked up; and, so far as possible, others were given a turn in the wagons from time to time to conserve their strength and enable the unit to advance at maximum speed.

"Away into the wee hours of the morning" the regiment advanced on foot, in wagons and, in the case of Company F, on horseback. It was tramp, tramp, tramp until "the gay song, the gibe, the story, the boisterous cheer all died a natural death, and nothing broke the stillness of the night except the steady tramp of the men and the rattle of the wagons." Finally, after a night march of thirty miles, the animals began to drop and die in harness from overwork and underfeeding, and the regiment was forced to halt at Maxwell's ranch on the Cimarron River. The major had preceded them to this point and "had beeves slaughtered" and other provisions ready to furnish a good breakfast. The Colorado Volunteers had marched sixty-seven miles since the morning before, and ninety-two in the previous thirty-six hours.[5]

After breakfast and a short rest, the command was again on the march early in the morning of March 10. A bitterly cold wind arose and increased in fury until it reached almost hurricane proportions. The line of march followed the base of the mountains, taking a circular course across the headwaters of the Cimarron. The condition of the stock grew progressively worse from the effects of the previous night of heavy driving. Major Chivington's big greys and saddle mule were left where they fell dead. Many other animals died, and the command was forced to slow its pace to avoid losing them all.[6] After a march

---

[5]Whitford, *Colorado Volunteers in the Civil War*, p. 78.
[6]Hollister, *History of the First*, p. 50.

of eighteen miles, they went into camp at the Reyado ranch in a storm of sand, gravel and dust. It was late at night before they were at rest in the heavy windstorm with no shelter available, since the tents had been left behind with the other baggage.

The regiment was on the march at sunrise next morning. Approaching Fort Union, the terrain became uniformly descending as they followed a little alkali stream flowing in a valley about four miles wide bordered on the east and west by low timbered ridges. When the fort came in sight it was seen that it was located about one mile from the west side of the valley, on a gentle rise in the ground. The outer earthworks, recently added by Colonel Canby's direction, consisted of a dirt parapet and ditch surrounding the original structure, which was a simple field work of moderate size, with bastioned corners and a slight abatis at exposed points.[7]

The First Colorado arrived at Fort Union just at dark. There the regiment was met by Colonel Slough, who had completed his journey by coach. The colonel took command, formed the troops in column and marched them into the post "with drums beating and colors flying." After several marchings and countermarchings, the tired and footsore men were finally halted in front of the commanding officer's quarters. Here they were harangued for two hours by the post commander Colonel Paul, Governor Conelly of New Mexico and others, who complimented them on their remarkable marches and successful arrival in time to save the fort. Finally at about nine o'clock they were allowed to march to their camp, just outside of the post. Some of the company officers were able to secure supplies for their men from the commissary and served a meal that night. Others were not so fortunate. The men of F Company, with no provis-

---

[7]Hollister, *History of the First,* p. 51.

ions available for their supper, went back to their old habits acquired at Fort Wise and raided the nearest sutler's store, where they secured cheese, crackers and champagne. Following their repast they went to bed in the corral with their horses.

The regiment remained at Fort Union until the 22nd of March, which gave the men a period in which to recuperate from the ordeal of their forced winter marches. Daily drill was held for the improvement of training and discipline, and the unit was resupplied and fully equipped with regulation clothing, arms and ammunition from the stores at the fort. Wagons were sent for the baggage left behind at Red River, and most of this equipment was recovered.

On March 14th an express arrived from Canby advising that the Union forces had captured a large train from the south with an escort of one hundred men. It was also stated that Sibley was in Santa Fe, where recruiting was considerably increasing his ranks, and that the Confederate strength was estimated at from twenty-five to thirty-five hundred. On the same day the wagons brought from Colorado were sent back to Denver in the charge of Captain Pollock, Quartermaster for Colorado Volunteers, since other transportation had been provided from the facilities of Fort Union.

When records were compared it appeared that Colonel Slough's commission antedated that of Colonel Paul. Accordingly, as the senior officer present in the area, Colonel Slough assumed command of all Union forces in the Northern District of New Mexico.[8] Paul had been planning to proceed south with a column to join Colonel Canby, leaving Fort Union on March 24 and taking a back road east of the Rio Grande valley. Canby's approval of the plan had been received, and Slough decided to

---

[8] Hall, Martin H., "Colorado Volunteers Save New Mexico for the Union" *Mid-America,* Vol. 38: New Series, Vol. 27: No. 4, p. 207.

carry it out. However, during preparations for the march, a dispatch was received from Colonel Canby cancelling the proposed junction of forces, and ordering that Fort Union be held and communications to the east maintained at all costs. Fort Garland was to be destroyed if necessary to prevent its falling into the hands of the Rebels. Paul was instructed to concentrate all Union troops in northern New Mexico at Fort Union and to remain at that post until reinforcements from Kansas, Colorado or California arrived.

Canby's orders to Paul suggested that, pending the arrival of reinforcements, the Union troops engage in partisan operations to harass the invading Texans and to prevent them from securing necessary supplies. When reinforcements arrived in sufficient numbers to enable him to conduct direct operations against the enemy, Paul was instructed to immediately notify Canby of his plans to provide for cooperation by the forces at Fort Craig. Shortly thereafter Canby learned of Slough's assumption of command and sent him substantially the same instructions.[9]

Colonel Paul had been greatly mortified to discover that Slough's commission was prior to his, and, bypassing intermediate commands, he wrote to the Adjutant General protesting the injustice in his loss of the command, which he had organized, to an inexperienced officer. He also asked for an appointment as brigadier general of volunteers to correct this condition and to avoid its repetition.[10]

Slough and Paul were soon in vigorous dispute over the interpretation of Canby's orders and the proper military action to be taken thereunder. Their differencs were probably intensified by Paul's jealousy and Slough's lack of tact. Slough was

---

[9]*Rebellion Records,* Series I, Vol. IX, p. 649.
[10]*Rebellion Records,* Series I, Vol. IX, p. 646.

obviously not strong in leadership. His failure to accompany
his men on their forced march and to share their hardships was
proof of that fact. Also, he was entirely without training or experience in military tactics or strategy, in contrast to both Canby
and Paul, who were professional soldiers. However, he knew
his men well enough to realize that they had come to New Mexico to fight, and that garrison duty at Fort Union would soon
bring them to the brink of mutiny or desertion. They could not
be handled like the regulars. He also seems to have grasped the
value of the offensive in the art of war; and, like many other
contemporary volunteer officers, he was anxious to defeat the
enemy without delay and to thus win military glory. Therefore,
he announced in no uncertain terms that he intended to move
against the enemy, taking not only his own regiment but most
of the other troops at the fort as well.

At this point in the discussion Paul began a series of written
communications with Slough, apparently in an effort to provide
a record to help in proving blame in case of disaster. In one of
his notes Paul stated that he had turned command over to
Slough only to facilitate the plan for a junction with Canby, and
that Slough's decision to move toward the enemy was in violation of Canby's order of March 16. Slough's answer pointed out
that, under Canby's order, he was to be governed by his own
judgment, and that, "if joined by sufficient force," he was
authorized to act independently against the enemy. He also refused to leave the garrison troops requested by Paul, stating
that he needed every available man to insure the success of his
operation.

This reply was a great disappointment to Colonel Paul, who
immediately addressed another communication to the commander of the First Colorado Regiment urging reconsideration.
The Colorado colonel had made up his mind to advance south-

ward toward the Confederates, and could see no point in further letter writing on the subject. Therefore, he made no effort to answer Paul's last letter. This so disturbed the former commander of the Northern District of New Mexico that he wrote again to the Adjutant General "to throw the responsibility of any disaster which . . . (might) occur on the right shoulders." In the expectation of such a misadventure he asked for reinforcements of four thousand men and several batteries of the best artillery.

At about noon on March 22, Colonel Slough moved out of Fort Union with a command of 1,342 men which included most of the available regular and volunteer troops, leaving only a very small force to garrison the post.[11] The advancing column consisted of the First Regiment Colorado Volunteers, 916 men; Captain W. H. Lewis' battalion (two companies) of the Fifth Infantry and Captain James H. Ford's independent company of Colorado Volunteers, 191 men; Captain John F. Ritter's battery of four guns, 53 men; and Lieutenant Ira W. Claflin's battery of four small howitzers, 32 men. The remainder of Slough's command, Captain George H. Howland's detachment of the First and Third Cavalry, with a strength of one hundred and sixty men, was already well in advance of the main body on a scouting expedition.

There was considerable confusion in getting the column on the road. The night before, some of the members of the First had made another raid on the sutler's cellar and secured a quantity of whiskey, wine and canned delicacies. A number of the culprits, knowing of the impending movement from the earlier published orders, had gone ahead to secrete some of the plunder. Prior to the departure of the main column, a squad of

---

[11]*Rebellion Records,* Series I, Vol. IX, p. 534

BRIGADIER-GENERAL HENRY H. SIBLEY
—*Courtesy, State Historical Society of Colorado.*

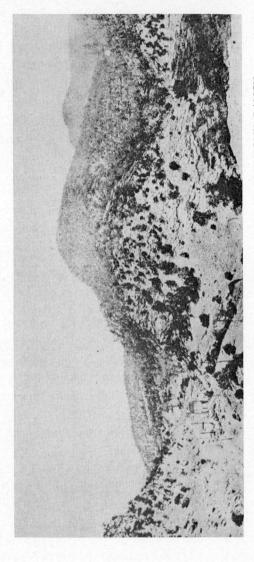

WESTERN ENTRANCE TO LA GLORIETA PASS, AT JOHNSON'S RANCH

—Courtesy, State Historical Society of Colorado.

regulars was sent to apprehend any men found with the stolen goods, but they had no desire to interfere with the wild "Pike's Peakers" and took care to find no missing property. The main body camped the first night out on a small stream only eight miles from Fort Union. A considerable portion of the command was scattered along the line of march drinking and burying loot.[12] Many other members of the First spent the night at a little Mexican village called Loma about five miles from the fort, carousing with the women and fighting with the men. The Fighting Parson decided that some of them had fared badly, judging from their appearance the next morning.

With their night of dissipation over, the Coloradoans were willing to submit to march discipline. The whole command was on the march early the next day, with the men of the First full of enthusiasm and well pleased at the prospect of action at last. Good progress was made for two days, and on the night of the 24th the column reached Bernal Springs, about forty-five miles south of Fort Union and forty miles east of Santa Fe. The main body camped here, while Company F proceeded eight miles farther and joined the advance cavalry detachment under Captain Howland at San Jose.[13]

It has been said that the Texans, when first informed of some newly arrived Colorado troops who were defending Fort Union, dubbed them the "Pet Lambs of Colorado," and so referred to them until the day of the second battle in Glorieta Pass. At Bernal Springs Slough's command was near the eastern approach to this pass, and at the same time Major Pyron, with Sibley's advance guard, had reached a point in the vicinity of the western

---

[12]Hollister, *History of the First,* p. 55.
[13]Hollister, *History of the First,* p. 58.

end of the pass. Thus the stage was set for a fierce and decisive, though brief, struggle between those two hardy groups of frontiersmen, "Baylor's Babes" and the "Pet Lambs of Colorado."

VIII

The Fight In Apache Canyon

IN HIS advance south from Fort Union, Slough was following
the Santa Fe Trail, which was the only practical wagon road
to the valley of the Rio Grande. Sibley used the two routes
which were available as far as the western end of Glorieta Pass.
The main body followed a reasonably adequate trail from Albuquerque to Galisteo, and thence northeasterly for fifteen miles
for a junction with the Santa Fe Trail at the western entrance to
the pass. The advance guard under Major Pyron used the Santa
Fe Trail all the way. Thus control of Glorieta Pass was the
strategic key to success for either side.

The elevation of the summit of the pass is seven thousand
five hundred feet. To the north it is flanked by rugged mountains up to ten thousand feet in height, while on its south it is
bordered by a great round mesa. The western approach was by
way of a relatively steep trail up the Apache Canyon, while the
road from the east wound through juniper and piñon studded
hills, with a final short, steep climb to the top of the grade. The

pass is very narrow at each end, but nearly a quarter of a mile wide in the center. On each side are abrupt, brush covered slopes from one to two thousand feet in height.

Upon arriving at Bernal Springs, Colonel Slough decided to send a rapidly moving, small column to make a night march southwesterly, resting by day and continuing the next night to Santa Fe. Here the detachment was to make a surprise attack on the enemy, destroying his supplies and spiking his guns, and then fall back on the main body. For this purpose he organized a provisional battalion of four hundred and eighteen men consisting of Captain Howland's regular cavalry, Captain Cook's mounted Company F and sixty men each of Companies A, D and E First Colorado, commanded by Captains Wynkoop, Downing and Anthony, respectively.[1] The infantry was assigned sufficient wagons to carry all of the men and to thus increase the mobility of the command. Slough seems to have been uninformed of the movements of the Confederates, and to have had no idea of the location and strength of the units in his path.

Major Chivington had been taken sick during the march on the 24th and forced to fall out and rest at a wayside store for several hours. Arriving late at Bernal Springs he learned of the colonel's plan and was assigned to lead the raiding column in place of Captain Wynkoop, who, as the senior captain, had originally been designated for this duty in the major's absence.

Late in the afternoon of the 25th the infantry section moved out of camp, riding in wagons. They met the cavalry at San Jose, and the entire column marched twenty miles farther to reach Koslosky's ranch at the crossing of the Pecos River at 10 P.M.[2] Here Chivington learned from the ranchmen that heavily armed and well mounted Confederate scouts had visited the place in

---

[1] *Rebellion Records*, Series I, Vol. IX, pp. 530-531 (Chivington Rept.).
[2] Hollister, *History of the First*, p. 59.

the early evening. With this evidence of the proximity of the enemy, the major considered that in spite of his orders for a night march, he was justified in halting to determine the approximate strength and location of the opposing forces. He immediately sent Lieutenant Nelson forward with twenty men from F Company under instructions to find and capture the Rebel scouts, and meanwhile the remainder of the command was allowed to rest until morning. Before daybreak Lieutenant Nelson surprised the Confederate outpost in a poker game at Pigeon's ranch, in the eastern entrance of the pass, and captured all of the group without firing a shot or giving alarm to the enemy.[3]

Just at daylight Lieutenant Nelson returned and reported that he had captured an enemy picket, consisting of seven men and two officers, including a Lieutenant McIntyre who had served on Canby's staff at Valverde and later deserted. "Good work, Lieutenant," the major said. "Have the prisoners brought here. I want to question them." From the captured scouts he learned that Sibley's advance guard was encamped at Johnson's ranch at the western end of Glorieta Pass with orders to move on Fort Union the following day. Nevertheless, the doughty major decided to continue his advance, as a reconnaissance in force without artillery.

The Fighting Parson broke camp at eight o'clock on the morning of March 26, and set out for the pass with his little command. His advance guard was thrown out well ahead, followed by the infantry, and the cavalry brought up the rear, marching in order of rank, which placed Company F as the second unit in the mounted column. As the command advanced leisurely, scouts kept coming back with information which confirmed the intelligence received the night before. The Union column passed the

[3]Chivington, "The Pet Lambs" *Denver Republican*, Apr. 20, 1890, p. 24.

ruins of the Pecos pueblo and the old Franciscan mission, and soon reached the ranch of Alexander Valle, a Frenchman who had been given the nickname of "Pigeon" due to his peculiar style of dancing at parties. Like Koslosky's it was used as a hostelry for travelers, and it was the largest and most convenient one on the trail from Las Vegas to Santa Fe. It was located in a very narrow canyon, the floor of which was entirely taken up by the ranch buildings, the road, and an arroyo which contains a small stream during some seasons of the year.

Marching past Pigeon's ranch the command reached the summit of the pass within a mile and a half, and began the descent into Apache Canyon at about one P.M. At a sharp turn in the road the advance guard came suddenly on the Rebel advance, consisting of a lieutenant and thirty men, who were surprised in a thicket and captured without firing a shot. One of the Union pickets came charging back to the main body to announce the approach of the enemy, crying "We've got them corralled this time. Give them hell, boys. Hurrah for the Pike's Peakers!" Immediately the ranks closed up, the cavalry took open order by fours, and the entire battalion advanced on the double quick, discarding knapsacks, canteens, overcoats and miscellaneous clothing and equipment as the men stripped for action.[4] The captured Rebels were disarmed and sent back to Colonel Slough's headquarters under guard, where they joined the previously captured prisoners. The major again threw out his advance and continued down the canyon.

On turning a short bend in the trail, they entered the canyon proper and observed the Texans coming up the road in force. The advancing column included two howitzers, which were escorted by a company of cavalry displaying a red flag with the

---

[4]Hollister, *History of the First*, p. 61.

lone star emblem. It was the advance guard of Sibley's brigade, under the command of Major Pyron, which had been marching for about two hours after leaving their camp at the western end of the pass. The Confederates were undoubtedly extremely surprised to discover, without any forewarning, that they were faced with a determined foe only a third of a mile away and eager for an encounter. The Rebel force halted at once, took up position and opened fire in an effort to exploit its advantage in artillery.

Major Chivington sized up the situation and immediately ordered his infantry to take cover on the slopes of the canyon. Under the spur of artillery bombardment with shells and grape shot flying at close range, the troops needed no urging, and one wing flew into either hill. Captain Howland's company of regular cavalry parted either way and filed to the rear in confusion, leaving Captain Cook's mounted company facing the enemy alone in the road.

The entire area was in confusion, with the regular cavalry officers plunging wildly from place to place and unable to exercise any control over themselves or their men. Chivington was placing his infantry in position on the sides of the canyon where they would be beyond the uphill range of the artillery, and Cook's cavalry awaited orders while the shells were screaming over them.[5]

By vigorous measures the major restored order in the command. The mounted units were all sent to the rear, where they were held in reserve in cover of a gorge in the mountain, and placed under the command of Captain Howland. The captain was ordered to keep a close watch on the enemy and at the first sign of his retreat to charge him with the entire force and cap-

[5]Hollister, *History of the First,* p. 62.

ture the guns if at all possible. Captains Wynkoop and Anthony advanced through the timber on the left side of the canyon with their companies deployed as skirmishers, while Captain Downing and his men performed the same maneuver on the right.

The progress of the troops was slow along the rough mountainside, but after some little time they gained the flanks of the enemy and proceeded to pour a volume of well directed small arms fire into his ranks. Then they advanced down the steep slopes driving in his supports. Since the Rebels were unable to reach their foe firing uphill, they soon found their position in the road untenable. Accordingly, they broke battery and taking their little red clout, retired rapidly down the trail for about a mile to a sharp left turn in the canyon, where their infantry was concealed in the rocks on either side. Crossing an arroyo approximately sixteen feet in width, which traversed the canyon wandering from side to side, they tore up the log bridge over the channel and set up their howitzers to command the road. The Rebel commander took up a strong position—a stream nearly twenty feet deep with vertical banks on his front and a high ridge at his back. He threw his supports high up the sides of the mountains to avoid a repetition of the Union flanking attack.

Since Captain Howland failed to carry out his orders to charge the enemy as he was leaving the field in a broken condition, the full benefit of the successful flanking attack was lost. The Federal forces followed the retreating Confederates cautiously down the road until they reached a projecting point of rock, under the cover of which they halted to prepare for another attack. The enemy was holding a very strong position which could be taken only by the exhibition of exceptional bravery and skillful maneuver. Nevertheless, the Fighting Parson proceeded at once with the execution of a plan for the assault of what amounted to a natural fortress. The regular cavalry was dismounted, every fourth man left to hold the horses, and the remainder assigned to serve as infantry under the command of Captains Wynkoop and Downing.[6] Once more Captain Downing was ordered to take his command up the steep mountain on the right to gain a position above the Texan supports, while Captains Wynkoop and Anthony executed the same movement on the left. Captain Sam Cook with his mounted company was placed in reserve under cover from artillery fire, with instructions to charge the enemy on the major's signal or the first sign of a Rebel retreat.[7]

The movements for the deployment of forces, which were carried out under enemy fire, were directly supervised by Chivington on horseback "with a pistol in each hand and one or two under his arms." He gave his orders with great energy, gnawing at his lips as he thought of his new responsibility, but with no apparent thought of personal danger. "Of commanding presence, dressed in full regimentals, he was a conspicuous mark for the Texan sharpshooters." One of the Confederates who was taken prisoner later stated that he had emptied his revolver three times at the major and ordered his company to fire a volley at him, but "he galloped unhurt through the storm of bullets."[8]

The flanking forces advanced slowly and cautiously along the rough mountainsides, but they reached their goal above the Rebel supports within about an hour. After a stubborn resistance, the Texans were driven in toward the center of the canyon. Sensing that the moment for another Confederate withdrawal was at hand, the major signaled to his reserve. "Quick as a flash of gunpowder," Company F dashed down the canyon, Captain

---

[6]Chivington, *The Prospective (Retrospective)*, pp. 28-29.
[7]Chivington, *First Colorado Regiment*, p. 7.
[8]Hollister, *History of the First*, p. 62.

Cook in the lead, with his sword "gleaming in the sunlight like a streak of lightning athwart the heavens."[9]

The ground was unfavorable for the action of cavalry. The deep trench, worn by the action of water, confined the attackers to the rough, narrow road between the trench and the hill, and forced them to approach the battery by column directed fairly at its face. At the bend in the canyon there was a high, steep, rocky bluff immediately to the front of the attacking column, upon which the enemy had posted a full company of infantry. The battery was mounted on a mound at the base of this hill. Although the advancing cavalrymen could not see beyond this point, it was obvious that there was ample opportunity for the concealment of a heavy support, and it was apparent that the bluffs and road beyond the bend were well garrisoned. To add to the difficulties the horses were weak and thin and they had a sixteen foot arroyo to jump.

Captain Cook was wounded in the first volley, receiving a one ounce ball and three buckshot in the thigh. He kept his seat in the saddle, but two hundred yards farther on his horse stumbled and he was thrown to the ground, spraining his ankle and getting another wound in the foot. He managed to limp to one side as the charge swept on down the canyon under the leadership of Lieutenant Nelson. Only one of the horsemen in the company failed to force his horse to make the jump across the arroyo at the site of the missing bridge. His horse fell back on him, rendering him a cripple for life.

Reaching the bend in the canyon, the Colorado cavalrymen were met by terrific bursts of small arms fire. Pausing slightly, they discharged a volley from their revolvers at the bluff above them, swept around the point, broke the center of the Texan

---

[9]Chivington, *The Prospective (Retrospective)*, p. 29.

line and ran over the enemy reserves.[10] The enemy artillery, having secured an early lead, proved to be too fleet footed to be overtaken, and escaped down the canyon. The confused enemy reserves left their post in the road, and fought like tigers at bay, from cover in the rocks along the slopes. The Union infantry under Captains Downing, Wynkoop and Anthony came charging down the sides of the canyon. Terrified at this impetuous attack, the Rebel forces broke and fled the field in a disorderly retreat, leaving many of their number prisoners in the hands of the Northerners.[11]

The Union forces had won a complete victory, but not without cost. Several of Captain Cook's men lay dead and there were a number of wounded, as well as some missing horses which had escaped when their riders were unhorsed. Within half an hour after the charge, the enemy had vanished and the firing had ceased. It was now sundown; and, lacking information of possible enemy reinforcements, the Northern troops hastily gathered up their dead and wounded and several of the enemy's, and fell back to Pigeon's ranch, where they camped for the night.[12] The main ranch building was converted into a hospital for both the Union and Confederate wounded.

Chivington kept his force on the alert throughout the night and maintained an outpost in the canyon, since he was apprehensive of a possible night or early morning attack from the main body of the enemy. Captain Lord and his company of dragoons left for the rear with the Texan prisoners and a report to Colonel Slough, giving the details of the engagement and urging that the reserves be brought forward to ward off a possible Rebel attack in force. On the morning of the 27th, after burying

---

[10]Hollister, *History of the First*, p. 64.
[11]Hollister, *History of the First*, pp. 64-65.
[12]*Rebellion Records*, Series I, Vol. IX, pp. 530-531.

the dead, the major fell back five miles to Koslosky's ranch where there was a more adequate supply of water, as well as a better position for attack or defense in case of an encounter with the enemy. The wagons were sent out, and brought back a supply of flour and corn previously stored by the Rebels near Pigeon's, which formed a welcome addition to the scanty available rations.

Although the numbers engaged in the Apache Canyon encounter were comparatively small, the fighting was furious; and, on the Union side, the action was carried forward with judgment and enthusiasm. The Northern forces suffered losses of five killed, thirteen wounded and three missing. In addition, Lieutenant Marshall of F Company was accidentally shot while breaking a prisoner's musket over a rock, and died within a few hours. Captain Cook, who was seriously wounded but made light of his injuries, was the only other officer casualty. The Confederate losses amounted to thirty-two killed, forty-three wounded and seventy-one prisoners, which included seven captured commissioned officers.

A paroled Texan prisoner wrote to his wife describing the fight in Apache Canyon in a letter which stated in part as follows:

On the 22nd six hundred of us were ordered to march to Apache Cañon to stand picket. . . . On the 26th we got word that the enemy was coming down the cañon in the shape of 200 Mexicans and about 200 regulars. Out we marched with the two cannons, expecting an easy victory; but what a mistake! Instead of Mexicans and regulars, they were *regular demons,* upon whom iron and lead had no effect, in the shape of Pike's Peakers, from the Denver City gold mines. . . .

As I said, up the cañon we went for about four miles, where we met the enemy coming at double-quick, but our grape and shell soon stopped them; but before we could form in line of battle their infantry were upon the hills on both sides of us, shooting us down like sheep. The order was given to retreat down the cañon, which we did about a mile. . . . This was no sooner done than up came the cannons, with the enemy at their heels; but when they saw us ready to receive them they stopped, but only for a short time, for in a few minutes they could be seen on the mountains jumping from rock to rock like so many mountain sheep. They had no sooner got within shooting distance of us than up came a company of cavalry at full charge, with swords and revolvers drawn, looking like so many flying devils. On they came to what I supposed was destruction; but nothing like lead or iron seemed to stop them, for we were pouring it into them from every side like hail in a storm. In a moment these devils had run the gauntlet for half a mile, and were fighting hand to hand with our men in the road. . . .[13]

Immediately upon learning of the engagement, Colonel Slough ordered the main body to join the advance; and, at eleven P.M. of the day following the fight, the command arrived at the Union camp at Koslosky's. The men in the colonel's detachment had heard of the action and were eager to meet the enemy themselves. While the troops slept, Colonel Slough and Major Chivington spent the remainder of the night estimating the situation and planning the next day's operations.

"Major," said the colonel, "you have been in close contact with the enemy. What do you advise?" "According to my best information," the major replied, "we are outnumbered nearly two to one; and the enemy's troops are all veterans. We cannot hope to defeat them in open combat; and, therefore, strategy must be employed." After considerable discussion of various possibilities, a plan was adopted under which Chivington, with a provisional battalion, would bypass the Apache Canyon road and gain the western entrance to the pass by a little used trail through the mountains. Meanwhile the colonel, with the main body, would advance slowly by the main road, with the hope that the enemy might be attacked simultaneously on his front and rear.

---

[13]Whitford, *Colorado Volunteers in the Civil War*, p. 94.

IX

The Battle of Glorieta

UPON THE beginning of hostilities in Apache Canyon, Major Pyron dispatched a swift messenger to Lieutenant Colonel Scurry, commander of the Confederate reserves at Galisteo, informing him that the advance was engaged in a sharp conflict with the enemy and requesting that reinforcements be hastened to his relief. This request met with instant response. Early the following morning, after an all night march, the entire Texan reserve with its supply train reached Pyron's camp at Johnson's ranch in the western entrance to Glorieta Pass.[1]

Expecting an attack at any time, Scurry examined the locality, decided it presented a very strong defense position, and stationed his men to command all approaches. The day having passed without an attack, he decided to advance through the pass, leaving his train behind under a small guard to facilitate

---

[1]*Rebellion Records*, Series I, Vol. IX, p. 542 (Scurry's report).

rapid movement. Scurry's plan of operations was based on a familiarity with the surrounding area. It was his intention to make a rapid march through the pass and to gain the level ground near the Pecos Pueblo, where he could exploit his advantage in veteran assault troops. Thus he expected to secure a victory similar to that which was won at Valverde, largely through his efforts.

Soon after sunrise on March 28, Scurry began his advance with portions of three Texan regiments, one independent company and a battery of three guns,[2] a force of approximately one thousand men. The troops were all fairly well rested and animated with the fullest confidence in the ability of their leader and his subordinate commanders. Further, both officers and men were veterans who had proven their worth in battle. Thus all ranks were imbued with the expectation of an early seizure of Fort Union and its vast supplies, which would insure their possession of the lower ranges of the Rocky Mountains. Including the wagon guards left at Johnson's ranch, Scurry's command comprised the main portion of Sibley's brigade, except for Green's regiment which had been held in Albuquerque for a few days "to check any movement from Fort Craig."[3]

In the meantime Slough had divided his forces in conformity with the plan of operations adopted on the previous night, and early in the morning his forces were on the march. Chivington was assigned a force consisting of Captain Lewis' detachment of the Fifth Infantry; Captain Ford's independent company of Colorado Volunteers and Companies A, B, E and H, First Colorado Regiment, a total of four hundred and thirty men. This unit was ordered to strike the enemy in the rear, proceeding

[2]*Rebellion Records*, Series I, Vol. IX, p. 543 (Scurry's report).
[3]*Rebellion Records*, Series I, Vol. IX, p. 509 (Sibley's report).

along a trail south of Apache Canyon which left the main road about three miles west of Koslosky's.[4] Lieutenant Colonel Manuel Chavez of the New Mexico Volunteers was assigned as guide for the anticipated toilsome and dangerous march.

A small group of cavalrymen was sent on a scouting mission toward Galisteo to avoid a possible surprise attack by any Confederate force which might decide to bypass the main road and strike from the south. The absence of these detachments, men assigned to guard and other duties, together with combat losses, reduced the effective strength of Slough's main body to approximately eight hundred men. His force consisted of Companies C, D, F, G, I and K of the First Colorado; a broken company of New Mexico volunteers; a small detachment of regular cavalry and two light batteries of regular artillery.[5]

The Union commander was marching to meet a confident, well armed and well led force of Confederate veterans which considerably outnumbered his command. Only about one fourth of his men had ever been under fire, and a portion of them were badly fatigued, having reached camp very late the night before after a sixteen hour march of thirty-five miles. In addition, the troops did not regard their colonel with any feelings of affection or confidence, due to his habitual austerity and lack of military experience. Probably it is very seldom that a fighting unit has ever faced battle under much more adverse circumstances.

In view of the longer distance and slower traveling conditions along Chivington's line of march, his battalion moved out first at a rapid pace. Slough followed more leisurely, sending his cavalry in advance with a supply train of over one hundred wagons and its escort in the rear. The different parts of this

[4]Chivington, "The Pet Lambs" *Denver Republican,* April, 20, 1890, p. 24.
[5]Whitford, *Colorado Volunteers in the Civil War,* p. 101.

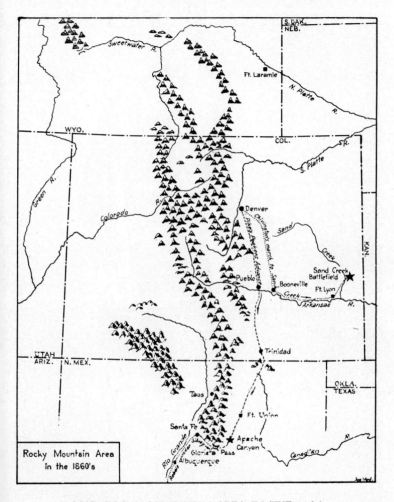

MAP, ROCKY MOUNTAIN AREA IN THE 1860's

CAPTAIN SAM H. COOK
Leader in the Charge at Apache Canyon
—*Courtesy, State Historical Society of Colorado.*

column arrived in the vicinity of Pigeon's ranch at various times between eight-thirty and ten o'clock in the morning. At this point the infantry and supply train were halted for a brief rest, while the cavalry was sent forward to reconnoiter. Company D was kept in line and under arms by its commander, Captain Downing, who sensed the imminence of battle. The rest of the infantry broke ranks and stacked their arms in the road while they visited the wounded in the hospital and filled their canteens from the last supply of water east of Johnson's Ranch. Soon after the men had broken formation, a picket rushed back from the advance with the information that the Rebels were in position for attack concealed in a thick grove of trees about eight hundred yards to the front. Immediately the bugles sounded the assembly, and the command was given to fall in and take arms. However, before the lines were re-formed, the enemy artillery was in position and grape shot and shell were cutting the cottonwood trees above the heads of the troops.[6]

The hostilities opened at nine-thirty in the morning, which was too early to fit into the Union plans since Chivington was far from his objective and unable to strike at the same time. It was also an upset in the Confederate plans, since Scurry was forced to accept battle on rough, broken, timber-covered ground which favored a defense by his outnumbered foes, in lieu of the open location on which he had planned.

Upon approaching Pigeon's, Scurry's advance discovered that the ranch was occupied by a considerable body of Union troops. He halted his command and formed his first line of battle on the most westerly of two parallel ridges, which extended across the canyon from an arroyo a short distance north of the road into the pine forest on the south. His cavalry was dismounted to join

---

[6]Hollister, *History of the First,* p. 68.

the foot troops on the battle line; and the artillery, under the
command of Lieutenant Bradford who had distinguished himself at Valverde, was placed in position on the front of the ridge,
opening fire at once.

The Union cavalry under Captain Walker, upon entering the
gulch between the two ridges, discovered the Texan guns and
battle preparations; and, moving into the timber on the left,
dismounted and formed a line of skirmishers on foot.[7] The
Union batteries, consisting of four guns each, were advanced
and took position on the ridge to the east of the Confederate
position. Captain Ritter's pieces were emplaced on the lower
northerly end of the hill near the road, and Lieutenant Claflin's
guns occupied the southerly end among the trees within sight
of the enemy across the gulch. Both batteries soon opened with
great spirit.[8]

Having been taken somewhat by surprise with the infantry
largely out of formation, there was considerable confusion for
a time. However, order was soon restored and the troops assigned to positions on the line of battle by Lieutenant Colonel
Tappan, who was placed in command of the Colorado Volunteers and regular artillery. Companies C and K were designated
as the support of the batteries, and took their positions in the
road under shelter of the hill. Company D was deployed to the
south and Company I to the north, and from there they advanced
as skirmishers along the flanks of the Texans. Company G was
held about a mile to the rear to form a reserve and to guard
the supply train. In the meantime Scurry had divided his command into three columns. One, under the command of Major
Pyron, was stationed on the right, near the southern end of the

[7]*Rebellion Records,* Series I, Vol. IX, p. 532 (Capt. Walker's rept.).
[8]Hollister, *History of the First,* p. 68.

ridge. One was assigned to Major Raguet and placed in the center near the artillery; and the third, under his personal command, held the northern end of the line beyond the road.

The fighting soon became general and furious along both sides of the battle line. The artillery fire was incessant, and its deafening roar was echoed through the mountains on all sides. This was accompanied by the continuous rattle of small arms and the cheering of the Federal troops, indicating that the battle was initially going well for the outnumbered Coloradoans. As a matter of fact, within a short time the Confederate battery faltered and finally ceased its fire. The Springfield rifles in the hands of the Union troops, which were highly superior to the muskets used by the Texans, had told with deadly effect on the Rebel artillery and its support. The Confederate artillery commander was carried off wounded. All of his horses had been killed and his men retreated in disorder.[9]

Lieutenant Kerber and his Company I endeavored to turn the left flank of the enemy, but Scurry discovered them advancing in an irrigation ditch. The left wing Rebel column charged these German-Americans, opposing the Union bayonets with pistols and machetes; and, after a desperate struggle, forced them to fall back, leaving many dead and wounded. At the opposite end of the Texan line, Major Pyron launched a heavy attack on Captain Downing's Company D, forcing it back with heavy losses.

Following these reverses, Colonel Slough, fearing an immediate charge all along the front by a superior and determined foe, ordered a withdrawal of about four hundred yards. Here a new defense line was formed following the high rocky ground north and south of the arroyo in the vicinity of the ranch house. Cap-

---

[9]Whitford, *Colorado Volunteers in the Civil War*, p. 107.

tain Downing and his company occupied a wooded, rocky bluff at the southern end of the line, and Lieutenant Claflin's battery was stationed on the western slope of this eminence. Initially, Captain Ritter's battery was placed in front of the other artillery position, but it was soon relocated northerly to an emplacement in the road. Artillery supports were strengthened by the commitment of Company G from the reserve; and the remnants of Company I held the northern flank with the support of the cavalry, leaving the command without any reserve.

As soon as the Union troops withdrew from their first ridge position, the Texans took it over, stationed their reorganized artillery on it, and again opened fire on Slough's command. The Union batteries responded with vigor, beginning an artillery duel which lasted for three hours and created a terrific cannonading which reverberated through the high slopes of the canyon and onto distant mesas. Finally the Rebel artillery was put out of action. The sharpshooters of Companies D and I had picked off most of the gunners, while the Federal artillery had dismounted one piece and damaged another.[10] Thus Scurry was forced to rely solely on his infantry and dismounted cavalry, and to attempt to carry the day by bold and repeated charges on the Union positions.

Due to the rough nature of the ground, cavalry was almost useless, and the opportunities for cover and concealment greatly reduced the value of artillery. Therefore, it was apparent from the start that the battle would be decided largely by rifles. Under these circumstances it appears that Slough was in error in not dismounting his cavalry at the start of the engagement. The mounted troops were held in reserve a great part of the day and it seems were never used effectively. Ovando J. Hollister, who

[10]Hollister, *History of the First*, p. 69.

was an enlisted man in Company F of the First Colorado, stated in his *History of the First Regiment of Colorado Volunteers* that "The regular cavalry was of no account at all, for whenever the Texans came in sight they would mount and fall back out of range. Walker's company never discharged a single rifle during the day."

When the Rebel artillery ceased its fire in the early afternoon, Slough sensed that Scurry would be forced to initiate a series of heavy assaults in an effort to force a decision. The Union commander, therefore, rearranged his troops, withdrawing some units to provide better defense positions and to avoid the possibility of encirclement by the superior forces of the enemy. A considerable portion of Company C was withdrawn from the support of Ritter's battery and assigned to strengthen the right flank. The cavalry formed on the left, with the special mission of preventing an enemy thrust around that flank which might endanger the wagon train.

By this time Scurry had received reinforcements to the extent of two companies of fresh troops, numbering approximately one hundred and fifty men. At the sound of the cannon they had deserted their post at Johnson's ranch, declaring that they had "enlisted to get glory by fighting, and not in guarding mules and provisions." The Confederate troops were rearranged in three columns on the ridge which had been captured from the Federals. The Rebel leader then ordered Major John S. Shropshire to launch an attack among the pines on the southern wing of the Union defense line. However, the attack was delayed; and, on visiting the troops on his right wing, Scurry discovered them to be leaderless. There was a section of Captain Cook's gallant Company F stationed immediately to the front of the proposed assault. A private of that company, George W. Pierce, had darted from the ranks, shot and disarmed Shropshire at the head of his column and made a prisoner of Captain D. W. Shannon at his side.[11] Scurry took over command and ordered a charge, which was repulsed.

In an effort to turn the right flank of the Union forces, Scurry next sent two columns under Majors Raguet and Pyron northeasterly across the arroyo and up a rugged slope to the top of a range of hills, with orders to attack Slough's positions in the vicinity of the ranch. However, the Colorado colonel had anticipated this maneuver, and strengthened his line by assigning additional platoons of infantry to the center and relocating his artillery to more effectively protect his right flank. Captain Ritter was sent across the arroyo to the north side of the narrow canyon, while Lieutenant Claflin left his position on the bluff to the south and set up his mountain howitzers in the road not far from Ritter's battery. From their superior positions the troops under Raguet and Pyron opened a heavy fire with their muskets and double-barreled shotguns, and then advanced rapidly, dodging from tree to tree and rock to rock, until they met the Federals at close quarters. On their part, Slough's men poured volley after volley into the ranks of the advancing Confederates, defending their positions stubbornly and falling back slowly onto a ridge of rocks extending northerly from the ranch.

About the middle of the afternoon, in an effort to exploit his success on the left, Scurry reinforced his attacking units with the remaining forces from the right and center of his line, which were assigned to attack positions in and near the road about three hundred yards west of the ranch. It was his intention to capture the Union batteries in the gorge to his front and to drive the enemy infantry from their positions on the rocky ledge. Scurry, Raguet, Pyron and their subordinate officers mingled

---

[11]Whitford, *Colorado Volunteers in the Civil War,* p. 110.

with the men in an effort to inspire them to repeat their gallant charge at Valverde, and to thus save their long and weary campaign which might otherwise well be lost. The men responded with alacrity, and with deafening Rebel yells they charged down the road and along its sides into the face of the Union batteries. The Federal guns opened on them at close range with grape, canister and shell "like a regiment of Mexican dogs roused by the stranger at midnight."[12] Five times they charged and five times the Coloradoans turned them back. At least twice they came to within forty or fifty yards of Claflin's guns, when he gave the order to cease firing and his supports rose from the ground, ran forward and fired a deadly volley into the faces of the enemy. Then, with fixed bayonets, they charged and put the Rebels to flight.

While the main body of the Confederates was making these frontal assaults on the Union line, a detachment of Texans gained possession of the higher ground to the north and poured a deadly stream of small arms fire into the flank of the Federal batteries, rendering their positions untenable. Accordingly, the entire Northern command withdrew in good order down the canyon to the eastern edge of the open field beyond the ranch where they formed their third line of battle with the supply train forty yards to their left. As soon as the Union forces were in position, the Texans made one last desperate charge in an effort to capture the batteries and supply train, but they were again repulsed and driven back in confusion.[13]

Colonel Slough was apprehensive concerning the fate of the detached force under Major Chivington from whom he had received no word since early morning. With this in mind, as well as the superior forces of the enemy and his own heavy losses, at

---

[12]Hollister, *History of the First*, p. 71.
[13]Whitford, *Colorado Volunteers in the Civil War*, p. 114.

five o'clock in the afternoon he ordered his command to disengage and fall back to its former camp at Koslosky's.[14] The retreat was carried out in good order, with artillery pieces and groups of well guarded wagons withdrawing one after another. Many of the officers and men were enraged at this development, and several of them approached their commander and vigorously upbraided him for his unpopular decision. However, the colonel stood firm, feeling the retrograde movement was not only necessary to protect the command, but that the purpose of his reconnaissance in force, "to annoy and harass the enemy," had been accomplished. Ritter's battery remained in position for some time after the order to retreat had passed along the line. Captain Downing, who had also remained behind, approached the guns and Ritter said, "Captain, you are the only ranking officer left on the field. What are your orders to me?" "Double shot your guns and keep on firing," was the quick reply. [15] However, finding that he was not properly supported, Ritter soon began his preparations for withdrawal.

Just at that time an ambulance was seen approaching from the Confederate lines. Upon reaching Captains Downing and Ritter, three Texan officers alighted and requested a truce until noon of the following day for the care of the wounded and burial of the dead. Captain Downing sent them blindfolded along the road to Koslosky's. Here they met Colonel Slough, who granted their request. Subsequently the armistice was extended to the morning of the second day. Actually, Colonel Scurry needed the break in hostilities for the recuperation of his men more than for the care of the wounded or burial of the dead, since his troops were too exhausted and crippled by the

[14]Chivington, *The First Colorado Regiment*, p. 9.
[15]Whitford, *Colorado Volunteers in the Civil War*, pp. 114-115.

struggle for any further fighting. The battle had lasted eight hours, and neither side had been able to take any rest or refreshment during that period.

The fighting in the gorge near the ranch building was extremely heavy and resulted in severe casualties to the Texans. There they lost three of their bravest and most accomplished officers, Major Raguet, Captain Buckholts and Lieutenant Mills. Several other officers were killed or wounded during the day. Colonel Scurry himself, whose magnificent courage and intrepid leadership won the admiration of the Union troops, had some narrow escapes. In reporting the battle to General Sibley, he stated that "all the field officers on the ground were either killed or touched."

On the Union side the work of the artillery was outstanding, and was probably the only factor that enabled the outnumbered, stubbornly fighting infantry to hold their own against well led, brave and determined veterans. The guns were well served throughout the day under the leadership of Captain Ritter and Lieutenant Claflin. No braver nor more skillful artillery officers ever fought in the American army. Just prior to the heavy fighting in the gorge Captain Ritter lost his two able lieutenants, Peter McGrath of the regular cavalry and Clark Chambers of Company C, First Colorado.

In the meantime, unknown to Colonel Slough, the detachment under Major Chivington had inflicted a crushing disaster on the Confederate rear areas, which was the compelling reason for Scurry's request for an armistice. Leaving the camp at Koslosky's soon after sunrise, this column marched past the old Pecos Pueblo and turned off the main road a mile further west where a trail leads southerly through the San Cristobal Canyon to Galisteo. They had not gone far on this trail when they heard the sound of artillery fire and knew that the engagement had begun. After following this route for approximately eight miles, the detachment turned right and marched eight miles farther west across country, over rocks and through dense thickets of piñon and cedar, towards Johnson's ranch. Lieutenant Flavia, with forty men of the regular cavalry, left the main body at the last turn, and continued down the San Cristobal trail.[16] His mission was to scout toward Galisteo and warn the major of the approach of any enemy troops which would threaten his rear.

The Fighting Parson and his men made all possible speed over the rough terrain to strike an early blow in aid of their outnumbered comrades engaged with the Texan main body. At about one in the afternoon, they reached the top of the mountain immediately above the Confederate rear guard, where they captured an enemy sentry. Lieutenant Colonel Chavez looked down on the camp more than one thousand feet below and remarked to the major, "You are right on top of them." However, before ordering the attack, Chivington spent more than an hour in careful reconnaissance of the situation below,[17] unobserved by the enemy. The ranch house with its outbuildings was in plain view, as well as the road leading from the canyon to Santa Fe and ravines to the right and left. They observed several abrupt knolls with a cannon mounted on the highest of them, the wagons and draft animals in a group at the center and about two hundred guards and teamsters leisurely moving about.

Satisfied that there was no insurmountable difficulty to prevent a successful attack, Chivington gave the order to descend the steep slope, the upper part of which had to be negotiated with ropes and straps. When they had completed about one fourth of the descent the enemy was made aware of their pres-

---

[16]Hollister, *History of the First*, p. 68.
[17]Chivington, "The Pet Lambs" *Denver Republican*, April 20, 1890, p. 24.

ence by the crashing of dislodged rocks which thundered through the brush to the bottom of the slope. Soon the Rebel cannon was manned by a crew of eight men who opened fire on the scattered Federals without effect. Aided by a flattening of the slope, which began about half way down the mountain, the Union forces soon reached the bottom where they again formed into ranks. Panic seized some of the teamsters and guards, who immediately took possession of the nearest horses and mules and fled down the road toward Santa Fe, while others retreated rapidly up the canyon running east from the ranch.[18]

Unaware of the small number of men in the camp and fearing an ambuscade, Major Chivington at first formed his men in line of battle near the ranch buildings in a position to resist an attack from any force which might be concealed in the vicinity. A quick reconnaissance of the surrounding area soon showed his fears to be groundless, and he divided his forces into two columns, sending one to capture the cannon and the other to seize the supply train. Captain Lewis, assisted by Lieutenant B. N. Sanford of Company H, First Colorado, was assigned the more dangerous mission of assaulting the artillery position. With their men, these officers ascended the steep knoll in the face of five rounds fired without effect, spiked the cannon and tumbled it with its carriage down the side of the hill, breaking the wheels.

After a short resistance, the outnumbered wagon guards lost heart and fled, leaving the Federals in possession of the entire Confederate supply train of eighty wagons. This prize included all of Sibley's quartermaster stores, camp and garrison equipage and ordnance supplies, in fact, everything he had for his campaign except for the items carried by the troops in their knapsacks and haversacks.[19] Although Chivington's attack was a

---

[18]Whitford, *Colorado Volunteers in the Civil War,* p. 118.
[19]Chivington, "The Pet Lambs" *Denver Republican,* April 20, 1890, p. 24.

complete surprise to Scurry, he had left a fair-sized force to guard his trains, and if the men had all remained at their posts, the Union maneuver would at least have been more difficult. The Rebel losses at Johnson's ranch amounted to twenty-seven killed, sixty-three wounded and seventeen taken prisoners; but there were no Union casualties.[20]

Since the Fighting Parson was in no position to transport the captured materiel over a road held by the enemy, he ordered its complete destruction. The wagons were assembled in groups, overturned, set on fire with their contents and kept under guard until the ammunition had all exploded and everything was consumed except the metal in the wagons. The draft and riding animals of the enemy, between five and six hundred in number, which were found in a ravine, were bayoneted, and the troops began the toilsome climb back up the mountain. While the Federals were occupied in their operation of destruction, a mounted Texan dashed out from behind the ranch house and sped up the road toward Pigeon's ranch, carrying the news of the disaster to Scurry. For his part, Chivington received a pessimistic account of the progress of the fighting at Pigeon's from five Union soldiers who had been captured and sent to the rear and later released by his attack.

It was sundown when the Union command reached the top of the mountain, and the Fighting Parson assembled his men with a great feeling of relief arising from the failure of the enemy to interfere with the most precarious part of their withdrawal. He looked back on the scene of desolation with a feeling of satisfaction mingled with a sense of sadness for the predicament in which he had been forced to place a gallant foe. At this point they met Lieutenant Cobb of Company C, First Colorado, who

---

[20]*Rebellion Records*, Series I, Vol. IX, p. 538 (Chivington's report).

had been detailed as aide-de-camp to Colonel Slough. He brought a message advising that the battle had gone badly for the Northerners, who had retreated to Koslosky's, and directing the major to join them there, if he could possibly escape the enemy.

By this time it was pitch dark and the Fighting Parson was faced with the necessity of traversing over six miles of rugged country, covered with a tangled mass of trees and brush, which in many places formed interlacing branches not over two feet from the ground. Further, in view of the information received from the prisoners released at Johnson's ranch and the message of Lieutenant Cobb, it appeared that the Rebels were in full control of the area around Pigeon's ranch. Therefore, a return by the same route used in the morning would place the force in great danger of interception by the enemy, either on the San Cristobal Trail or the main Santa Fe Trail. In this emergency there was no available guide, due to the refusal of Lieutenant Colonel Chavez to accept the responsibility of attempting to take any other route than the one used in the advance.

While Chivington was conferring with his aides, a Mexican Catholic priest rode up on a white horse and greeted the officers in Spanish. Colonel Chavez replied in the same tongue. After a short conversation, he turned to the major and said: "This is Padre Ortiz of the Pecos Pueblo, who is well known to me. He offers to lead us over the mountains to our camp by a shorter road paralleling Glorieta Pass. He says that we must avoid our old trail which is in the hands of the Texans. I believe we should use his services." Chivington agreed and the march was resumed. Leading his own horse, the Fighting Parson walked behind the mounted priest, and the remainder of the command managed to follow. In intense darkness, over rocks and ridges, through narrow defiles and over a pathless route, their guide conducted them in safety to the main road near the Pecos Pueblo. Here they halted briefly, fearing the proximity of the enemy, but there was no sign of danger, and they continued their march. Finally, at ten P.M., hungry and tired, they came within sight of the Union camp fires, without knowing however whether they belonged to friend or foe. One of the officers said, "Major, is this our camp, or is it the Rebel camp?" Chivington replied, "If it is not ours, we will soon make it ours; close up ranks, fix bayonets as silently as possible, forward double-quick!"[21]

The hail of the sentry soon apprised them by his accent that the location was indeed occupied by Yankees, and the major marched his little command into the camp, where they stacked arms. When the news of the disaster to the enemy train spread through the command the men went wild with joy. After struggling all day with a superior foe and withdrawing from the field, the knowledge that the Rebels must now retreat or starve was almost beyond belief.

The records and official reports are at variance concerning the losses of the two armies in the Battle of Glorieta. The reports of both Colonel Slough and Lieutenant Colonel Tappan seem to have placed the Union casualties far below the correct figures. From an actual tabulation of the names of the known killed and wounded and reliable estimates of the missing, as taken from the records of the Colorado Adjutant General, newspaper files of 1862, Hollister's *History of the First* and other reliable sources, it appears that the losses suffered in the two battles near Glorieta by the Colorado volunteers alone amounted to forty-eight killed, sixty-five wounded and twenty-one prisoners in the hands of the enemy. To these figures should be

---

[21]Hollister, *History of the First*, p. 72.

added the not inconsiderable casualties sustained by the other units and detachments, amounting to approximately twenty-five per cent of the Union forces. In the absence of more accurate information, it can only be said that the losses of Colonel Slough's command on the 28th of March were at least equal to one fifth of the number of Union troops engaged. The best estimate of the Confederate casualties was secured from their surgeon's book discovered at Albuquerque, which showed two hundred and eighty-one killed, two hundred wounded and one hundred prisoners, or a total of five hundred and eighty-one for the two engagements.[22]

---

[22]Hollister, *History of the First*, p. 76.

X

The Rebel Retreat

CHIVINGTON'S attack on the Confederate rear at Johnson's ranch was fatal, not only to Scurry's advance, but to the entire Texan campaign. Although Scurry reported to Sibley that he had won "another victory," he mentioned the destruction of his train, and asked for more ammunition. He delayed at Pigeon's ranch for two days following the battle, without blankets or rations; and, at the end of that time, retreated to Santa Fe in search of supplies.[1]

Hearing of the engagement, Sibley hurried to Santa Fe to take personal charge of the main body. Upon receipt of urgent requests from Colonel Green in Albuquerque for support to protect the limited Confederate supplies from capture by Federal troops advancing from Fort Craig, Sibley ordered a retreat from Santa Fe without delay.[2] Although his final decision to abandon

[1] *Rebellion Records*, Series I, Vol. IX, p. 542 (Scurry's report).
[2] *Rebellion Records*, Series I, Vol. IX, p. 510 (Sibley's report).

the campaign was not made until later, this was, in effect, the beginning of the Confederate evacuation of the area. The Pike's Peakers had saved the Far West for the Union, but their decisive defeat of the enemy does not appear to have been appreciated by the department commander.

Although not appointed brigadier general until May, Canby was sometimes accorded this title, and he must have anticipated promotion in the absence of defeat. In any event, it seems he was wary of a possible Confederate resumption of the initiative. Although there was no further word on the reports of the year before of a Rebel force assembling in north Texas, he apparently was still fearful of a possible attack from that quarter. In any event, on March 29, the day following the battle, Colonel Slough received positive orders to retire at once to Fort Union "to protect it at all hazards and to leave nothing to chance." Disgusted with this denial of the opportunity to pursue and destroy the defeated enemy, Slough ordered the march of his command to Fort Union, and at once forwarded the resignation of his commission. He may also have been thinking of a possible court-martial, since Canby considered his advance on the Confederates to be a breach of orders. Later in the war he served as a brigadier general in command of the Military District of Alexandria, Virginia.

When the victorious Union forces reached Fort Union they found that the post was in no danger. Within a few days orders were received for all possible reinforcements to join General Canby, who had left Fort Craig on April 1 and was approaching Albuquerque. Leaving a small garrison at the fort, the expedition set out for the south on April 5, with Colonel Paul in command and Colonel Slough still leading the First Colorado Regiment. Although the Colorado troops had been disgusted with previous orders, a brief address by Major Chivington outlining the ob-

jectives of the new orders resulted in a raising of morale. With
the cavalry in advance they marched rapidly toward a junction
with Canby. On the night of the 12th Slough received word
that his resignation was accepted, and his parting address was
published to the regiment on parade.[3]

Meanwhile the Confederates had completed preparation for
a rapid retreat down the Rio Grande valley to Texas. Assembling a small store of supplies and a few wagons from local resources, the Texans evacuated Santa Fe on the 5th and 6th of
April, leaving their more seriously sick and wounded behind.
As Canby approached Albuquerque on the 8th, he found Sibley
already in control of the old part of town along the river bank,
with his cannon in place at different points in the area. Artillery
duels and sharp skirmishes continued for two days. Finally
Canby concluded that he could accomplish no useful results
with his small force, and retired northeasterly to the Sandia
Mountains. Marching by night for fifteen miles, he eventually
went into camp at Tijeras in Carnuel Canyon, and settled down
to wait for the arrival of reinforcements from Fort Union.

Canby's withdrawal left Sibley free to continue his retreat
unhindered. He had buried some of his original brass artillery
pieces in Santa Fe. Having exhausted his ammunition for these
guns, he buried the remainder in Albuquerque, keeping only the
six cannon he had captured at Valverde. The carriages of the
buried guns were pressed into service as transportation. On the
12th and 13th of April the Confederates evacuated Albuquerque. One column crossed the river and proceeded down the west
bank to Las Lunas. The remainder of the force followed the
east bank, and went into camp on the ranch of Territorial Governor Connolly near Peralta, across the river from Las Lunas.

---

[3]Hollister, *History of the First*, p. 86.

Sibley remained here almost two days, occupying the governor's large residence and with his men encamped behind the protection of high adobe walls which enclosed the cultivated portion of the ranch.[4]

Starting long before daylight on April 13, Colonel Paul's command made a forced march of forty-two miles from Galisteo over desert and rough terrain to join General Canby at his camp in Carnuel Canyon. After fourteen hours on the trail, the thirsty and exhausted troops arrived at about dusk, having left many dead horses and mules along their route of march. Upon arrival, Lieutenant Colonel Tappan presented to the general a petition, signed by all the officers of the unit, requesting the appointment of Major Chivington as the colonel of the First Colorado Regiment. Canby agreed, and, by a field order dated the next day, the requested appointment was made, subject to approval of the Governor of Colorado, which was later received. This action won approval from all ranks. Almost from the beginning of the campaign, Chivington had been the real leader of the regiment by reason of his personality, popularity and superior ability.[5]

Setting out on the 14th, Canby marched thirty-six miles, going into camp late at night without the enemy's knowledge, although the Texans at the governor's ranch were only about a mile away. Chivington's men had insured secrecy by capturing the Rebel pickets. Soon after camp was made, Lieutenant Colonel Chavez, who was serving as guide and scout for the First Colorado, reported to the Fighting Parson. "I have been all through the enemy's camp," he said, "and found no commissioned officers on duty. They are all up in the governor's ranch house holding a big *baile* with the local *muchachas,* and drinking heavily.

---

[4]Whitford, *Colorado Volunteers in the Civil War,* p. 130.
[5]Whitford, *Colorado Volunteers in the Civil War,* p. 130.

Your splendid regiment, my colonel, could easily take the camp and capture all the officers." Chivington took this information to Canby and offered the services of his regiment for an immediate attack. With his usual caution the general refused, saying, "Night attacks are very dangerous, and especially so for the attacking party." After some further discussion, Canby agreed to consider the matter and to advise the colonel if he decided to attack.

There was no further word from the general during the night. At sunrise next morning, Canby's man lit a fire to make some coffee for the general. At about the same time the Union buglers sounded reveille. In reply the Rebel band played "Dixie," and all thoughts of any surprise were at an end.[6] The Confederates soon trained their battery on the Federal camp and began firing. Canby and Chivington were standing near the general's head-quarters mule team discussing the situation when a solid shot from an enemy six-pounder took the head off one of the mules. Calmly the general announced. "I think we had better retire to a safer position."

At this point a small Confederate supply train was seen approaching from Albuquerque, with an escort of one officer and thirty men. Turning to the Colorado commander, the general said, "Now, Colonel, you have been so anxious for something to do, capture that detachment, taking such force as you may deem sufficient."[7] The Fighting Parson detailed Company H and the horsemen of Company F, which included only thirty-two men still with usable mounts, and those in poor condition as a result of recent forced marches. Although the Texans put up a sharp fight, they were soon defeated with a loss of six men killed, three wounded and the remainder of the escort made

[6]Hollister, *History of the First*, p. 92.
[7]Chivington, "The Pet Lambs" *Denver Republican*, April 27, 1890, p. 24.

prisoners. The Pike's Peakers captured seventy mules, seven wagons, ten to fifteen horses and one howitzer.

Canby divided his forces into two sections, one, including the First Colorado, under Colonel Paul, and the other under his personal command. Paul was sent forward to a position in an open space near the river, where he lost several men from artillery fire. Chivington protested to Paul against maintaining this exposed position, and was advised that the general's orders were to clear the woods without bringing on a general engagement. The Fighting Parson replied, "If I were under such orders I would clear the woods of the Rebels, and if in doing that I brought on a general engagement, fulfilling the first paragraph of my order would be my excuse for so doing."[8]

After some further discussion Chivington was ordered to attack with one battalion, with the support of a second battalion if necessary. Accordingly, Major Wynkoop was sent forward with the First Battalion, deploying his men as skirmishers. Later Chivington supported the attack with the Second Battalion, and the two units drove the Confederates from the woods and silenced their battery. This action forced the enemy from the ranch into a grove of trees along the river, where they were joined during the day by reinforcements from the main column on the opposite bank.

Indecisive skirmishing and exchanges of artillery fire continued until night, with some advantage for the Federals. At ten o'clock in the evening, without any hindrance from the Union forces, Sibley withdrew all his troops from the eastern side of the river, leaving some sick and wounded behind; and by morning his entire force had advanced five miles down the west bank of the river. There is evidence that Canby was well aware that

---

[8]Chivington, "The Pet Lambs" *Denver Republican,* April 27, 1890, p. 24.

this enemy movement was taking place, and still made no effort to interfere. Thus ended the last battle between the Confederates and Federals in this campaign, and there was considerable disgust in the ranks of the Colorado Volunteers. Canby's actions at Peralta and during the remainder of his "pursuit" of Sibley's column, which resulted in the escape of the remnants of the Rebel force, were never forgiven by the Union people of New Mexico, nor by many of his soldiers. It was intimated by many that Canby deliberately allowed Sibley to escape because he was Canby's brother-in-law, or due to misplaced sentiment toward a former comrade-in-arms. One of the Colorado soldiers who served in the campaign probably expressed the general feeling when he later wrote: "Of what avail our forced marches? Our regiment has made great efforts and sacrifices to meet the vile traitors, and to see them escape when actually within our grasp, from the stupidity or treachery of our general, effectively kills our enthusiasm if it goes no further."[9]

In Canby's defense, it should be noted that he probably thought it better for the Confederates to make their escape providing their own supplies than for him to take them prisoners and be required to feed them from his scanty stock of provisions. He intimated as much to Chivington when he disapproved of a night attack at Peralta. He also has been quoted as saying that he considered one honest man's life to be worth ten of theirs, which would logically account for his refusal to fight except under superior advantages.

During the 16th and 17th of April the two commands proceeded south on opposite sides of the stream, often within easy artillery range of each other.[10] However, Canby was never able to get far enough in advance to cross the swollen stream in the

---

[9]Hollister, *History of the First*, p. 95.
[10]Chivington, *First Colorado Regiment*, p. 10.

face of enemy artillery fire. On the night of the 17th they camped
almost opposite and within sight of each other. However, at
daybreak, Canby discovered that the enemy was gone, although
many of his camp fires were still burning. In order to avoid further contact with the Federal troops, Sibley had taken an old
path twenty miles west of Fort Craig, which passed through the
San Mateo Mountains and returned to the river thirty miles
below the fort. Setting fire to most of his remaining wagons,
and leaving his sick and wounded, he packed his scanty supplies
on the backs of mules, took his ambulances and set out before
dawn in a blinding sandstorm.[11]

For ten days the Confederates followed the trail over one
hundred miles of mountain and desert, enduring great hardships and suffering from lack of food and water. They abandoned nearly all of their ammunition and almost everything else
not carried on their persons. When Sibley finally reached the
river he was met by a supply train which had been sent from
Mesilla, and the demoralized remnants of the Sibley Brigade
were enabled to make their way back down the river to Texas.
Sibley arrived in El Paso during the first week in May, with his
command still strung out behind him for fifty miles up the valley of the Rio Grande. The results of the struggle through the
desert went a long way in justifying Canby's delaying tactics.
He could not have inflicted much more loss on the Rebels in
hard fought engagements.

In this desperate retreat Sibley's men were unmolested by
Union troops, except for Captain Paddy Graydon and his independent company of New Mexico Volunteers, which served as
a scouting unit for the Federal forces. This organization, which
seems to have been of an irregular or partisan nature, was com-

[11]Chivington, "The Pet Lambs" *Denver Republican*, April 27, 1890. p. 24.

posed of men who had lost heavily by the Texan invasion. Its only cost to the government was for occasional rations and supplies, but the services of the men in the company were invaluable in their operations as spies, scouts and foragers. They had been a thorn in Sibley's side during his advance north, but now their activities were largely limited to gathering intelligence, salvaging discarded property and rescuing abandoned sick and wounded.

Many of Sibley's men died on this terrible march, but he insisted on dragging along the six guns he had captured at Valverde. However, the possession of these trophies was of scant solace to the Confederates, in view of their disastrous losses in the campaign. According to General Canby's report to the Secretary of War, Sibley left behind him, "in dead and wounded, and in sick, prisoners and missing, one-half of his original force.[12]

In contrast to the Confederate debacle, the benefits of the campaign to the Union cause were considerable, since the successful operations of the Colorado troops saved the government the necessity of dispatching large reinforcements from the east. An army of five full regiments and two artillery batteries, with all necessary supplies and equipment, had been concentrated at Fort Riley, Kansas to march to the relief of New Mexico. When news of the victory at Glorieta and Confederate retreat from Santa Fe was received, these forces were diverted to the hard-pressed eastern theatre of operations.

As the Union troops marched south, the volunteers in the command became impressed with Canby's qualities of leadership and gradually lost some of their bitter disapproval of his actions at Peralta. The men usually observed him riding near the head of the column, attended by his staff and an escort of a few cavalrymen. His figure was tall and straight and he was

[12]Whitford, *Colorado Volunteers in the Civil War*, p. 136.

dressed in rough civilian clothes. With a hard and weatherbeaten face, an unlighted cigar in his mouth and a chin covered with a two weeks' growth of grizzly beard, he did not present the smart and polished appearance often affected by military men. Nevertheless, with his commanding presence and his dignified and self-possessed manner, his whole appearance tended to inspire confidence and respect from his followers. At least some of his officers and men came to the conclusion that he was a man of patience, foresight and judgment, and that, although cautious, he was possessed of great physical and moral courage.[13]

After an exhausting march on the previous day, through a sandstorm and without forage, Canby rested in camp on the 19th to rehabilitate his stock. The command had been divided into two provisional brigades, one composed of volunteers under Colonel Chivington, and the other including the regulars under Colonel Paul. The two units were camped in separated but adjoining areas. Early in the afternoon, Canby, with his interpreter and a local citizen of Mexican ancestry, called at Chivington's tent. "Colonel," the general announced, "your troops have been stealing this man's chickens;" and the Mexican shouted, *"Gallinas! Gallinas."* The Fighting Parson asked Canby how he knew what troops were involved, and was advised that the guilty parties wore the uniform of the volunteers, which was different from that of the regulars. Chivington pledged his word to find the stolen chickens, if there were any in his camp.

A short time later, after a thorough search of his area, the colonel reported to his commander that he had found no chickens in the volunteer camp. The general then stated, "I have suffered more annoyance over this petty thieving since your command joined me than I have in twenty years' service in the Regu-

[13]Hollister, *History of the First*, p. 102.

lar Army. This pillaging must be stopped." Just at this point the Mexican recognized the general's striker, rushed into Canby's tent crying, *"Mis gallinas,"* and brought out the stolen chickens. Canby was soon convinced that the regular troops had been foraging in volunteer uniforms to throw suspicion on Chivington's men; and additional evidence of this fact was provided when the colonel discovered pork stolen from local Mexicans in the regular officers' mess. A few months later in Santa Fe the general presented his senior volunteer officer to Mrs. Canby, saying, "My dear, I want to introduce to you this Methodist preacher of Colorado, Colonel Chivington, who once caught me in the very act of being a chicken thief."

On the 20th the Union force crossed over to the west side of the stream and marched leisurely down the river, arriving at Fort Craig on the 22nd of April. Thirty straggler and convalescent Confederates came in and surrendered on the 19th, and seventy-five more on the 21st. They were given the oath of allegiance and released to return to their homes. Some doubt concerning this procedure was expressed in the ranks, where there was a feeling that "their oaths amounted to nothing," and that "we will undoubtedly meet these fellows again whenever we have another engagement."[14]

Upon arrival of the command in the vicinity of Fort Craig, a permanent camp for the First Colorado was established at Valverde seven miles to the north, since the accommodations at the fort were adequate only for the regular troops and the two independent companies of Colorado volunteers. General Canby immediately issued an order placing Colonel Chivington in command of the Military District of Southern New Mexico, with headquarters at Fort Craig and instructions to make sure that

---

[14]Hollister, *History of the First*, p. 102.

the enemy had left the country and did not again pass up the river. Two days later the general and his staff, accompanied by a heavy escort, returned to department headquarters at Santa Fe.

Canby had been met by one commissary train from Fort Union at his camp on the night of the 20th. This provided the men with a welcome change from the monotonous diet of rotted bacon and bread, which, without any soda, salt, coffee or sugar, had formed their ration on the long march south. However, the new supplies were soon exhausted, and for the next six weeks the troops half starved on a ration of six ounces of flour per day each. The trains of needed supplies from the north were delayed by the spring season of high water, which overflowed the river banks and made the roads impassable. Finally, when the first train of twenty wagons did arrive, it was discovered to the astonishment of Colonel Chivington that it carried nothing but whiskey and vinegar.[15]

Adequate commissary supplies became available early in June, and a month later the men of the First received another piece of good fortune which is prized by all soldiers. On July 4th Major Fillmore, Assistant Paymaster of Volunteers, arrived from Denver and paid off the regiment for its first eight months of federal service. Further, having a surplus of funds available, he proceeded to pay the regulars at Fort Craig, many of whom had received no pay for twenty-two months. He brought word that, through his solicitation, the War Department had agreed to pay the drafts issued by Governor Gilpin to defray the costs of raising the regiment.

Also on July 4th, Colonel Howe of the Third Cavalry arrived at Fort Craig and relieved Colonel Chivington in command of the Southern District of New Mexico. He was an old man and

---

[15]Chivington, "The Pet Lambs" *Denver Republican*, April 27, 1890, p. 24.

somewhat infirm, and had asked for an assignment where there would be no fighting. Accordingly, since the Rebels had been driven out of New Mexico, he was assigned to Canby. The Fighting Parson had previously applied for a leave of absence for a trip to Denver to establish recruiting offices to replace the losses in his regiment, and from there to Washington to request service for the unit in an active theatre, as well as a transfer of the regiment from the infantry to the cavalry arm. Under these circumstances he was prepared to leave as soon as possible for Denver by way of Santa Fe, and was, therefore, well satisfied to be replaced in command of the district.

About this time it was learned that the sutler for the regular troops was due to arrive from the north with stores, including tobacco. This was an item which had been unknown by any of the troops at the fort or Camp Valverde for many weeks, and, as a result, both officers and men were cross and irritable. The Pike's Peakers had decided to raid the sutler's train, but the colonel heard of the plan. He assembled the regiment, told the men he knew of their plan and disapproved of it. However, he promised them that if they abandoned their raid, they would have one-half of the tobacco before the train passed through their camp. They readily agreed to this proposal. Chivington rode down to the fort and made a request for tobacco to the officer in command of the regulars. When he was told that there was only enough tobacco for the regulars and that the volunteers must look to their own sutlers, he replied: "It is only a question, sir, as to whether we will have half or all of it. If we have to use force we will take every ounce of tobacco your sutler has, and you will never get one chew, nor any of your men, of that tobacco. We have come down here, done the fighting and marching, endured the privation, relieved you from the grasp that the enemy had upon you, and we don't intend now that we will be cut off with anything less than fair, even-handed dealing."[16] The officer sent for his sutler, explained the situation, and said, "Give Colonel Chivington an order on your wagon boss for one-half of the tobacco he has in his train."

Within a few days, when an overland mail coach passed through on its way to Santa Fe, Colonel Chivington mounted his horse and proceeded to department headquarters, accompanying the coach and its escort. In Santa Fe he advised General Canby of dispatches received from Colonel Carleton at Tucson that he was on his way to Fort Craig with a contingent of California volunteers, which would be available to relieve the First Colorado. With this assurance, the general issued an order for the Colorado colonel to proceed to Denver to open recruiting stations and to superintend the filling up of his regiment. The Fighting Parson left at once for Denver, riding in an ambulance drawn by four mules. There was no escort, and only the colonel, the driver and a Dr. Cass of Denver were in the party. However, they traveled fast and eluded the Southern guerilla bands operating between Fort Union and Pueblo.

Having obtained an order from Headquarters, Department of Kansas, authorizing the trip, the Fighting Parson left for Fort Leavenworth, where, with the help of Senator Lane of Kansas, he managed to get authority to proceed to Washington. Ostensibly this journey was on business connected with recruiting. Once in Washington, he had to wait several days, but was finally able to see Secretary of War Stanton, who refused to transfer the First Colorado to the eastern theatre of war, but granted the request for its conversion from infantry to cavalry. Stanton was impressed with the Colorado colonel and suggested that he stay in Washington as a brigadier general to help train the fresh

---

[16]Chivington, "The Pet Lambs" *Denver Republican,* May 4, 1890, p. 15.

troops coming in. Chivington replied, "I would rather command the First Cavalry of Colorado than to command the best brigade in the Army of the Potomac."[17]

On the way back to Colorado, Chivington stopped at department headquarters, which had been moved to St. Louis, and submitted his authority for conversion of the regiment to General S. R. Curtis, Department Commander. Somewhat to the colonel's annoyance, the general delayed compliance with the War Department orders until he had secured the concurrence of Colorado Governor John Evans, who had succeeded Governor Gilpin. Since Chivington had discussed the proposed change in status with the governor before leaving for Washington, the necessary approval was granted. Conversion of the regiment with authority for the issue of necessary equipment was provided for in Special Order No. 36, Headquarters Department of the Missouri,[18] dated November 1, 1862, which also specified that the regiment would rendezvous in Colorado Territory, with headquarters at Denver.

In the meantime the soldiers of the First Regiment were not too well pleased with the abusive attitude of their new district commander. Matters came to a head when one of the men of Company A was placed under arrest for leaving his post. Somewhat worried at possible results, he managed to get an interview with Colonel Howe. As soon as the district commander realized the nature of the incident in question, he broke into a tirade, saying, "Smart, smart, hellish smart. Won't have nothing to do with it. Hate the volunteers, hate'm, hate'm, hate'm!" Awed at this outburst, the soldier asked concerning the punishment, and the colonel replied, "Oh, shooting affair, shooting affair. Leave

---

[17]Chivingon, "The Pet Lambs" *Denver Republican,* May 4, 1890, p. 15.

[18]Apparently the Dept. of Kansas had been superseded by the Dept. of the Missouri.

the room sir, leave the room. Hate the volunteers. Hell, hell, hell!" When word of this interview reached the men of the regiment, they were soon on the border of mutiny. The Colorado soldiers would never sit idly by while one of their comrades was executed for what they considered to be a minor infraction of the rules. In this emergency Captain Downing approached Howe and dropped some broad hints that the Pike's Peakers were in the habit of hanging officers who didn't suit them. "Hell, hell, hell," said the colonel, "Love the volunteers, always loved the volunteers."[19]

During their stay in southern New Mexico the Colorado volunteers had some experience with marauding Indians. Although not strictly on the warpath, it was customary at all times for the various local tribes to raid the ranches and run off sheep, cattle and other stock. They seldom killed the Mexicans, who practically occupied the status of tenants of the savages, raising sheep and cattle for the use of the Indians. Bold and dexterous in their operations, they would often seize a flock of sheep almost from under the walls of a military post, and with an hour's start, escape all pursuit. On one occasion a detachment of the First Colorado followed a band of Navajos to the west, and after a skirmish recovered a flock of stolen sheep. On another occasion Lieutenant George Shoup, with a detail of forty-five men from Company C of the Second Colorado Regiment (later Company L of the First Colorado Cavalry), followed a party of Comanches from New Mexico for a distance of three to four hundred miles, passing through villages with thousands of warriors, and recovered ninety mules, more by diplomacy than by fighting.

Shortly after Colonel Chivington left for Colorado, the First Colorado Regiment began to move by stages to Fort Union, hav-

[19]Hollister, *History of the First*, pp. 126-127.

ing been relieved in southern New Mexico by California troops. From this point the various companies were gradually moved north, and early in January 1863 the entire regiment completed concentration at Colorado City. Companies C and D of the Second Colorado Regiment were transferred to the First to provide the twelve companies required for a full cavalry regiment. Captains Downing and Anthony were promoted to majors to conform to the cavalry organization, which included three majors in each regiment. A number of minor promotions were also made to complete the full officer and noncommissioned officer authorizations.

Thus reorganized and equipped as a new cavalry regiment, but with ranks thinned by a year of hard service, the First proceeded to Denver. On the 13th of January the unit marched through the city under escort of the Third Colorado Regiment, and was enthusiastically received by a large crowd of citizens. The ceremony of welcome was concluded when the Fighting Parson addressed his troops with a few forcible remarks. It was obvious that he possessed the sincere admiration and affection of his men, which was only increased by his success in securing them the opportunity of serving as mounted troops.

XI

Terror on the Plains

WHEN the First Colorado Regiment started its march south in February 1862, there was no military force left in the Territory of Colorado for defense against Confederate guerrillas or hostile Indians. However, on the 17th of February, the Secretary of War authorized Colonel Jesse H. Leavenworth to raise the Second Regiment of Colorado Volunteers. Recruiting for the unit was started in May and completed early in the summer, following which the regiment was available for the protection of the territory throughout the remainder of the year. During the summer the Indians kept the recruits in practice.[1]

With the return of the First Colorado Cavalry in January 1863, General Curtis was enabled to redistribute his scanty forces to more effectively protect the extensive area in his depart-

---

[1]Bancroft, *Nevada, Colorado and Wyoming*, p. 459.

ment. Therefore, Colonel Dodd, who had replaced Colonel Leavenworth, was ordered to Fort Leavenworth with the Second Colorado; and later the unit was sent to Fort Larned to protect the Santa Fe trail against raids by Texans and hostile Indians. In the meantime, Colonel Chivington had been appointed Commander of the Military District of Colorado, which covered all of the Territory of Colorado with the exception of a strip adjacent to the Kansas line. To protect the settlements in this area, the colonel had the major portion of his own regiment and a few miscellaneous units. Some of the troops from the First Colorado were assigned to duty in eastern Colorado and western Kansas under the commanding general of the adjacent Military District of the Plains. Throughout the spring and summer of 1863 there was considerable raiding by bands of Indians, but these depredations were generally confined to the theft of stock and other movable property and did not present any great hazard to the people of the territory.[2] Nevertheless, Colonel Chivington kept his few forces well occupied in endeavoring to discourage this practice and in recovering some of the stolen property. By the following spring this situation began to change for the worse.

The 7th of April, 1864, was a fine spring day in Denver, and a comparative calm had descended on the headquarters of the Military District of Colorado. In the outer office Captain John Maynard, the acting assistant adjutant general of the district, was making a perfunctory check of the current strength reports submitted by the commanders of the troop units assigned to the district. The two enlisted clerks, relieved of his immediate supervision, stared out the window. The district commander was in the inner office, perusing the latest dispatches with information relative to the general unrest of the plains Indians and the con-

---

[2]Howbert, Irving, *Memories of a Lifetime in the Pike's Peak Region*. New York: G. P. Putnam's Sons, 1925, p. 100.

tinuance of their more or less minor depredations along the
routes of travel.

Suddenly the door was thrown open and a roughly dressed
civilian hurriedly entered, loudly announcing, "The Indians are
on the warpath and we need protection." At this juncture the
doorway to the inner office was immediately filled with the figure of a giant with a bushy black beard and a high forehead,
dressed in a blue uniform which had obviously seen hard service,
although it was neat, clean and in good repair. The colonel fixed
his piercing black eyes on the intruder.

"Well, sir," he asked in his deep, rumbling voice, "what is
the reason for this disturbance?" Somewhat awed by the formidable figure of the district commander, the newcomer gave his
name as Routh and explained that he was a herdsman employed
by Irwin, Jackman and Company, a firm hauling freight under
a government contract. He stated that a band of Cheyenne Indians had attacked the camp of the contractor in the Bijou Basin,
forty miles southeast of Denver, and driven off one hundred and
seventy-five head of cattle, which had been under his charge.
Faced with this evidence that the Indian attacks were spreading
to his district, the colonel turned to his assistant adjutant general.
"Captain," he said, "I believe that Lieutenant Eayre is at Camp
Weld and available for field duty. Please send for him at once."

Within an hour Eayre arrived, and was briefed on the situation. "Lieutenant," said the district commander, "take a detachment of about seventy-five men and proceed to the camp in the
Bijou Basin. Pick up the trail of the raiders, recover the stolen
stock if possible, and return it to the owners. Above all, avoid a
fight with the Indians if you can. So far their depredations have
generally been confined to the theft of stock, arms and ammunition. There is considerable evidence that the tribes are in alliance
for a concerted attack on the settlements and routes of travel

and that they are accumulating mounts, food and other supplies for the undertaking. However, as long as they refrain from full scale war, we must do the same. I don't want it ever said that an Indian war was brought about by the action of troops under my command."

Lieutenant Eayre was delayed in organizing his expedition by lack of transportation. However, at four P.M. on April 8, he set out with fifty-four men and two twelve pounder mountain howitzers from his own unit, the Independent Battery Colorado Volunteer Artillery, twenty-six men of Company D First Colorado Cavalry, and several supply wagons. He camped the first night on Running Creek, where he met Routh, who had gone ahead and was waiting to act as his guide. On the 14th, moving down the Big Sandy, he struck a broad Indian trail, from which it appeared that the raiders were driving at least a hundred head of cattle to the northwest. He followed this trail to the headwaters of the Republican, where his scouts reported an Indian camp in a defile about a mile ahead.

The lieutenant sent a column to the village to question the savages on the stolen cattle, but the Indians fled on the approach of the troops. One man stood his ground, however, and fired on the soldiers, seriously wounding one of them. Convinced by these actions that the band was hostile, Eayre occupied and burned their village. He then proceeded down the Republican, on the trail of the fleeing red men, and his scouts recovered and brought back nineteen head of stock, which Routh identified as part of the stolen herd. Due to exhaustion of his animals, the lieutenant returned to Denver, where he reported that the cattle had been stolen by Cheyennes, who were encamped on the Republican, and that they were planning hostilities against the whites.[3]

---

[3]The account of this expedition taken from *Rebellion Records,* Series I, Vol. XXXIV, Part 1, pp. 880-882 (report of Lt. George S. Eayre).

An even more alarming incident took place a few days after Lieutenant Eayre left Denver in search of the stolen cattle. W. D. Ripley, a ranchman from the Bijou, came into Camp Sanborn on the Platte River northeast of Denver, where a detachment under Captain George L. Sanborn was stationed to guard the Overland Trail. Ripley reported that Indians had been committing depredations along the Bijou, and that they had recently run off a herd of his horses, leaving him without any stock. The captain immediately ordered Lieutenant Clark Dunn to take forty men from Companies H and C First Colorado Cavalry, find the raiders, recover the stolen stock and take any firearms in the possession of the Indians. Leaving at daylight on April 12, the lieutenant divided his command and searched the bluffs on the south side of the river most of the day. Finally, with only fifteen men in his party, he found the trail of the raiders leading toward the river. Coming out of the sand hills near Fremont's Orchard[4] at about four o'clock, he discovered a party of twenty-five savages on the north bank. They were apparently preparing to steal a herd of grazing horses and mules, which were owned by the government and under the control of the Army Quartermaster in Denver.

Although his horses were nearly exhausted after traveling seventy-five miles in arid country, Dunn advanced at a gallop and cut the Indians off from the government herd, which was on the south bank. A small group of savages began to drive another herd of horses into the sand hills to the north, and the rest of the band disposed themselves in a threatening attitude. As the troops came close to the Indians, Ripley told Dunn that they were the raiders, and, pointing to the herd being driven off, that there was his stock.

---

[4] A grove of cottonwoods, which to Fremont resembled an apple orchard.

The lieutenant, who was a conscientious officer, was well aware of his heavy responsibility. Therefore, since he did not desire to bring about an Indian war by any act of aggression on his part, he dismounted and walked alone toward the chief, in an effort to obtain the stock without resort to violence. Dunn asked for the return of the horses, and the chief replied with a scornful laugh. The lieutenant then said that he would be compelled to disarm the band, and at the same time reached forward as if to take weapons from one of the Indians. They immediately opened fire, wounding four soldiers, of whom two later died, and Dunn ordered the fire returned. In a short time the red men fled and were pursued for fifteen miles, when the lieutenant was forced to return to camp due to the exhaustion of his horses. The Indians, who had been reinforced during the fight, were armed with rifles and pistols, in addition to their bows and arrows, while the troops were equipped only with pistols and sabres. Dunn estimated the raiders' casualties at from eight to ten killed and twelve to fifteen wounded.[5] This incident marked the beginning of a long series of unceasing and viciously savage attacks on the white settlers and trains by the federated plains tribes, extending throughout the entire spring, summer and fall of 1864.

---

[5]Account of this affair taken from *Rebellion Records*, Series I, Vol. XXXIV, part 1, pp. 883-885 (reports of Capt. Sanborn and Lt. Dunn). It varies considerably from the description given by Grinnell, George Bird, in *The Fighting Cheyennes*. Norman: Univ. of Oklahoma Press, 1956, pp. 140-142. Grinnell's account, and much of the rest of his book, is based on the Indian version of events as related by old warriors, probably in many cases years after the occurrences. (See Preface, p. X). Dunn was not sure of the tribe of the raiders, although their equipment seemed to be that of Cheyennes. However, according to Grinnell, the Cheyennes admit that they were the tribe involved. Since Dunn had no interpreter, it is assumed he talked to the chief with the sign language, at least in part.

It should be noted that these attacks, with their attendant savage atrocities, did not arise from any provocative acts by the settlers. Their only offense was occupation of lands which the Cheyenne chiefs had relinquished by treaty. There is no record that shows any settler of Colorado to have been guilty of injury or aggression to any Cheyenne or Arapaho prior to the Sand Creek engagement.[6]

In his efforts to provide for the safety and protection of the settlements in his district, Colonel Chivington was fortunate in receiving the full support of the representative of the civil authority in the area, Governor John Evans, who had been appointed chief executive of the territory in the spring of 1862. Although the governor was an able administrator, he is known primarily as a great philanthropist. Educated in medicine, he later made a fortune in real estate. He was a founder of Northwestern University in Evanston, Illinois and the University of Denver, and made large contributions to both schools. He also made many substantial gifts to a number of churches in Denver and other parts of Colorado.

Under applicable law, the governor, by virtue of his office, was ex-officio superintendent of Indian affairs within the territorial boundaries. In this capacity he had labored diligently for more than a year prior to the outbreak of full scale hostilities in an effort to avoid war with the Indians.[7] Beginning with the early spring of 1863, and continuing throughout the year, the warriors had been actively raiding the settlers and wagon trains. These raids involved wholesale theft of stock, arms and ammunition, large quantities of which were apparently being secured

[6]Dunn, *Massacres of the Mountains,* p. 429.

[7]*Senate Report 156,* 39th Cong., 2d sess., Report of Joint Special Committee to Inquire into Condition of Indian Tribes. Washington: U. S. Govt. Print. Off., 1867, pp. 78-87 (Reply of Governor Evans).

for use in future widespread bloody attacks. Word of these Indian activities on the borders of Colorado was received by Governor Evans in April 1863, when Agent Loree of the Upper Platte
Agency advised that the Cheyennes and Arapahoes were dissatisfied, and threatening hostilities.[8] After the New Ulm massacres
by the Sioux in Minnesota, a branch of the tribe was driven out
on the plains by the military. Angered by their defeat, the Sioux
approached the Cheyennes and Arapahoes, who were nursing
certain grievances concerning the terms of their recent treaties
with the government. As a result, the three tribes became the
leaders in forming an alliance of the plains Indians in a war to
drive the white settlers from the country while their soldiers
were occupied in the east; and, ultimately, the confederation
was expanded to include the Comanches, Kiowas and Prairie
Apaches.[9] In the meantime, anticipating an easy victory, the
Sioux, Cheyennes and Arapahoes became threatening, and
warned the whites to leave the area.

The Cheyennes and Arapahoes were of the same basic stock,
and the two tribes were always closely associated both in peace
and war. However, the formation of a confederation to include
four other tribes, with hunting ranges extending from North
Dakota to western Texas, appears beyond the usual war plans
of the plains Indians, who normally took the warpath in small
groups of a dozen or less. There was a widely held belief among
westerners loyal to the Union that the uniform hostility of the
plains tribes was inspired by Southern emissaries; and this belief

[8]*Senate Report 156,* pp. 45-46 (Testimony of Governor Evans).

[9]*Senate Document 142, Vol. 3,* 38th Cong., 2d sess., Report of Joint Committee on Conduct of War (section entitled "Massacre of Cheyenne Indians").
Washington: U.S. Govt. Print. Off., 1865, p. 106 (Deposition of Col. Chivington); Hall, *History of Colorado,* Vol. I, pp. 327, 330.

was not without a reasonable basis.[10] As one of the grounds for this belief, Chivington and Dunn refer to the case of George Bent, half-Cheyenne son of William Bent, an early day Indian trader. Having served with the Confederates under Price in Missouri, young Bent gave his parole after capture, joined the Cheyennes, took part in their depredations and was reported and believed to be a Rebel emissary to them.

After receiving instructions from Washington to negotiate treaties with the tribes in his area, Governor Evans appointed two agents to arrange a meeting with the Cheyennes and Arapahoes. One of them, Elbridge Gerry, was an educated man who had chosen a life in the wilderness, and the other was a French trader, Antone Janice. Both were married to Arapaho women and were well known to the Cheyenne and Arapaho chiefs. The governor sent them out on the plains to summon the two tribes to a treaty council to be held at the Big Timbers on the Arikaree fork of the Republican River about the middle of September, 1863.

Having received word of the reluctant consent of the Indians to meet him, the governor set out for the treaty ground, with an escort of one company of the First Colorado Cavalry and several wagons loaded with presents and materials for a feast. As the cavalcade approached the designated meeting place in smart military formation to impress the red men, Governor Evans and his associates scanned the area for a view of their savage guests. At first there was no sign of human presence, but on closer approach, "Little" Gerry was observed sitting alone. The governor asked for information, and Gerry replied, "Not one redskin has shown up and I don't expect any. They agreed to come in a

---

[10]*Sen. Doc. 142, V. 3*, p. 106 (Dep. Col. Chivington); Dunn, *Massacres of the Mountains*, p. 424.

pretty shifty and evasive manner, and I don't think they ever intended to be here."

Hoping that a few bands of Indians might be persuaded to visit the treaty ground at least for presents and a feast, Evans sent Gerry out again to search for the tribes. He located a large group of Cheyennes on Beaver Creek, forty miles to the east, where they were conducting their fall buffalo hunt. He talked to the chiefs several times, and they all replied in a sullen manner, giving excuses that the papooses were sick and that the squaws and warriors were busy with the hunt. Bull Bear, Chief of the Cheyenne Dog Soldiers, asked Gerry what the Great Father wanted of the Cheyennes. Gerry replied that if they would settle down peaceably on a reservation, the Great Father would build wooden tepees for them and teach them to farm. The Indian chief then demanded, "Does the Great Father want us to live like white men?" "Yes," said Gerry, "that is what he wants." Scornfully the red man answered, "You tell white chief Indian maybe not so low yet."

Gerry then tried bribery on the savages, offering a horse to each of them who would accompany him to meet the governor. A few, including Bull Bear, were willing to accept, but the majority were in an ugly mood, influenced by thoughts of plunder or fear of the Sioux, and threatened to kill any warrior who went with the white man. After an absence of several days, Gerry returned to Governor Evans with an account of his fruitless efforts. All prospects for negotiation having ended due to the recalcitrant attitude of the savages, the governor and his escort returned to Denver, and Gerry left for his ranch on the Cache La Poudre. Soon thereafter, the thefts of stock and attacks on wagon trains increased. It was obviously not peace the Indians wanted, but war and plunder.

On November 7 Governor Evans was secretly visited by Robert North, a white man married to an Arapaho squaw and living among the Indians. North told him that the chiefs of the Arapahoes, Sioux, Cheyennes and Kiowas held a big medicine dance fifty miles below Fort Lyon on the Arkansas, where they pledged themselves to a combined attack on the whites in the spring.[11] The governor immediately sent instructions to Major S. G. Colley, Indian Agent for the Upper Arkansas, to issue the Indians no more arms or ammunition until further notice. Four days later he wrote to the Indian Bureau advising that he had just held a council with Roman Nose, "Chief of the Northern Band of Arapahoes," who had professed an undying friendship for the whites, but had peremptorily demanded a reservation on the Cache La Poudre as the sole condition of a treaty. The governor was advised by Interpreter John Smith and Agent S. G. Colley, who were both present at the meeting, that, in their opinion, Roman Nose was in fact active in the league planning war against the whites.[12]

Colonel Chivington was appalled at the outbreak of full scale war which followed the attack on Lieutenant Dunn, and with good cause. The savagery of the enemy with whom he had to

---

[11]*Senate Report 156*, pp. 45-46 (testimony of Gov. Evans). Grinnell, in *The Fighting Cheyennes* (p. 135), says that Evans seems to have accepted North's statement without investigation and that it apparently made him lose his head. However, Governor Evans testified (*Sen. Rept. 156*, pp. 78-87) that he had received reports from Agent Loree that the Sioux, Arapahoes and Cheyennes were negotiating an alliance against the whites, and they refused to meet him in treaty council. Further, at the council in Denver, these reports were all verified when Black Kettle and other chiefs admitted that they had gone into an alliance and made war on the whites (*Sen. Rept. 156*, pp. 87-90, setting forth the minutes of the council).

[12]The above account of Governor Evans' dealings with the Indians and securing information of their activities has been taken from McMechen, Edgar C., *Life of Governor Evans*. Denver: Wahlgreen Publishing Co., 1924, beginning p. 112.

contend is almost incomprehensible to those whose knowledge of Indians is limited to present day civilized descendants of former raiders. Contrary to the portrayal often encountered in our literature, the American Indian of those days was not, in effect, a white man with a darker skin and rude customs arising only from his lack of educational advantages. Further, his mental processes, ideals and reactions to circumstances were not those of a white man. The plain fact was that the aboriginal Indians were cruel savages, or at best in some tribes, semi-savages. The nomads of the western plains, in particular, were so fiendishly cruel that other contemporary tribes regarded them with a feeling of awe and respect which almost amounted to fear.[13]

Although the savages sometimes had specific grievances which led them to attack the white man, the frequent outbreaks of war on the western plains were occasioned by the fact that warfare was the natural way of life for the plains Indians. In summer, when the grass was green with forage for their ponies, the young warriors naturally went on the warpath, attacking other tribes before the coming of the white man, and in many cases thereafter. From infancy a plains boy had it dinned into his ears that bravery was the path to distinction, that old age was evil and it was a fine thing to die young in battle.[14] Among the Cheyennes this feeling was very strong; and they fought, not only for the approval of their fellows, but also for the pure enjoyment of warfare. Every young man lived in a society in which he could never be recognized as a full-fledged warrior and honored member of the tribe until he had made his "coup" or military exploit. Although the element of danger was supposed

---

[13]Rister, Carl Coke, *Border Captives*. Norman: Univ. of Oklahoma Press, 1940, p. 196.

[14]Lowie, Robert H., *Indians of the Plains*. New York: McGraw-Hill Book Co., Inc., 1954, p. 106.

to be included in an exploit, many tribes regarded the killing of a woman or child as a feat entitling the perpetrator to war honors.[15] The truth was that these Indians enjoyed savage torture and killing, and would inflict suffering and massacre on members of other tribes, as well as the whites, entirely without provocation.[16]

The military spirit was further encouraged by the existence of the warrior or soldier societies, which included in their membership most of the able-bodied ambitious men of the tribe. Although these groups, which cut across the various tribes, were theoretically of equal importance, particular societies were in the ascendency over others at various times. Among the Cheyennes the Dogs were of conspicuous importance during historic times. Although, unlike the societies of some other plains tribes, the Cheyenne groups were not segregated into membership by ages, the most active society members were the younger men. Accordingly, the famous Cheyenne Dog Soldiers, who were so active in raiding the frontier and in fighting the troops, were made up of the main body of the young and vigorous men of the tribe. As was the case with young men of most of the plains tribes, warfare and raiding were their pride and esteemed manner of life.[17]

In the course of the war of 1864, many women were carried off to a fate more horrible than death, men were burned at the stake and put through other diabolical tortures. To exaggerate the fiendishness of the attacks would be impossible. Yet, incred-

---

[15]Lowie, *Indians of the Plains,* p. 108

[16]Tibbles, Thomas Henry, "Buckskin and Blanket Days" *Saturday Evening Post,* Aug. 31, 1957, p. 61. (Where such a massacre is described in a true story of adventure in 1856). (Original diary of T. H. Tibbles).

[17]Seymour, Flora Warren, *Indian Agents of the Old Frontier.* New York: D. Appleton-Century Co., Inc., 1941, p. 57.

ible as it may seem, there were white civilians and soldiers who later upheld and defended the perpetrators.

To meet the military requirements of this war, the district commander was forced to rely primarily on the major portion of his own First Colorado Cavalry, which, except for a few miscellaneous units, constituted the entire body of troops under his command. Strength reports for the month of March, 1864, gave the total personnel of the district as 2093 officers and men, of whom only 1310 were "present for duty." Until carbines were finally received in May, most of the units were armed with only revolvers and sabres. The available forces were only sufficient to escort the mails, garrison the posts and camps, and provide detachments for the periodic pursuit of raiding bands of Indians.[18]

One of the most successful of these pursuits occurred in May, when Major Downing, guided by an Indian trader named Ashcraft, surprised a band of Cheyenne raiders in a fortified camp at Cedar Canyon sixty miles north of the South Platte. He attacked at daylight with a detachment of forty men; and, after a fight of three hours, defeated them and destroyed their camp, capturing one hundred horses, killing twenty-six and wounding thirty of the hostiles, with a loss of one soldier killed and one wounded.[19] The command ran out of ammunition and was unable to pursue.

---

[18]Chivington, *First Colorado Regiment*, p. 13.

[19]*Senate Report 156*, p. 69 (testimony of Major Downing) ; Bancroft, *Nevada, Colorado and Wyoming*, p. 461. Grinnell (*The Fighting Cheyennes*, p. 143) gives the Indian version that the people in the camp "did not know there had been any trouble with the whites; the men were all away and only old women and children were in the camp." This seems almost incredible, particularly in view of the total absence of the younger women who were the mothers of the children.

Anticipating a possible Confederate attack on the Federal posts along the Arkansas River in southeastern Colorado, General Curtis, the department commander, in apparent disregard of the requirements of the Indian war, instructed Colonel Chivington to concentrate all of his available forces near Fort Lyon. During the early part of June this movement was completed, with the exception of one company of the First, which was camped on Cherry Creek, fifteen miles from Denver, under orders to join the remainder of the regiment on the Arkansas.

Late in the afternoon of the 18th of June, a rider was seen rapidly approaching the eastern outskirts of Denver, urging his tired horse forward with whip and spur. He halted in front of the military headquarters, threw the reins over the head of his mount and hurriedly entered the office. "The red devils have massacred a whole family on Running Creek!" he cried. Under questioning by Captain Maynard, he stated that the raid had been on the Van Wormer ranch twenty-five miles to the east. The savages had murdered Hungate the ranch foreman, his wife and two children, scalped and mutilated all the bodies, burned the ranch house and had driven or carried off all the stock and other movable property.[20] It was later learned that the attackers were a party of Arapahoes under Roman Nose. The mangled bodies were brought to Denver and placed on public view, and there was great excitement verging on panic at this evidence that the horrors of savage warfare had been brought close to the city. Governor Evans, after conference with Colonel Chivington, placed the city under martial law and began organization for defense. Telegraphic authority was secured from General Curtis for the district commander to hold in the north, for defense against hostile Indians, the one company of the

---

[20]*Sen. Doc. 142, V. 3, p.* 107 (Dep. of Col. Chivington); Hall, *History of Colorado,* Vol. I, p. 332.

First Colorado Cavalry which was still in the vicinity of Denver.[21] However, this authority came too late for the organization of an effective pursuit of the raiders.

In this emergency, with nearly all available troops on duty elsewhere, the militia was ordered to organize for service as home guards. To stimulate the formation of militia units, Governor Evans published a proclamation urging all citizens to organize to repel the savages, specifying that they would be entitled to all property of hostile Indians which they might capture, and expressing the expectation that the federal government would pay them for their services, since the territory was unable to do so.[22] Several companies were raised and assigned to duty patrolling the road between Denver and Julesburg.

After two months of increasingly savage attacks, culminating in the Hungate massacre on Running Creek, it appeared that there would be no peace on the plains until the hostile Indians received a decisive punishment for their depredations. Nevertheless, Governor Evans took one more step in his long efforts to restore peace to the area, or at least to limit the scope of the hostilities and to protect any of the red men who might still entertain friendly feelings toward the whites. Messengers were sent to the Indians of the plains with a proclamation by the governor, in his capacity as the superintendent of Indian affairs. This message, which was dated June 27, 1864, directed all friendly tribesmen to assemble at Forts Lyon, Larned, Laramie and Camp Collins for safety and protection, and warned them that all hostiles would be pursued and destroyed.[23] There was no response. Accordingly, early in August, a public proclamation was issued by which all citizens of Colorado, singly or in groups,

---

[21]Bancroft, *Nevada, Colorado and Wyoming*, pp. 461-462.
[22]Hall, *History of Colorado*, Vol. I, pp. 326-327.
[23]*Rebellion Records*, Series I, Vol. XLI, Part 1, p. 964.

were empowered by the governor to go in pursuit of the hostiles. Under this document, they were authorized to kill and destroy such savages wherever found, and to seize for the use of the pursuers any property of these Indians, carefully avoiding those, if any, who might have assembled at those posts designated in the governor's proclamation.[24]

Throughout the entire spring and summer, the hostiles kept up a continual series of extremely destructive raids, capturing wagon trains, destroying ranches and settlements, torturing and killing their victims, and leaving large areas deserted and in ruins.[25] Travel on the Overland Trail was extremely heavy that year, including, according to a record kept at Fort Laramie, nineteen thousand persons who passed that post en route to the Pacific settlements. The number of these travelers who fell at the hands of the savages will never be known, although the Coloradoans counted two hundred victims, at least fifty of which were their own people.[26] Although the scanty available military forces in the plains and mountain area put forth strenuous efforts, and conducted pursuits in widely separated locations, they were seldom able to catch the raiders, who were adept at covering their trail and always moved with great speed.[27]

As the season wore on, conditions grew critical in Colorado. The interruption of traffic on the river trails led to a scarcity of food, much of which was normally imported from the east. Prices rose in proportion, until flour sold at twenty-five dollars

[24]*Senate Document 142, Vol. 3*, p. 47.

[25]*Rocky Mountain News*, April 14, 15; May 4; July 23; Aug. 1, 9, 13, 15 and 25, 1864.

[26]Bancroft, *Nevada, Colorado and Wyoming*, p. 463.

[27]*Rebellion Records*, Series I, Vol. XLI, Part 1, p. 830; Part 2, pp. 661, 673 (Report of Major Colley), 810 and 845.

per hundredweight. Finally, the Indians cut the Overland Trail and held it from the middle of August until late in September. No mails or stagecoaches traveled the road during this period. Freight continued to move in armed convoys, but conditions soon grew so difficult that this traffic also stopped, leaving the savages in control.[28] All summer the attacks continued unabated, even extending to the valley of the Little Blue, east of Fort Kearney, where a savage massacre took place in an area previously considered relatively safe.[29]

In many of these raids, women and children were carried off as captives of the red raiders to suffer indescribable torments, since the customs of the plains Indians with reference to their prisoners were fiendish in the extreme. A white woman captured by a war party was the common property of all till they reached their village, when she became the special property of her captor, who could sell or gamble her away when he chose.[30] When she resisted, she was often "staked out," that is, four pegs were driven into the ground and a hand or foot tied to each to prevent struggling. "Instances are known to have occurred in the wars under consideration, where women after ravishment by perhaps a dozen or more, were lassoed by their merciless captors and compelled to fellow on foot—they being mounted. When, from sheer inability to keep up, the hapless victims fell behind, to make their sufferings more acute and therefore more enjoyable to their captors, the horses were urged to great speed, the women thrown to the ground, and dragged

---

[28]*Rocky Mountain News*, Aug. 11, 15; Sept. 3, 10, 1864.
[29]*Sen. Doc. 142, Vol. 3*, p. 63; *Rebellion Records*, Series I, Vol. XLI, Part 2, p. 672.
[30]Rister, *Border Captives*, p. 25.

to death. In other cases the brutes, having satiated their appe-
tities, hacked them literally to pieces."[31]

Throughout the summer, Governor Evans forwarded urgent
pleas to both the civilian and military authorities of the government asking for troops to alleviate the defenseless condition
of the territorial inhabitants, but none could be spared in view
of the needs of the war in the east. He then appealed for authority to call the militia into federal service, or to raise a regiment
of one-hundred-day volunteers. Finally, on August 13, the War
Department authorized the raising of such a regiment for use
in protecting the settlements and punishing hostile Indians.
Recruiting for the new unit, which was designated as the Third
Colorado Cavalry, proceeded rapidly; and, within a few weeks,
between eight and nine hundred men were enlisted. Officers and
men were generally citizens of a high type, including many
farmers, merchants and professional men who would have been
exempt in case of a draft. Upon recommendation of Colonel
Chivington, Governor Evans appointed, as colonel of the new
regiment, Lieutenant George Shoup of the First Colorado Cavalry, who had served with distinction in the New Mexico campaign.

Near midnight on August 20 Governor Evans was awakened
by a loud knocking. Upon reaching the door he was met by a
man who had obviously been riding far and fast. It was his
former agent, "Little" Geary, who excitedly announced: "Governor, there is no time to lose. I have been warned by Indian
friends that within the next two nights all the settlements from
the Platte to the Arkansas will be attacked at one time by separate war parties of hostiles. Between eight hundred and a thousand Cheyennes and Arapahoes are now encamped at Point of

---

[31]Hall, *History of Colorado,* Vol. I, pp. 336 and 337.

Rocks, in preparation for this raid." The governor wasted no time. He sent for Colonel Chivington. After a short conference, Evans immediately issued orders placing the militia and all the recruits under the district commander, and dispatched messengers in all directions with warnings of the impending attack. Chivington, on his part, at once drew on his available forces to reinforce the troops in the vicinity of the threatened localities. The entire area was thus placed on guard; and, when the raiders appeared on schedule, they found the settlers had either fled to the protection of the larger settlements or were prepared to defend themselves. The Indians killed one man at Fort Lupton and two or three others near the head of Cherry Creek, and stole many cattle and horses, including one hundred and fifty head from Gerry's ranch.[32]

During the middle part of August the various companies of the Third Colorado Cavalry were mustered into federal service,[33] and went into camp to drill and wait for issuance of equipment. Within a short time a number of mounts and saddles and a limited supply of arms, ammunition, uniforms and equipment were made available by local procurement, or from district warehouses, under authority of the department commander.[34] With these items four companies of the Third were partially equipped and made ready for field duty, and Colonel Chivington dispatched them at once to points along the Overland Trail. A portion of the militia assisted in patrolling the route above Denver, and the First Regiment continued to guard the Arkansas River road. These operations resulted in the re-

---

[32]Description of this incident from Howbert, *Memories of the Pike's Peak Region*, pp. 110-113; and *Rebellion Records*, Series I, Vol. XLI, Part 2, p. 809.

[33]*Rocky Mountain News*, Aug. 13 and 23, 1864.

[34]*Rebellion Records*, Series I, Vol. XLI, Part 2, p. 695.

establishment of communications with the Missouri River during October, as well as the surrender of a small group of Cheyennes and Arapahoes who had previously refused to enter into a treaty with the government.

XII

The Raiders Offer A Truce

IT WAS late in the afternoon of September 4, 1864. The garrison at Fort Lyon had completed its daily retreat and guard mount with a lack of ceremony which was typical of the time, place and troops involved. Regardless of his personal preference, Major Wynkoop, the post commander, was sufficiently astute to realize that, after three and one half years of war, his volunteer troops could not be expected to take part in elaborate military formations at this desolate outpost without serious damage to their morale and efficiency.

The new sentry assigned to patrol the parapet along the north wall of the structure stopped from time to time to scan the distant prairie for signs of Indians. The fort, which was on the north bank of the river, was far from an imposing structure, with its three foot thick walls of stone and adobe mud and heavy wooden gates covered with iron. At intervals along the parapet, several small howitzers were mounted at embrasures in the walls. Inside, along the walls, were the headquarters, barracks, warehouses, stables and other essential buildings, also built of stone and adobe, with flat dirt roofs and dirt floors. In the center of the enclosure were the flag pole and parade ground.

As the sentry reached the east wall of the fort, he glanced to the northeast and observed a party of horsemen approaching at a rapid pace. Soon he was able to discern that there were three Indian braves in the party. When they arrived to within about one hundred yards of his post, he called, in a loud voice, for them to halt, enforcing compliance by the tone of command and by the raising of his musket to the shoulder. When the corporal of the guard arrived, he sent for an interpreter, and it was soon learned that the visitors were Cheyenne warriors bearing a message for Major S. G. Colley, the Indian agent stationed at the fort, from Chief Black Kettle and the tribal council.

The savages were brought into the fort under guard and interviewed, through an interpreter, by Major Wynkoop and Agent Colley to whom they delivered a letter, which had been written by George Bent at the request of the principal Cheyenne Chief, Black Kettle. This message read as follows:

Cheyenne Village
Major Colley: August 29th, 1864.

We received a letter from Bent, wishing us to make peace. We held a council in regard to it. All came to the conclusion to make peace with you, providing you make peace with the Kiowas, Comanches, Aarapahoes, Apaches and Sioux. We are going to send a messenger to the Kiowas and to the other nations about our going to make peace with you. We heard that you have some (prisoners) in Denver. We have several prisoners of yours which we are willing to give up providing you give up yours. There are three war parties out yet, and two of the Arapahoes. They have been out some time and expected in soon. When we held this council there were few Arapahoes and Sioux present. We want true news of you in return. That is a letter.

BLACK KETTLE AND OTHER CHIEFS.[1]

_____
[1]*Senate Report 156*, p. 79.

At the time this letter was prepared, Black Kettle was encamped with the main body of his tribe in a large village near
the headwaters of the Smoky Hill River, one hundred and
forty miles northeast of Fort Lyon. Summer was nearing a
close and the hostile warriors had begun to turn their thoughts
to peace. In prior years it had been the normal custom for them
to make war, with varying degrees of intensity, during the
summer when the grass was green and game was plentiful, and
to make peace in the fall. Further, Black Kettle had received a
message from Colonel Bent, a former agent for the Cheyennes,
warning him that the white men were in a vengeful mood, that
new troops were being raised and that punishment for the
raiders would soon be on the way. With this information and
the early approach of the fall season, it was decided by the
tribal council that the time had come to arrange for a cessation
of hostilities; and the message to Colley followed.

This letter was conclusive evidence of the responsibility for
the summer long reign of terror conducted by Black Kettle and
his Cheyennes, in league with the other plains tribes. Moreover,
it contained a demanding offer for peace only on terms pre-
scribed by the hostiles, including a requirement that the government conclude a peace with each of the other warring tribes.
Obviously, the red men considered themselves masters of the
situation, but winter was approaching when lack of feed
rendered their ponies nearly useless for transportation. Their
lodges were crowded with plunder and the lodge poles fringed
with scalps. They wanted to go into winter quarters where they
could enjoy the fruits of war without danger of attack by the
troops, which they had heard were gathering for that purpose.
The reference to prisoners was the master bargaining point,
since the red men had learned that white men were extremely
sensitive to the welfare of their women and children.

Oblivious to the inconsistencies in this letter and genuinely concerned with the fate of the prisoners mentioned, Major Wynkoop felt it to be his duty to make a suitable response[2] He apparently had a childlike belief in the good faith of the plains Indians and their desire for true peace. This belief even continued in later years, when he was agent for the Cheyennes and they usually took the warpath in the summer and made peace in the fall if possible. After discussion with Colley and some of his officers, he turned to Captain R. A. Hill, of the First New Mexico Infantry, and announced: "Captain, I believe we should take action on this message. I will leave tomorrow with the cavalry and proceed to the Smoky Hill to open negotiations for peace and to try to bring back the women and children now held as prisoners. You will be in command of the post with your New Mexico infantry as garrison until my return."

Wynkoop started early the next morning with one hundred and twenty-seven mounted men and two small artillery pieces. Late in the afternoon of the fifth day he reached his destination, where he was soon surrounded by six to eight hundred warriors.[3] The red men had no fear of the troops, who were at their mercy and could be destroyed at any time. Therefore, the hostiles took charge of the negotiations, while their women hovered around the cannon and spiked them with beans. Placed in an extremely perilous position due to his own folly, Wynkoop, who was by this time an experienced field officer, became uneasy and took early occasion to extricate his troops. Following preliminary talks with Black Kettle, he managed to withdraw for twelve miles to a strong position, while the chiefs held a

[2]*Senate Executive Document 26,* 39th Cong., 2d sess. Washington: U. S. Govt. Printing Off, 1867, pp. 83-103 (Testimony of Major Wynkoop).
[3]*Senate Executive Document 26,* pp. 83-103.

council among themselves regarding his request for the release of the captive women and children.

The following day the chiefs came to his camp and surrendered four white prisoners, a Miss Roper and three children, the small daughter, son and nephew of Mrs. Lucinda Ewbanks, all of whom had been captured by the Cheyennes at the raid on the Little Blue. Three others, including Mrs. Ewbanks, who was not released until the following May, were stated by the Indians to be with another band at too great a distance to be immediately delivered to the troops. One other captive, a Mrs. Snyder, had hanged herself to escape the indignities and cruelties which had been practiced on all of them. The daughter and nephew of Mrs. Ewbanks died in Denver a short time after their release as a result of ill treatment by the savages.[4]

Major Wynkoop told Black Kettle and the other chiefs that he had no authority to arrange terms for a peace; but he invited them to accompany him to Denver for a conference with the governor, promising them protection on the journey and a safe return. This invitation was accepted, and Black Kettle and the other chiefs representing the Cheyennes and some of the Arapahoes left for Denver, where a council was held at Camp Weld on the 28th of September.[5]

The whites were represented at the council by Governor Evans, Colonel Chivington, Colonel Shoup, Major Wynkoop, Simeon Whiteley, United States Indian agent who acted as secretary, John Smith, interpreter for the Upper Arkansas Agency, and a number of private citizens. The Indians attending were Black Kettle, head chief of the Cheyennes; White

---

[4]*Senate Report 156*, pp. 90-91 (Statement of Lucinda Ewbanks).

[5]*Rocky Mountain News*, Sept. 24, 29, 1864. Description of Wynkoop's march to Smoky Hill and negotiations with Indians taken from *Sen. Executive Doc. 26*, pp. 83-103 (Testimony of Major Wynkoop).

Antelope, central chief of the Cheyennes; Bull Bear, chief of the Cheyenne dog soldiers; Left Hand's brother Neva, a subchief of the Arapahoes; Bosse, representing Arapaho Chief Left Hand, and several minor chiefs of both tribes.

The council opened with an address by Black Kettle, displaying a keen intelligence and a surprising grasp of the factors which led to the conflict between the two races, and expressing an earnest desire for peace. He did not deny the Cheyennes had been responsible for bloody raids against the white settlements and trains, but placed all blame on the young men, who would not follow the wise advice of their elders. He acknowledged the receipt of the governor's circular of the early summer, in which all friendly Indians were invited to assemble near military installations. He also claimed that he had held a council in relation thereto as soon as he could get his people together, and that the letter to Major Colley followed as a result.

All the chiefs present admitted that their people had been, and still were, engaged in open warfare with the whites, and that they had previously spurned the governor's efforts for peace. Although they denied allying themselves with the Sioux, their statements were a clear indication of concerted action against the whites by all of the plains tribes. Their attitude is shown by the following extract from the records of the council as taken down by Agent Whiteley:[6]

Black Kettle: On sight of your circular of June 27, 1864, I took hold of the matter, and have now come to talk to you about it. . . . I want you to give all these chiefs of the soldiers here to understand that . . . we have made peace, that we may not be mistaken by them for enemies. . . .

Governor Evans: I am sorry you did not respond to my appeal at once. . . . Hearing last fall that you were dissatisfied, the Great Father at Washington sent me out on the plains to . . . make it all right. I sent messengers out to tell you I had presents, and would make you a feast,

[6]*Senate Report 156*, pp. 87-90.

but you sent word to me that you did not want anything to do with me, and to the Great Father at Washingon that you could get along without him. . . .

Black Kettle: That is true.

Governor Evans: Again, whatever peace they make must be with the soldiers, and not with me. Are the Apaches at war with the whites?

White Antelope: Yes, and the Comanches and Kiowas as well; also a tribe of Indians from Texas, whose names we do not know. There are thirteen different bands of Sioux who have crossed the Platte, and are in alliance with the others named.

Governor Evans: Who committed the murder of the Hungate family on Running Creek?

Neva: The Arapahoes, a party of the northern band, who were passing north. It was Medicine Man, or Roman Nose, and three others. . . .

Governor Evans: Who killed the man and boy at the head of Cherry Creek?

Neva (after consultation): Kiowas and Comanches.

Governor Evans: Who stole the soldiers' horses and mules from Jimmy's camp twenty-seven days ago?

Neva: Fourteen Cheyennes and Arapahoes together.

Governor Evans: What were their names?

Neva: Power Face and Whirlwind, who are now in our camp, were the leaders.

Colonel Shoup: I counted twenty Indians on that occasion.

Governor Evans: Who stole Charlie Autobee's horses?

Neva: Raven's son.

Governor Evans: I suppose you acknowledge the depredations on the Little Blue, as you have the prisoners then taken in your possession?

White Antelope: We (the Cheyennes) took two prisoners west of Fort Kearney, and destroyed the trains.

Black Kettle admitted the truth of all the governor's charges, with the sole exception of the alliance between the Cheyennes and the Sioux, but it was amply clear that such an arrangement existed. Bull Bear stated that the Sioux had planned to clean all the whites out of the country, but failed to mention that this was also the plan of the Cheyenne and Arapahoes and that they had been active in its attempted fulfillment ever since the spring of the previous year.

Governor Evans told the assembled chiefs that, since war had begun, the negotiation of peace was in the hands of the military, and matters passed to Colonel Chivington, as the senior army officer present. The council closed with the colonel's advice to the Indians that peace could only be secured by the surrender of the hostile tribes, which was expressed as follows:

I am not a big war chief, but all the soldiers in this country are at my command. My rule of fighting white men or Indians is to fight them until they lay down their arms and submit to military authority. They are nearer Major Wynkoop than anyone else, and they can go to him when they are ready to do that.

The Fighting Parson's decision not to negotiate on any terms other than complete surrender was reinforced by the following telegram from General Curtis, which was sent on the very day of the council, apparently under apprehension that it might result in a premature peace:

I shall require the bad Indians delivered up; restoration of equal numbers of stock; also hostages to secure. I want no peace till the Indians suffer more. . . . I fear the Agent of the Indian Department will be ready to make presents too soon. . . . No peace must be made without my direction.[7]

Following the close of the council, Major Wynkoop returned to his post, and the Indians to their villages. Wynkoop held a conference with the chiefs before they left the vicinity of Fort Lyon, and told them to bring in their bands so they could be kept under his observation until he could hear from department headquarters with instructions as to precise terms of peace. About the middle of October, Left Hand and his band of Arapahoes came in to Fort Lyon and surrendered some of their summer's plunder to Wynkoop. However, neither Black Kettle nor any substantial number of his Cheyennes ever made even a token effort to comply with Chivington's requirement that they

[7]*Senate Executive Document 26*, p. 173.

must surrender and lay down their arms as a condition of peace.[8]

Fort Lyon was not within the Military District of Colorado, but was a part of the adjacent Military District of the Plains, and both districts were included in the Department of Kansas. General Curtis, the department commander, disapproved of Wynkoop's actions in endeavoring to arrange a peace with the hostile Cheyennes and Arapahoes without proper safeguards. He also felt that Wynkoop's trip to the Indian village was foolhardy, that he had allowed Indians to approach the fort contrary to explicit orders, and that, in making the trip to Denver, he had left his assigned post of duty without proper authority. Therefore, by Special Orders No. 4, dated October 17, 1864, Major Scott J. Anthony of the First Colorado Cavalry was ordered to take command at Fort Lyon and to investigate and report on Wynkoop's actions toward the Indians.[9]

On November 2, when Major Anthony arrived and took com-

---

[8]*Senate Executive Document 26*, testimony of Capt. S. S. Soule (p. 9) that most of the Indians encamped near Fort Lyon at the time in question were Arapahoes, testimony of Lt. Joseph Cramer that very few of the Indians attacked at Sand Creek were at any time encamped at Fort Lyon (p. 63); *Senate Document 142, Vol. 3*, testimony of Maj. Anthony (p. 17) that he found 650 Arapahoes encamped near Fort Lyon when he took command, confirmed by Anthony's report (pp. 70-71) made before the attack occurred, and similar testimony of Major Colley (p. 31). Only John Smith, in his testimony before the Joint Committee on the Conduct of the War (p. 5), testified that the Indians who tried to make at least a token surrender, and were fed for a time as quasi prisoners of war, included Cheyennes under Black Kettle; and the entire case that the Sand Creek attack was made against friendly Indians under the protection of the military rests solely on his prejudiced testimony. Grinnell refers to the Sand Creek incident (*The Fighting Cheyennes*, p. 176) as an "unprovoked attack on an unsuspecting community that had been promised protection by government officials, and on the faith of that protection had put themselves in the hands of the troops." He gives no citation, but only Smith's testimony provides any support for his conclusions.

[9]*Senate Document 142, Vol. 3*, p. 70 (report of Major Anthony). Grinnell states (*The Fighting Cheyennes*, p. 161) that it was a complaint from Chivington to Curtis that resulted in Wynkoop's relief. He cites no sources on this point, and I have found no authority to verify this statement, which Grinnell

mand at Fort Lyon, he found a band of six hundred and fifty Arapahoes, including Chiefs Little Raven and Left Hand, who were encamped about a mile from the post. Apprehensive concerning the proximity of such a group of savages, who until recently had been and probably still were hostile, he immediately arranged for a conference with their leaders, who offered to take any action he might suggest in an apparent desire to stay near the post. Anthony agreed to let them remain and be treated as prisoners of war if they surrendered all of their arms and stolen property. The chiefs accepted these terms and turned over some twenty head of horses and mules and a few worthless arms, following which they persuaded Anthony to provide them with food as Wynkoop had done.[10]

After ten days Anthony decided that conditions were not compatible with the safety of the post. The idea that these Indians were "prisoners of war" and thus entitled to rations was at best a fiction. They had never surrendered the most of their arms and he would have been unable to exert any real force over them with his small garrison, if such an action became necessary. Therefore, he called the chiefs together for a conference in an open area near the entrance to the post. "Tell them," he told the interpreter, "that I cannot feed them any longer. The Big War Chief has ordered me not to give them food, since they have been at war with the whites and have not made peace. They can go out on the prairie and hunt buffalo. Tell them to take back their rusty muskets and worn out bows and arrows, and leave at once." After this message was trans-

---

seems to feel has some sinister meaning, as might be expected from the obvious bias his book displays on behalf of the Indians. Actually, there is no apparent reason why Chivington should not have reported any facts which he might have learned concerning Wynkoop's apparent partiality for the Indian viewpoint, even though Wynkoop's station was outside of Chivington's command.

[10]*Senate Document 142, Vol. 3*, p. 18 (Anthony's testimony).

lated to the Indians, they accepted their weapons, gathered their people and sulkily left the vicinity of the fort.

A short time later, Left Hand and a small group of his band, amounting to eight lodges or about forty individuals, left the main body of Arapahoes under Little Raven and joined Black Kettle and a considerable number of his Cheyennes, who were encamped on Sand Creek thirty-five miles northeast of Fort Lyon.

Following a heavy snowstorm, with its reminder that winter had begun, a delegation of fifty or sixty Cheyennes, with Chiefs Black Kettle and War Bonnet, came in to Fort Lyon, arriving just before the Arapahoes left. Anthony met them outside the post and they told him they wanted peace. The post commander replied that he had no authority to conclude a peace with them, and that he would not permit them to come near the post, but that they might camp on Sand Creek if they chose.[11]

Black Kettle's band of Cheyennes was devotedly attached to Wynkoop, who seemed willing to forgive their transgressions; but they hated and despised Anthony for his lack of sympathy for their ways. They knew he would attack them if he had the strength to provide some chance of victory; and at one time they sent word that, "if that little red-eyed chief (Anthony) wants a fight, we will give him all he wants." On his part, Anthony was only awaiting the arrival of reinforcements, and considered it his duty to temporize with the Cheyennes in the meantime.[12]

---

[11]The account of Anthony's dealings with the Indians at Fort Lyon is taken from his testimony before the Joint Congressional Committee on the Conduct of the War, *Sen. Doc. 142, V. 3*, pp. 17-18.

[12]Hall, *History of Colorado*, Vol. I, p. 334. Grinnell states (*The Fighting Cheyennes*, p. 167) that Anthony was lying to the Indians when he said he would let them know if he received authority to make peace, and that he was merely trying to keep them where he could get at them if he wished to attack. It seems clear from the record that the Cheyennes were never in doubt as to Anthony's attitude toward them, which is clearly set forth in his report of Nov. 6, 1864 (*Sen. Doc. 142, V. 3*, pp. 70-71), made before there was any thought of battle or controversy.

XIII

Battle At Sand Creek

URING the long weeks of late summer and early fall the men of the Third Colorado Cavalry waited impatiently for action. Their one-hundred-days' enlistment was nearly half expired when a supply train arrived from the Missouri River under escort of the militia, and they were issued their allotment of horses, arms and equipment, largely of inferior quality. Discipline had suffered from the long period of idleness in camp and the monotony of patrol duty. They had enlisted for the single purpose of putting an end to the war which was strangling the economic life of the territory; and, after months of relative inactivity, they began to clamor to be led against the hostile Indians or disbanded.[1]

Meantime, with the war still on, communication with the east being maintained with great difficulty, and no signs of any large scale surrender by the warring tribes, Colonel Chivington

---

[1]Hall, *History of Colorado,* Vol. I, p. 345.

decided to act. His plans were laid in such a manner as to not only strike a blow that would bring the raiders under control, but which would also teach them that they could no longer play the game of summer warfare followed by a winter of peace without punishment. In this he was acting in full accord with the desires of General Curtis, whose final instructions sent by telegram to the district commander were: "Pursue everywhere and chastise the Cheyennes and Arapahoes; pay no attention to district lines. No presents must be made and no peace concluded without my consent."[2]

With the approaching expiration of the term of enlistment for the Third Regiment, the available time for action was growing short. Therefore, the Fighting Parson issued orders for the concentration of the unit in the Bijou Basin, near the edge of the plains about fifty miles southeast of Denver. The movement began on October 17, and, by night of the 21st, seven companies had assembled at Camp Evans, the new headquarters of the regiment, near the center of the basin.[3]

On October 28, Colonel Shoup left Major Hal Sayr in command of the camp and returned to Denver, where the district commander outlined the plan of campaign to him under orders of secrecy. Shoup at once dispatched orders to Sayr to be prepared to march immediately, and left for the camps of the two companies still on patrol duty north of Denver to start them marching south to join the remainder of the regiment. In order to increase his striking force Chivington also formed a provisional battalion, consisting of detachments of Companies C, E and H of the First Colorado Cavalry, under command of Lieutenant (later Captain) Luther Wilson, who was ordered to start his

[2]Dunn, *Massacres of the Mountains*, p. 423.

[3]Perrigo, Lynn I., "Major Hal Sayr's Diary of the Sand Creek Campaign" *The Colorado Magazine*, Vol. XV, No. 2, March 1938, p. 51.

men marching south at once to a junction with the Third Regiment.

In the meantime, with inadequate facilities, Major Sayr was struggling to prepare the men of the Third for extensive field service and to protect them from the worst effects of early winter. The first storms along the base of the mountains were accompanied by a drop in temperature, which caused intense suffering among the poorly sheltered troops. In addition to these problems Sayr was faced with the continuing necessity of attending to the large volume of administrative detail which seems to have always harassed military field commanders.

At four o'clock in the afternoon of November 13, the major sat alone in his tent, checking the latest "Return of Quartermaster Stores, Camp and Garrison Equipage," which had been prepared for forwarding to District Headquarters. There was a knocking on the canvas wall. "Come in," said the major, and the tent flap was thrown open to admit a dispatch rider, whose muddy boots and tired eyes gave evidence that he had been riding long and hard. "Express from Denver City, Sir," said the soldier, handing him an envelope and saluting. He was dismissed, and Sayr opened the packet which contained orders from Colonel Shoup to proceed with the entire command, at all possible speed, to a rendezvous with the remainder of the regiment at Boone's ranch on the Arkansas.

Next morning Sayr broke camp and, after a vast amount of work, got the main body of his troops on the road. However, due to a shortage of transportation, he was forced to leave Company H behind, as well as two loads of commissary stores, all of his quartermaster stores, the hospital stores, and a part of the tentage of Company B. The troops marched twelve miles that day, and, at seven P.M. they went into a very cold camp on Squirrel Creek, where there was very little fire wood. The supply wagons began arriving two hours later and continued to come in all night. A number of animals died and a few had to be abandoned. Next day they marched twenty-three miles to Fontaine-qui-bouille Creek, where they encountered warmer weather. The transportation arrived at eight P.M. without the commissary supplies, and more animals had to be abandoned.

On November 16, Sayr reduced his day's march to ten miles, which brought him to a ranch. Here he secured a good supply of hay and corn for his suffering stock. Although he was forced to leave more animals, he sent seven wagons back to bring up Company H and the abandoned supplies. For the next two days they continued on in more clement weather; and, in the early afternoon of the 18th, after marching ninety miles in five days, Major Sayr brought his entire command, with all its supply train except the commissary wagons, to the rendezvous point on the Arkansas. Here he established Camp Fillmore and settled down to wait for the remainder of the expedition. Company E of the the First Regiment had preceded him to that location. Company G of the Third Regiment, which had been in camp near Pueblo since it was mustered into the federal service, also joined the command on the 18th. On the 21st Colonel Shoup arrived with Companies C, D and F of the Third, and the remainder of Lieutenant Wilson's battalion of the First.[4]

Several days before the troops had left Denver, General Connor, Commander of the Military District of Utah, visited the headquarters of the Military District of Colorado. He did not state the reason for his call, but, from the nature of his conversation, Colonel Chivington gained the impression that he had been sent by the Secretary of War to report on whether or not the campaign against the Indians was being prosecuted with due

---

[4]Perrigo, "Sayr's Diary of the Sand Creek Campaign," p. 54.

diligence and efficiency. Later this viewpoint was strengthened just as the colonel was leaving Denver to join the expedition in the field. The district commander had mounted his horse in front of District Headquarters, and was prepared to depart with his personal aide, Lieutenant B. N. Sanford, and a small detachment, when General Connor approached and remarked, "I think from the temper of the men that you have, and all I can learn, that you will give these Indians a most terrible thrashing if you can catch them; and if it was in the mountains and you had them in a canyon with escape cut off, you could catch them; but I am afraid on these plains you won't do it." Chivington expressed his confidence of coming to grips with the hostiles; and, in response to the general's request, promised to advise him by telegraph concerning the results of any engagement.

Finally, just as the colonel was about to ride off and the general had started to walk away, he turned and said, "Colonel, where are these Indians?" Chivington replied, "General, that is the trick that wins in this game, if the game is won. There are but two persons who know their location, and they are myself and Colonel George L. Shoup." "Well, but I'll not tell anybody," Connor protested. "I am sure of that," rejoined the Fighting Parson. General Connor then commented, "Well, I begin to think that you will catch the Indians."[5]

On the evening of November 23, Colonel Chivington, accompanied by members of his staff and his personal aide, arrived at Camp Fillmore and assumed command of the expedition. A brief inspection of all units was held just before dark. Thereafter, marching orders were issued, and at nine the next morning the troops were on the road. The expedition proceeded steadily down the Arkansas at a maximum rate of advance, with the men

---

[5]Chivington, "The Pet Lambs" *Denver Republican,* May 18, 1890, p. 18.

on the march from daylight to between seven and eight o'clock every night. By the time supper was eaten and the horses cared for, it was ten o'clock, and reveille sounded at four the next morning.[6]

To preserve secrecy of his movements and prevent information of his operations from reaching the Indians, the Fighting Parson stopped all traffic on the Arkansas Road, taking travelers into temporary custody, and left detachments of guards at all ranches and settlements. The command reached Fort Lyon a short time before noon of the 28th, to the complete surprise of the garrison. Chivington immediately threw a picket around the fort, with orders to prevent anyone from leaving without proper authority, and went into camp one mile below the post.

After completing arrangements for establishing the camp, the expedition commander and his principal subordinate officers left for the fort. They were met at the gate by Major Anthony, who exclaimed: "Damned glad you have come, Colonel! I've got a band of hostiles only about forty miles from here and have been waiting for assistance in dealing with them."[7] The group of officers proceeded to Post Headquarters, where they were joined by Major S. G. Colley of the Upper Arkansas Indian Agency. Chivington asked Anthony, "What about these hostile Indians you mentioned, Major?" "There is a band of about one thousand encamped on Sand Creek forty miles to the north," Anthony replied, "Mostly Cheyennes under Chief Black Kettle with a few Arapahoes, and another group of about two thousand more Cheyennes on the Smoky Hill, sixty to seventy miles further north.[8] To the best of my knowledge, all are hostile." He

[6]Howbert, *Memories of the Pike's Peak Region*, p. 121.

[7]*Senate Executive Doc. 26*, pp. 211-212 (testimony Lt. Richmond).

[8]*Sen. Doc. 142, V. 3*, pp. 21-22 (Anthony's testimony that he first estimated the Sand Creek camp at 1000 and later at 700); and pp. 70-71 (Anthony's rept.

then went on to explain that they had admitted depredations, and that he had rejected their offer of peace on their own terms. He also said he was apprehensive that Black Kettle's band might attack the post, and that his sentinels had fired on some of them when they tried to come into the fort contrary to his orders. He added he was only waiting for reinforcements to mount an attack on both groups of hostiles.

The Fighting Parson turned to the Indian agent and asked: "What is your opinion of these Indians, Major Colley? When at peace they fall under your jurisdiction." "I have done everything in my power to make them behave themselves," Colley replied, "but for the past six months I have been able to do nothing with them. In my opinion, they should be punished for their hostile acts."[9]

"I am marching to Sand Creek tonight," said the colonel. Anthony then offered to accompany the expedition with a provisional battalion of one hundred and twenty-five men, stating, "I have been ordered by General Blunt to fight hostile Indians wherever I find them. However, to secure decisive results, our campaign should include the defeat of the main body of Cheyennes on the Smoky Hill." Chivington replied that while this was desirable, this operation would have to depend on the outcome of the first attack.

"My recommendation," said Anthony, "is to surround the Sand Creek camp so that none may escape to warn the main body; and then, as soon as the first action is concluded, to push on to the Smoky Hill without delay. Further, by first surround-

---

of Nov. 6, 1864 stating that Indians told him that 600 were camped near Sand Creek and that 2000 were 75 miles further north). He doubtless gave Col. Chivington his best information.

[9]*Sen. Doc. 142, V. 3,* pp. 104-105 (dep. Col. Chivington); *Sen. Ex. Doc. 26,* p. 178 (dep. Col. Shoup stating Colley told him no lasting treaty could be made till all these Indians were severely punished).

ing the village, we will give our friends and agents in the camp an opportunity to escape before any fighting begins. Chief One Eye is there acting as a spy in my employment, on a salary of one hundred and twenty-five dollars a month and rations. Left Hand and Black Kettle are there, and I consider them to be personally friendly. John Smith is probably also there with a soldier, ostensibly to trade, but actually to act as a spy at my request. All of these should be saved, and in order to get them out safely, notice should be given in advance of an attack."[10] "Black Kettle," replied Colonel Chivington, "is the prinicipal chief of the Cheyenne nation, which has been engaged in bloody war with the whites since April. His claim of friendship seems to have arisen with the ending of the summer season and the approach of cold weather when Indians fight at a disadvantage. However, it is not my intention to attack without warning. Actual operations must, of course, depend on conditions which we find on arrival, but I propose to first immobilize the Indians, if possible, and then to offer them a parley on terms of surrender. Such terms would include the delivering up for punishment of all savages guilty of hostilities, the return of all stolen property, the surrender of all firearms and the giving of hostages to insure against further hostilities."[11]

Chivington and Anthony then proceeded with the detailed planning of the expedition. Anthony agreed to furnish two additional howitzers and all necessary rations and other supplies to supplement stocks brought from Denver. Chivington decided that his wagon train, with all reserve supplies and all baggage, tentage and other equipment that could not be carried by the men, would be left at the fort. Lieutenant C. M. Cossit, the post

---

[10]*Senate Document 142, V. 3*, p. 29 (testimony of Major Anthony).

[11]Substantially General Curtis' terms for surrender as set forth in his telegram to Col. Chivington of Sept. 28th, 1864. See Note 7, Chapter XII.

quartermaster, was summoned and directed to provide the supplies required for the campaign. The colonel and his staff then left with Cossit to make arrangements to secure the necessary items.

Many of the junior officers stationed at Fort Lyon had served under Major Wynkoop. They had accompanied him to the Cheyenne village, and they had taken part in his efforts to arrange a surrender, or apparent surrender, of the hostiles. They approved all his actions, and some felt that, as a result, the status of Black Kettle and his immediate band had been changed from "hostile" to "friendly." In addition, they felt that by failing to attack the troops when they made their trip to the Cheyenne village on the Smoky Hill, these Indians had saved their lives and created an obligation on the part of Wynkoop and his men to protect them from punishment. In addition to his largely nominal authority as principal chief of the tribe, Black Kettle had a personal band which normally accompanied him on their nomadic wanderings. For some obscure reason these officers seemed to feel that, in addition to Black Kettle whose influence they thought had saved them on the Smoky Hill, this personal immediate following was also entitled to their gratitude.

The attitude of these officers became apparent when Major Anthony called in several of his aides to complete the planning for the organization of a force to proceed at once for Sand Creek with Colonel Chivington's column. Captain S. S. Soule and Lieutenants Joseph Cramer and James D. Cannon were ordered to form a provisional battalion by assembling detachments from Companies D, G and K of the First Colorado Cavalry. "Since we will probably proceed to the camp on the Smoky Hill after defeat of the band on Sand Creek, you will provide your men with three days of cooked and twenty days of uncooked rations," Anthony announced. All three officers objected vigorously. Captain Soule requested that Colonel Chivington be advised that the Indians on Sand Creek were friendly; and Lieutenant Cramer stated, "I will obey your orders, but only under protest. I feel that it would be murder to attack those Indians, since I consider that the men of Major Wynkoop's command owe their lives to this same band." Anthony replied, "I have made no pledges that would compromise my honor. It appears that Black Kettle is himself presently friendly to the whites; but, as to any other members of his band, I have grave doubts. However, we do not intend to punish those who are not hostile. I have been assured by Colonel Chivington that, if possible, provision will be made for the escape of our friends and agents in the camp. The object of the expedition is to surround the camp, recover the stolen stock and kill the Indians who have been committing depredations during the last spring and summer." "On those grounds," said Cramer, "I am perfectly willing to go.[12] The meeting then broke up, and Cramer left for the commissary to arrange for supplies for his company. Here he met Colonel Chivington and his staff, who had concluded their business with Lieutenant Cossit and were about to leave.

Still disturbed at the prospect of an attack on the Sand Creek camp, Cramer approached the colonel and said, "Sir, I believe that an attack on Black Kettle and his band would be murder in view of the obligations that we of Major Wynkoop's command are under to those Indians. Major Wynkoop pledged his word to them as an officer and a man, and all officers under him are indirectly pledged in the same manner. I feel that you are placing us in a very embarrassing circumstance by requiring

---

[12]*Senate Executive Document 26,* p. 47 (testimony of Lt. Cramer).

us to fight the same Indians that saved our lives." "The Cheyenne nation," replied the Fighting Parson, "has been waging
bloody war against the whites all spring, summer and fall, and
Black Kettle is their principal chief. They have been guilty of
robbery, arson, murder, rape and fiendish torture, not even
sparing women and little children. I believe it right and honorable to use any means under God's heaven to kill Indians who
kill and torture women and children. Damn any man who is in
sympathy with them."[13] Turning on his heel, he left the room
followed by his staff.

The additional men provided by Anthony formed a needed
reinforcement. The detailing of troops for garrison duty and
posting guards along the Arkansas Road had reduced the
available strength of the Third Regiment to about five hundred
men. Since Wilson's and Anthony's battalions each numbered
one hundred and twenty-five men, the strength of the expedition
was now approximately seven hundred and fifty. The fire power
was augmented by four twelve pound howitzers manned by
detachments from the cavalry companies.[14]

Chivington's preparations proceeded rapidly. Field rations,
consisting of bacon and hard tack, were issued and placed in the
saddle bags. The expedition formed in column of fours, and
moved out at eight o'clock on the night of November 28, head-
ing across the trackless prairie, with only the north star to point
the way. Their route lay across grass covered, rolling plains. It
was a clear starlit night, but there was a bitter chill in the air.
About midnight, the guide, Jim Beckwith, a mulatto trapper,
who was stiffened and blind from age and cold, was no longer

[13]*Senate Executive Documents 26*, p. 47 (testimony of Lt. Cramer).
[14]*Sen. Doc. 142*, V. 3, p. 102 (deposition of Col. Chivington).

able to distinguish the course. Anthony's half-breed guide was brought forward as a substitute.[15]

All night long the troops alternated pace. It was walk, trot, gallop, then dismount and lead. Three men rode half a mile in advance of the column, the half-breed guide and two officers, one of such gigantic stature as to dwarf the men beside him. For the past four days and nights, most of the men had spent long hours on the march, with a minimum of sleep, and were so tired that they could scarcely stay awake in the saddle. Nevertheless, the personality of their indomitable commander permeated all ranks and inspired belief that at last they were being led to decisive action.

They proceeded as silently as possible, with Colonels Chivington and Shoup both keeping a sharp eye on the guide, until they reached a place within eight or ten miles of the Indian camp. At this point the guide turned to Chivington in an effort to persuade him that any further advance might alarm the savages and cause their flight. He announced: "Wolf he howl, Injun dog he hear wolf and dog howl too; Injun he hear dog and listen, hear something and run off." The huge officer tapped the butt of his revolver in a suggestive manner and replied: "I haven't had an Indian to eat for a long time. If you fool with me and don't lead us to that camp, I'll have you for breakfast." The march was resumed with no more talk of "wolf" or "dog," and at early dawn they reached a ridge with a view up a valley to the northwest. The guide pointed out an Indian camp in the valley to the two officers, and was at once sent to the rear.[16] Chiv-

---

[15]Chivington, John M. "Sand Creek" (address delivered Sept. 13, 1883), as published in *Denver Republican* Oct. 5, 1894 with story of Col. Chivington's death on Oct. 4, 1894.

[16]Chivington, "Sand Creek" *Denver Republican,* Oct. 5, 1894.

ington had accomplished a feat extremely rare in military an-
nals, the surprise of a hostile Indian camp by white troops.

Carefully the Fighting Parson studied the terrain, and formed
his plan of operations. Off in the distance, about a mile to the
northwest, an Indian village of approximately one hundred and
thirty lodges was scattered irregularly for about a mile along the
northern bank of a dry creek bed, at a loop known as the South
Bend of the Big Sandy, generally referred to as Sand Creek. In
spite of the cold weather and distance, a faint hint of the fetid
odor of the camp was evident on the early morning breeze. Immediately to the west, south of the camp, and on the opposite
side of the creek bed, was a herd of from five to six hundred
ponies. North of the village, barely visible in the early light, was
another smaller herd. Turning to Colonel Shoup, Chivington
said, "We must secure their horses without delay. Send your
best mounted battalion to the south of the village and capture
the herd in that location. No shot must be fired unless the savages fire first." The expedition commander then sent for Lieutenant Wilson, and ordered him to immediately seize the herd
north of the camp without opening fire unless first attacked.[17]

It was between daybreak and sunrise, and some of the Indians
were beginning to move about. Hearing the rumbling of hoofs,
a squaw reported that a herd of buffalo was near. Others
ran out of their lodges to investigate, and discovered that the
noise was made by a large body of approaching troops. Soon
the camp was in confusion, with men, women and children running about securing arms for a fight, or preparing for flight. At
the same time the two detachments of mounted men were gal-
loping toward the pony herds in an effort to cut them off, and
several Indians were hurrying to the same locations. Upon ob-

---

[17]Chivington, "Sand Creek" *Denver Republican*, Oct. 5, 1894.

serving the large force opposing them, the savages riding south hesitated, and then made all possible speed back to their camp. The larger herd was soon captured and driven off under a small guard, but Lieutenant Wilson's assignment proved to be more difficult.[18]

Meanwhile, the remainder of the command was brought up and formed in line of battle, with Anthony on the left and the Third Regiment less one battalion on the right. Chivington rode along the line, saying, "Men, remember the murdered women and children on the Platte." He was followed by Colonel Shoup, who told his men, "Boys, you have been anticipating that you would have no opportunity to fight, but your chances look good."[19]

The Fighting Parson awaited the outcome of the maneuver for the seizure of the Indians' mounts. It was his intention, after securing their means of transportation, to engage them in parley on terms of surrender. However, the northerly herd of ponies took alarm and ran for the camp. In trying to cut them off, Wilson's men were forced to run in close to Black Kettle's lodge, where firing broke out.[20] It was soon apparent that they were heavily engaged, after capturing approximately half of the four hundred or more animals in the herd. With a fight against the savages starting before their eyes, the men of the Third were becoming increasingly difficult for their officers to hold in line. Accordingly, and with no prospects of avoiding a full scale

---

[18]*Senate Report 156*, p. 67 (testimony of Capt. Wilson).

[19]Shaw, Luella, *True History of Some of the Pioneers of Colorado* (hereafter cited as *True History of Pioneers*). Hotchkiss (Colorado): W. S. Coburn, John Patterson and A. K. Shaw, 1909, p. 81.

[20]Chivington stated ("Sand Creek" *Denver Republican*) that the Indians began the firing, which is confirmed by testimony of Pvt. Alexander Safely (*Sen. Ex. Doc. 26*, p. 220). However, Lt. (then Capt.) Wilson testified (*Sen. Rept. 156*, p. 67) that he was forced to open fire to carry out his mission. Apparently the firing broke out simultaneously on both sides.

engagement, Chivington ordered a general advance in support of Wilson's hard pressed troops.[21] The men surged forward, seething with long pent up fury and bent on dealing retribution for the long reign of terror, replete with murder, torture and rape.

Anthony's battalion advanced along the south bank of the creek to cover the left flank, and Lieutenant Wilson was assigned to the right flank. Led by their giant commander, who rode through their ranks shouting words of encouragement, the main body of troops formed by the Third Regiment advanced rapidly toward the center of the village, firing as they came. They were

---

[21]Grinnell gives the Indian side of the attack (*The Fighting Cheyennes*, pp. 176-180), as told to him by George Bent, who was in Black Kettle's camp at the time. On page 177, he quotes Bent as saying that, after running out and observing the approaching troops, he looked toward the chief's lodge and "saw that Black Kettle had a large American flag up on a long lodgepole as a signal that the camp was friendly." There was also some evidence at the various hearings on whether or not a flag was flown in the village, and much has been made by various writers of this alleged circumstance, although the mere hoisting of a flag could hardly be considered as changing the status of the camp. Of course, savages would always like to pose as "friendly" when attacked, in an effort to avoid punishment for their depredations. As to the sworn evidence, the record of the Joint Committee to Inquire into the Condition of the Indian Tribes includes the testimony of John Smith (p. 41) and Robert Bent (p. 96) that Black Kettle ran up an American flag with a white flag underneath, and the testimony of Major Talbot (p. 68), Major Downing (p. 70), Capt. Wilson (p. 67) and Dr. Birdsall (p. 72) that they saw no flags. The evidence received by the military commission included testimony by Lieut. Cramer, who was not friendly to Col. Chivington, (p. 50) and by Lieut. Decatur (p. 200) that they saw no flags during the fight, as well as evidence by Pvt. N. D. Snyder (p. 77) and Pvt. Geo. M. Roan (p. 142) that they saw a flag. Hall states (*History of Colorado*, p. 347) that the preponderance of the evidence received by Senator Doolittle's committee *(Sen. Rept. 156)* is against the statement that Black Kettle raised a flag over his lodge. It certainly seems that Capt. Wilson, whose men had to run in close to Black Kettle's lodge in pursuit of the horse herd, would have seen a flag flying there. From all the evidence, it must be concluded that, if a flag was flown, it was not sufficiently conspicuous to impart any knowledge to the attacking troops that the camp claimed to be friendly by reason of its display.

soon joined by the battalion which had captured the larger pony herd, and the entire group advanced on the camp.[22]

With some men out of action to serve as guards for the captured horses and on other special assignments, the strength of the attacking force was reduced to about seven hundred. The exact number of Indians is unknown, but based on the common estimate of three warriors to a lodge, it appears that there were about four hundred fighting men. There may have been more, since, as an advance base of a tribe at war, the camp at Sand Creek contained an unusually high percentage of males.[23] In any event, including the squaws without young children who stayed and fought with the men, Chivington was opposed by approximately five hundred hard fighting Indians. Had he not captured their ponies, which were superior to the mounts of the troops, they would have been extremely difficult to defeat, since they were excellent horsemen.[24] As it was, all odds were against a successful defense by the red men. Although they were well armed, in some cases better than the soldiers, they were unaccustomed to fighting on foot, and were opposed by a relentless foe in superior numbers and equipped with artillery. Nevertheless, they fought fiercely and skillfully in conformity with the reputation of their warlike tribe.

Early in the engagement, one hundred warriors formed a line northwest of the village, which covered the escape of noncombatant women and children. The direction of the attack left routes open for them to leave the danger area, either westward up the valley of Sand Creek or northward over the hills to the Smoky Hill River. The straggling ponies driven into camp by Wilson's men were caught, and many of the squaws and most

---

[22]Howbert, *Memories of the Pike's Peak Region*, pp. 123-124.
[23]*Sen. Doc. 142, V. 3*, p. 102 (deposition of Col. Chivington).
[24]Howbert, *Memories of the Pike's Peak Region*, p. 124.

INDIANS ARRIVING FOR COUNCIL AT CAMP WELD, SEPTEMBER 1864
Lawrence Street Methodist Church in Center

—Courtesy, State Historical Society of Colorado.

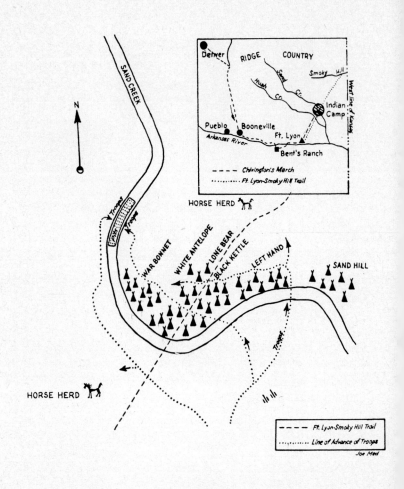

SAND CREEK ENGAGEMENT

of the children took them and fled. As the main body of troops approached the village, a large number of these refugees were seen in the distance, hurrying northward on their horses.[25]

Crossing the creek, Shoup's men proceeded along the north bank to the edge of the village, where they met the Indians, and the battle began in earnest. Colonel Chivington sat on his horse in the thick of the fight, calmly directing his troops, but did not fire a shot himself. Many of the savages were armed with rifles, many had revolvers, and all had bows and arrows.[26] The warriors in the defense line were well armed and put up a stiff fight. They turned back the first charge of Shoup's advance force, and the soldiers fell back to reorganize for another assault. The artillery had been brought up when the attack started, and two of the howitzers were in place on a ridge within range of the line of Indians. Chivington ordered them into action, and the first salvo made a breach in the line. The soldiers then attacked on the front and both flanks, forcing the defenders back. Leaving a number of their dead on the field, the savages retreated slowly up the creek, fighting as they went.[27]

Meanwhile, a number of other Indians had retired upstream three quarters of a mile to a point where the banks rose from three to ten feet on each side of a sandy creek bed about three hundred yards wide. Here they took refuge in pits or trenches which apparently had previously been dug for just such an emergency.[28]

As the Indians fell back, some took cover in the tall grass and sagebrush, but most found shelter in the rifle pits. Bullets filled

[25]Howbert, *Memories of the Pike's Peak Region*, p. 124.

[26]*Sen. Doc. 142, V. 3*, p. 102 (deposition of Col. Chivington).

[27]*Rebellion Records*, Series I, Vol. XLI, Part I, pp. 948-950 (Chivington's report on the battle of Sand Creek).

[28]*Sen. Doc. 142, V. 3*, p. 102 deposition of Col. Chivington); *Sen. Ex. Doc. 26*, p. 207 (testimony of Maj. Talbot).

the air in all directions, and many hand-to-hand combats took place all over the field. Black Kettle was wounded in one of these encounters, but managed to kill his opponent.[29] Several squaws were shot while fighting beside the men, using spears, bows and arrows and muskets with as much dexterity as the warriors; and several children were struck by stray bullets.[30]

The Indians fought stubbornly, falling back from one position to another under sharp attack by the troops, until, finally, outnumbered and hard pressed, they abandoned organized resistance and dispersed in all directions. Ultimately, all of the savages left in the fight retired to the creek banks, and occupied the rifle pits from which they fired at the troops in relative safety. The various companies of soldiers became disorganized early in the battle and fought in small groups whenever a few Indians were encountered. After a time the engagement extended up and down the creek bed for about three miles above the camp, with the savages firing constantly from their shelters along the creek and the troops replying with a continuous fusillade, shooting at every Indian that came within range of their guns.[31]

The fighting continued until late in the day, when Chivington became apprehensive of a counterattack by a large body of savages thought to be approaching from the Smoky Hill encampment, and ordered his scattered forces to reassemble in the Indian camp.[32] As the returning troops marched down the creek, they were repeatedly fired on by the warriors hidden behind the

---

[29]Shaw, *True History of Pioneers*, p. 87. In this book the author relates the story of the Sand Creek engagement as told by John Patterson and A. K. Shaw, who served as soldiers in the Third Regiment.

[30]Casey, Lee Taylor, "Col. John M. Chivington—Soldier" *Rocky Mountain News*, March 3, 1929.

[31]Howbert, *Memories of the Pike's Peak Region*, p. 125.

[32]Howbert, *Memories of the Pike's Peak Region*, p. 127.

banks. The soldiers returned this fire, but the savages were so well protected that the shots were generally ineffective. Just above the camp, where the heaviest fighting had taken place early in the day, the soldiers observed the bodies of many dead Indians, including a few squaws.[33]

---

[33]Howbert, *Memories of the Pike's Peak Region*, p. 128. Grinnell says (*The Fighting Cheyennes*, p. 173) that two-thirds of the Indians killed were women and children, and it is true that several witnesses who were unfriendly to Col. Chivington so testified. However, in this account, considerable reliance has been placed on Howbert, who was a soldier in the Third Regiment and a prominent citizen of Colorado Springs for many years. After describing how he covered most of the battlefield during the day, Howbert says (*Memories of the Pike's Peak Region*, p. 157), "During that time, I saw much of the battle, but not once did I see anyone shoot at a squaw or child, nor did I see anyone take a scalp, although it is true that in some instances this was done, for, as I returned to camp, I saw a number of dead Indians whose scalps had been taken, among them a few squaws." As to the sworn testimony, *Sen. Doc. 142, V. 3* includes evidence by John Smith (p. 9) that one-half of the dead were men and testimony by Col. Chivington (p. 103) that very few women and children were killed. *Sen. Rept. 156* sets forth evidence by Edmond Guerrier, a half-Cheyenne living among the Indians, (p. 66) and by Cpl. Amos Milsch (p. 76) that two-thirds or more of the dead were women and children; as well as testimony of Pvt. Asbury Bird (p. 72) that one-half of those killed were women and children, and of Sgt. Lucien Palmer (p. 75) that only one-third of the bodies were those of women and children. On the other hand, at the same hearing, Maj. Downing testified (p. 70) that he had counted 200 bodies, which included only 12 to 15 women and a few children. *Sen. Ex. Doc. 26* contains evidence from Lt. Cramer (p. 50), Lt. Cannon (p. 111) and J. P. Beckwith, the guide (p. 70), that two-thirds of the dead were women and children, as well as testimony by Lt. Decatur (p. 195) that he had counted the bodies under orders of Lt. Col. Bowen and found only a small number of women, and by Pvt. Snyder (p. 77) that about one-half of the dead were women and children. A number of other witnesses did not give any evidence on the number of women and children killed, although some said that there were "many." It should be noted that, of the above listed eleven witnesses, six testified that one-half or less of the dead were women and children. Therefore, it cannot logically be concluded that the records clearly show that two-thirds of the dead were women and children. From all the circumstances, it appears that probably not over one-fourth of the dead were women, most of whom were killed fighting the troops, and that there were few children killed and most of them by accident. This conclusion arises from the fact that the noncombatants had every opportunity to escape, as testified to by Robert Bent, the guide, (*Sen. Rept. 156*, p. 96) who was in sympathy with the Indians since his mother and brothers were in the camp at the time of the attack. Further, Howbert says (*Memories of the Pike's*

When the troops completed their concentration at about four
o'clock in the afternoon, the fighting came to an end, after having continued without cessation since sunrise. Chivington immediately formed his command in a hollow square with the animals on the inside. Supper was provided from the field rations
carried by the men, and the exhausted soldiers were soon sleeping soundly, with their guns in their arms as ordered by the expedition commander. To eliminate the use of the Indian camp as a
base for further hostile operations, Chivington ordered it destroyed, and the lodges beyond the area occupied by the troops
were set on fire in the early evening.

An examination of the camp before its destruction gave abundant evidence of the hostile character of its occupants. The
troops found a large quantity of food staples, wearing apparel
and other belongings which obviously formed a part of the loot
secured in attacks on wagon trains and ranches.[34] That evening
Dr. Caleb S. Birdsall, Assistant Surgeon of the Third Regiment,
was dressing soldiers' wounds in a lodge which had been pressed
into service as a first aid station, when a soldier appeared in the
entrance. "What do you think of these, 'Doc,' " he said, exhibiting a half dozen scalps which he held in his hand. The doctor
examined them closely and noted that, on one or two, the skin
and flesh attached to the hair was quite moist. "They are undoubtedly white scalps," he replied, "and at least one of them
was taken from the head not more than ten days ago."[35] A great
many white scalps were also seen in the village by Dr. T. P. Bell,

---

Peak Region, p. 124) that many noncombatants did escape, and Anthony testified
(Sen. Doc. 142, V. 3, p. 22) that, while the women and children were escaping,
the men stood under the creek banks and fought the troops all day.

[34]Howbert, Memories of the Pike's Peak Region, p. 130; Sen. Rept. 156, p. 67
(affidavit of Capt. Wilson).

[35]Sen. Executive Document 26, pp. 202-204 (testimony of Dr. Birdsall).

Surgeon of the Third Regiment, who expressed the opinion that some were quite freshly taken, including one that was not over five to eight days old.[36] In many cases the texture of the hair and its length indicated that the scalps were those of women and children.

Near midnight an alarm was sounded, and the men turned out and formed line of battle to repel attack. Occasional shots were heard, and in the light of the still blazing tepees, the soldiers could see on all sides what appeared to be hundreds of ponies running back and forth. No riders were visible; but, in conformity with their usual custom, it was thought that the savages were concealing their bodies by lying over on the far side of their mounts as they circled their intended prey. However, it developed that what had appeared to be ponies were the numerous dogs of the camp, which had lost their masters and were running about wildly. Nevertheless, it was evident that there were Indians all around, since the pickets had been fired on and driven in on all sides.[37]

During the entire day following the engagement, the troops remained in the Indian encampment, on the alert and prepared for defense. The wagon train arrived about noon, and the vehicles were formed in a hollow square for additional protection. Many Indians were seen hovering about the camp, and skirmishing went on all day, resulting in the death of about a dozen savages and one or two soldiers, whose bodies were brought in badly mutilated.[38]

In the afternoon the Fighting Parson held a conference with his staff and subordinate commanders to determine the further course of the campaign. Some of the officers proposed an attack

---

[36]*Senate Executive Document 26*, p. 223 (testimony of Dr. Bell).
[37]Howbert, *Memories of the Pike's Peak Region*, p. 129.
[38]Perrigo, "Sayr's Diary of the Sand Creek Campaign," p. 55.

on the main body of Cheyennes, supposedly still encamped on the Smoky Hill sixty or seventy miles away. After a short discussion, Chivington announced: "With all our advantages of surprise, artillery and the capture of the enemy's mounts, we had a stiff fight against forces about equal to ours in numbers. Without these factors, the result would have been very doubtful. After a long, hard march to the Smoky Hill, we would be faced with superior numbers of well armed and mounted, hard fighting warriors thoroughly alerted to our presence. Therefore, I feel that this idea must be abandoned as impractical. I have received a message from Major Colley at Fort Lyon suggesting an attack on a band of hostile Arapahoes, who are on the Arkansas below the mouth of Sand Creek. We have already punished the Cheyennes, and tomorrow we will march on those Arapahoes."

Chivington's losses amounted to seven killed, forty-seven wounded, of whom seven afterwards died, and one missing.[39] The casualties of the Indians cannot readily be ascertained, due in part to their custom of carrying off their dead for burial with tribal rites to insure passage to the "happy hunting ground." It is known that Black Kettle, with two hundred of his warriors and their families, escaped to the main Cheyenne village on the Smoky Hill.[40] Considering this and other available information, it appears that about two hundred and fifty Indians were killed, including two hundred warriors and a few noncombatant women and children.[41] The Cheyenne chiefs who died in the fight were

---

[39]*Senate Document 142, V. 3,* p. 102; Dunn, *Massacres of the Mountains,* p. 401.

[40]Ward, Josiah M., "Chivington at the Battle of Sand Creek" *Denver Post,* Jan. 30 and Feb. 6, 1921.

[41]Anthony estimated the Indian dead at 125, Howbert at 250 to 300, Shoup at 300, Sayr at 400, Decatur at 450 and Maj. Downing and Col. Chivington at 500 to 600. Indian sources indicate a loss of 148. It seems that the Indians carried

White Antelope, Standing Water, One Eye, War Bonnet, Spotted Cow, Two Thighs, Bear Man, Yellow Shield and Yellow Wolf. Arapho Chief Left Hand was wounded.

During the second night on the battlefield the troops were kept constantly on the alert, and there were occasional exchanges of shots around the defense perimeter. On the morning of December 1 the command set out down the valley of Sand Creek; and, on the following day, the dead and wounded were dispatched to Fort Lyon. Soon after reaching the Arkansas they found the trail of a large body of Indians moving down the valley. The savages, a band of Arapahoes under Little Raven, head chief of the tribe, were apparently traveling in great haste, having discarded camp kettles, buffalo robes and other possessions along their route of march. Chivington detailed three hundred of his best armed and best mounted men to go forward by forced marches in pursuit of the hostiles. However, after a night

off their wounded, as well as many of the dead, since no wounded savages were left on the field (*Sen. Rept. 156*, p. 72—testimony of Dr. Birdsall). Grinnell states (*The Fighting Cheyennes*, pp. 173-174) that no prisoners were taken, except for two half-breeds; and it has generally been considered that such was the case. However, eight Indians fell into the hands of the troops alive, and all but one were sent to Fort Lyon and properly cared for (*Sen. Doc. 142, V. 3,* p. 103—dep. of Col. Chivington). These captives included the two renegade half breeds, Charles Bent and Jack Smith, who had deserted their fathers' people to join the savages in their murdering raids. Jack Smith was assassinated after capture by a soldier who later deserted (*Sen. Rept. 156*, p. 70—testimony of Maj. Downing). It appears that Col. Chivington issued no orders regarding the taking of prisoners (*Sen. Rept. 156*, p. 70—testimony of Maj Downing, and p. 67—testimony of Capt. Wilson). Most of the noncombatants had escaped, and the failure to take any of the combatants as prisoners was due in large part to the fact that any effort to make a prisoner of even a badly wounded Indian was a very hazardous undertaking (Howbert, *Memories of the Pike's Peak Region*, p. 156; *Sen. Doc. 142, V. 3,* p. 103—deposition of Col. Chivington). However, it is undoubtedly true that a number of the men of the Third Regiment, whose friends and families had been the victims of murder, torture and rape at the hands of the savages, were not inclined to grant quarter to a defeated opponent, whether or not the offer to surrender would be followed by treachery after the soldier was put off guard.

and day of rapid marching, almost every trace of the Indians had disappeared and the chase was finally abandoned near the Kansas line.[42]

Since the term of enlistment of the Third Regiment had already expired and his stock was exhausted, Chivington reluctantly ordered a return march to Denver on December 7. Leaving Colonel Shoup in command, the Fighting Parson proceeded rapidly to Denver to reassume his duties at District Headquarters. Colonel Shoup and his men traveled leisurely back, reaching Denver on December 22, when they went into quarters at Camp Weld. The returning soldiers were enthusiastically welcomed as heroes by the citizens of Denver;[43] and the Colorado legisla-

---

[42]*Rebellion Records*, Series I, Vol. XLI, Pt. 1, pp. 948-950.

[43]*Rocky Mountain News*, Dec. 22, 1864. Grinnell says (*The Fighting Cheyennes*, pp. 173, 175) that Chivington's troops returned to Denver, where they were received in triumph, exhibiting over 100 scalps that were taken and the trophies from the captured camp. I have found no direct confirmation for this statement, but it is probably correct to say that some of the men exhibited scalps, since a number of the soldiers undoubtedly took scalps in conformity with the usual custom in Indian wars of the time. However, it appears that all of the men did not take scalps, judging from the statement of Howbert (*Memories of the Pike's Peak Region*, p. 157) that he saw no one take a scalp, although he saw a number of scalped bodies, and similar evidence given in *Sen. Rept. 156* by Capt. Wilson (p. 67), Maj. Downing (p. 70) and Dr. Birdsall (p. 72). As to the other trophies mentioned by Grinnell, one of them was probably an Indian blanket fringed with the scalps of white women, which was found in the Indian camp (Chivington "Sand Creek"). A related, but more important point, is the alleged extensive mutilation of bodies by the soldiers, as referred to by Grinnell (*The Fighting Cheyennes*, p. 173). On this point there are three witnesses who saw no mutilations other than scalping, Lt. Decatur (*Sen. Ex. Doc. 26*, p. 199), Maj. Downing (*Sen. Rept. 156*, p. 70) and Dr. Birdsall (*Sen. Rept. 156*, p. 72). Seven witnesses referred to a small amount or a few cases only, Pvt. Snyder (*Sen. Ex. Doc. 26*, p. 78), Pvt. Louderback (*Sen. Rept. 156*, p. 56), Capt. Wilson (*Sen. Rept. 156*, p. 67), Lt. Cramer (*Sen. Rept. 156*, p. 73), Cpl. Milsch (*Sen. Rept. 156*, p. 75), Maj. Anthony (*Sen. Doc. 142*, V. 3, p. 26) and Robert Bent (*Sen. Rept. 156*, p. 96). However, there were only three witnesses testifying to extensive mutilations, Lt. Conner (*Sen. Rept. 156*, p. 53), John Smith (*Sen. Rept. 156*, p. 60) and Sgt. Palmer (*Sen. Rept. 156*, p. 75). Based on this record, there is no justification for a finding that there was a general practice on the part of the troops of mutilating the bodies of the dead. In this

ture passed a resolution expressing the gratitude of the people of the territory to Colonel Chivington for his actions in the Sand Creek campaign.[44]

The members of the Third Colorado Cavalry were mustered out of federal service on December 29, 1864. They could well be proud of their part in the forced march of three hundred miles, in winter weather and over rough terrain, with the resulting surprise and defeat of a large body of hostile savages, which constituted an almost unparalleled military exploit.[45] Accordingly, the officers and men of the regiment returned to their homes satisfied with the work that had been done, and with the belief that a small amount of additional warfare carried resolutely to the hostile tribes would put a permanent end to the

---

connection, it should be noted that the men of the Third Regiment, who were enlisted for a short term, and only to fight Indians, were not as disciplined as the soldiers of the First Regiment, who were largely three year veterans. Accordingly, and since many had personal grievances against the Indians arising from savage attacks made on their families and friends, a number of individuals in the Third undoubtedly sought revenge by mutilating the bodies of the enemy, and probably, in some instances, even were guilty of killing noncombatants just as the Indians had done. In addition to revenge as a motive, many of the frontiersmen of that day were convinced that the only way to fight Indians was just as they fought (Dunn, *Massacres of the Mountains*, p. 426). The red men had no fear of death, but scalping and mutilation filled them with terror, since it was their religious belief that the spirit in the next world would have the same injuries that were inflicted on the body here (Dunn, *Massacres of the Mountains*, p. 426). Thus, those men who fought at Sand Creek as the Indians fought were largely responsible for the fact that most Indian warfare after Sand Creek gave the Colorado settlements a wide berth (Dunn, *Massacres of the Mountains*, p. 427). Regrettable as their actions may seem to us now, they were at war and fighting for survival against a savage and ruthless foe. Further, before we cast the first stone, let us pause and consider some of our own relatively recent actions, when we, the people of the United States through our commander-in-chief, unleashed what was probably the most colossal massacre in history by dropping atomic bombs on Hiroshima and Nagasaki. This resulted in the death and mutilation of thousands of women, children and other noncombatants, and may adversely affect generations of Japanese yet unborn.

[44]Bancroft, *Nevada, Colorado and Wyoming*, p. 466.
[45]*Rocky Mountain News*, Dec. 17, 1864.

Indian troubles in Colorado.[46] Following the release of the Third, General Curtis was required to further reduce his strength by mustering out the major portion of the First Colorado Cavalry and several other units under War Department Circular 36.[47] This included Colonel Chivington, who was released on January 6, 1865. Although the three year term of service had expired for the First Colorado Cavalry, authority was given to keep on active service a small portion of the regiment, which was designated as the "Veteran Battalion First Cavalry of Colorado," and placed under command of Lieutenant Colonel Samuel F. Tappan.[48]

---

[46]Howbert, *Memories of the Pike's Peak Region,* p. 133.

[47]Letter Gen. Curtis to Gen. Halleck, Dec. 30, 1864. (Exhibit attached to rept. Joint Comm. on Conduct of War, *Sen. Doc. 142, V. 3*).

[48]Tappan, S. F., *Autobiography.* Ms., Kansas Hist. Soc., Topeka.

XIV

History Perverted

IN THE previous chapter the simple, straightforward story of the Sand Creek engagement was set forth in conformance with the official reports of Colonel Chivington and his subordinate commanders, with a certain amount of additional detail taken from the writings of Howbert and Sayr and other reliable sources. However, strange as it may seem, this is not the version of the affair often accepted by numerous otherwise well informed writers. The basic facts have been well obscured by the vast welter of charges and countercharges resulting from the bitter century-long controversy.

In justification of my description of the engagement, I can do no better than adopt the explanation given by Major Nankivell for his treatment of the Sand Creek affair in his work on the history of Colorado military units.[1] The major's reasoning was

---

[1]Nankivell, John H., *History of the Military Organizations of the State of Colorado 1860-1935*. Denver: W. H. Kistler Stationery Co., 1935, p. XXIII (of Introduction).

that official reports and contemporary publications are much more likely to be reliable than accounts written at a later date, which are open to the suspicion of having the aim of justifying certain individuals or events. He also pointed out that this reasoning is particularly applicable to the reports submitted by Colonel Chivington and the unit commanders in his expedition, which were prepared immediately after the battle, when they had no knowledge of the bitter controversy that was to arise over the affair. He further concluded that "subsequent research reveals that these reports came very closely to being an accurate record of the events of that day at Sand Creek." Nevertheless, in view of the widely held belief that the Sand Creek campaign was an unjustified assault on friendly Indians, it seems desirable to briefly discuss the available evidence on this matter.

The full benefits of the battle of Sand Creek were never secured, since the War Department was preventd by political pressure from continuing the campaign against the defeated savages. Nevertheless, it was a truly decisive battle. The vindictiveness of the soldiers' attack and the heavy loss in Indian dead, which included approximately one-fifth of the total warriors in the tribe, showed the savages the white man's strength, and broke the power of the Cheyennes.[2] Further, word of this relentless attack spread among all the plains tribes and filled them with terror. The Cheyennes and Arapahoes, with all possible speed, left Colorado for Kansas and Indian Territory and stayed there. Once, somewhat later, a party of Sioux raided into Colorado; but on learning that Colorado troops had been sent to pursue them, "they scampered off as though the evil spirit were at their heels."[3]

[2]Ward, "Chivington at the Battle of Sand Creek."

[3]Dunn, *Massacres of the Mountains*, p. 427; Letter Gen. Curtis to Gen. Halleck, Jan. 30, 1865 (exhibit attached to rept. Joint Cong. Comm.—*Sen. Doc.*

In spite of the obvious benefits of the campaign, there were a number of persons who were determined that the facts would be suppressed and Colonel Chivington discredited for his part in the battle. Chief among these individuals were Indian Agent S. G. Colley and John Smith, his interpreter at Fort Lyon, who suffered heavy financial losses from the attack. Colley, Smith, and Colley's son D. D. Colley, were operating as partners trading with the Indians. They were making huge profits and swindling the government by using, in lieu of trade goods, property furnished for Indian annuities.[4]

Another grievance that Smith may have held against the troops at Sand Creek related to his son Jack Smith, who was assassinated after having been made a prisoner. However, the son was, in fact, a murderous renegade of the same stripe as Colonel Bent's son Charles. This was well known to John Smith, as may be seen from the following remark which he made on hearing of his son's death: 'Well, it serves him right. I sent him east and had him educated. Instead of coming back and trying to help civilize the Indians, he led them into deeper and lower savagery. So he could expect nothing else.'[5]

Smith and Colley were joined in the vindictive attack by the considerable number of personal enemies which the Fighting Parson had made by his lack of diplomacy and his failure to compromise on matters of principle. During his war service, the element of jealousy added to these enemies, since a few of the officers were resentful of his popularity with the men and his obvious superiority as a military leader. Numbered among the latter category were Lieutenant Colonel Tappan, who was passed

---

142, V. 3) stating that, following the Sand Creek affair, "There is no new feature in these Indian troubles except that Indians seem more frightened."

[4]*Senate Report 156*, p. 93 (affidavit of Col. Wm. Bent).

[5]Shaw, *True History of Pioneers*, p. 96.

over when Chivington was promoted to colonel, and Major
Wynkoop, who resented Chivington's refusal to support the
major's efforts to make peace with the hostiles on their own
terms.

Another factor which gained support for those endeavoring
to falsify the facts on Sand Creek was the vast amount of jealousy and animosity existing among the various volunteer officers
and units in the western area. Referring to this condition, General Curtis, in a report to the chief of staff of December 30,
1864,[6] stated, "There is so much political and personal strife in
our service it is almost impossible to get an honest, impartial
determination of facts . . ." Since this report was written just as
the Sand Creek controversy was beginning, it may have been
one of the principal matters on which such a determination of
facts was needed.

The final and almost incredible circumstance that influenced
the course of the controversy was the intense bitterness which
at the time prevailed between the State and Anti-State political
factions in the territory. Those who favored admission of Colorado into the Union had proposed Colonel Chivington as the
new state's first representative in Congress, and Governor Evans
was later suggested as United States senator. The members of
the Anti-State faction, who were largely political office holders
led by United States Marshal A. C. Hunt, were determined to
defeat statehood at any cost, and to thus perpetuate themselves
as Washington appointees. The barbarities alleged to have been
committed at the battle of Sand Creek were seized on and used
relentlessly by the Anti-State faction in the prosecution of its
designs against the leaders of the State movement. Hall reports
that "this state of feeling had much to do with the crimson

---

[6]*Sen. Doc. 142, V. 3* (attached exhibit).

coloring which incarnated the news, and has been handed down to the present day;" and that it was these supposed barbarities which "were employed at every turn of events with added exaggerations to accomplish the ruin of Evans and Chivington."[7]

Out of this welter of personal and political animosities, the enemies of the colonel were able to arrange one military and two congressional investigations of the Sand Creek campaign. The results, although inconclusive, tended to cast some reflections on the conduct of the Fighting Parson and his men. In fact, many historians, failing to fully analyze the records of the three hearings and attending circumstances, have taken portions of these records at face value, and reported the affair as an unjustified massacre of peaceful, helpless Indians, largely women and children.

The contention over the nature of the campaign seems to have begun at Fort Lyon, when Colley and Smith received the news of the battle and its results on their partnership operations. On the third day after the fight, the sick and wounded arrived at the fort, having been sent there for medical care while the expedition continued its pursuit of hostile bands. One of the more serious cases was that of Major Presley Talbot, who remained at Fort Lyon for several weeks recovering from a wound. During this time he occupied a room adjoining the quarters of Major Colley.[8] Colley and Smith became friendly with the major and frankly discussed the battle, and its effect on their business, while in his presence. They told him that they had suffered great losses due to interruption of their operations by the campaign. They also said they had sustained direct damages by the destruction or loss of property which they had received in trade and which was still in the camp at the time of the attack. They

---

[7]Hall, History of *Colorado*, Vol. I, p. 355.
[8]*Sen. Rept. 156*, p. 68 (affidavit of Maj Talbot).

repeatedly cursed Colonel Chivington and Major Downing, whom they held responsible for their financial reverses.[9]

Private David Louderback, who later testified that the battle was an indiscriminate massacre, was assigned as a nurse to Major Talbot. He also appears to have been employed or interested in the trading business. He was in the Indian camp with Smith on a trading mission when the attack occurred, and he performed clerical work for the partners while serving as Talbot's nurse.[10] On one occasion Smith entered Talbot's room and asked Louderback, "Is the claim ready?" "Here it is," replied the soldier, "and I have sworn to it as a correct statement of account." Smith read the document and showed it to Talbot. It was a claim against the government in favor of John Smith and S. G. Colley in the amount of six thousand dollars, covering the value of one hundred and five buffalo robes, two white ponies and a wagon load of goods, all stated to have been lost or destroyed at Sand Creek. The Indian trader said, "This is only the first of our claims for property lost during that unnecessary attack on peaceful Indians. We have other demands and will collect twenty-five thousand dollars before we are finished. Damn Colonel Chivington!"[11]

After nursing his grievances against the colonel for a few weeks, Colley decided to take action which would give him revenge and possibly facilitate the payment of his claims by the government. On December 20 he sent a letter to Senator Doolittle of Wisconsin, a member of the Joint Congressional Committee on the Conduct of the War. In his communication, he made the following statements which were later shown to be completely at variance with the facts:

[9]*Sen. Rept. 156*, p. 68.
[10]*Sen. Rept. 156*, p. 68.
[11]*Sen. Exec. Doc. 26*, pp. 207-211, 218-219; *Sen. Rept. 156*, p. 68.

SAND CREEK BATTLE FROM ROBERT LINDNEUX PAINTING
Indication of flags is questionable

—*Courtesy, State Historical Society of Colorado.*

SAND CREEK BATTLEFIELD IN 1933
—*Courtesy, State Historical Society of Colorado.*

I had 250 lodges near this place under my protection and that of Fort Lyon. All the chiefs and their families were in camp and doing all they could to protect the whites and keep the peace when Colonel Chivington marched from Denver, surprised the village, killed one-half of them, all the women and children, and then returned to Denver.[12]

The people of Colorado first learned of the concerted effort to condemn the actions of their troops on December 30, with the publication of a dispatch from Washington stating that the Fort Lyon affair, "in which Colonel Chivington destroyed a large Indian village, and all its inhabitants," was to be investigated by Congress. It was with great amazement and indignation that they read in their papers that "letters received from high officials in Colorado" said "that the Indians were killed after surrendering and that a large portion of them were women and children."[13] The identity of the "high officials" remained undisclosed, but undoubtedly they were persons actuated by political ambition or personal animosity to Colonel Chivington or Governor Evans. The program of these "high officials" and other interested parties to discredit the battle of Sand Creek and those who took part therein was pushed forward with lurid and distorted publicity in the eastern press. The congressional hearings were scheduled before the Joint Committee on the Conduct of the War, and the War Department issued orders to General Curtis to inquire and report on the campaign. Somewhat reluctantly, the general ordered Major Wynkoop to Fort Lyon to conduct a preliminary investigation, and telegraphed instructions for a more formal inquiry to Colonel Moonlight, who had succeeded Colonel Chivington in command of the Military District of Colorado. On January 13, 1865, this telegram was followed by an informal letter, in which Curtis enclosed a clipping from the

[12]*Congressional Globe,* part 1, 38th Cong., 2d sess. Jan. 9, 1865, p. 158.
[13]*Rocky Mountain News,* December 30, 1864.

Intelligencer of January 7, which set forth a copy of Colley's letter to Senator Doolittle of December 20.[14] The general commented that the clipping was probably a part of the occasion of the War Department order for an investigation, and said that he supposed a military commission had better be ordered.

On January 15, 1865, Wynkoop submitted his report,[15] which is indeed a remarkable document. Attached to the report, in ostensible support of the conclusions therein, are the affidavits of Agent S. G. Colley, his interpreter John Smith, Captain R. A. Hill, Lieutenant James D. Cannon, Lieutenant W. P. Minton, Private David Louderback and R. W. Clark, a civilian. Of these seven, only Lieutenant Cannon actually took part in the battle, although Smith, Louderback and Clark were in the Indian camp engaged in trade when the attack occurred. The reason that the supporting affidavits included the statement of only one of the hundred and twenty-five officers and men from Fort Lyon who took part in the attack should not be hard to find. Undoubtedly Wynkoop had difficulty in finding any others whose statements would, even in a slight degree, conform to his preconceived intentions as to what his report would show.

Smith's affidavit stated, in effect, that Chivington had attacked a band of friendly Indians, and massacred between sixty and seventy, of whom two-thirds were women and children, and that the bodies of many of the slain were horribly mutilated by the soldiers. The other affidavits were similar, but briefer. Some of the affiants had no personal knowledge of the incident, and, therefore, stated that they were told of the matters referred to by others. All of the documents were in very general terms, with little detail as to why the Indians were described as "friendly," and none as to the conditions which made the affair a "mas-

---

[14]*Rebellion Records*, Series I, Vol. XLVIII, p. 511.
[15]*Rebellion Records*, Series I, Vol. XLI, Part 1, pp. 959-972.

sacre." None of the affiants referred to any orders or actions by Colonel Chivington or any other officer of the expedition which authorized or condoned the slaughter of noncombatants. Nor did they refer to any knowledge by any officer of mutilation of Indians' bodies, except possibly after such mutilations had already occurred.

However, Major Wynkoop did not allow himself to be limited by any of these circumstances. In his report, he stated: "Every one of whom I have spoken to, either officer or soldier, agree in the relation that the most fearful atrocities were committed that ever was heard of. Women and children were killed and scalped, children shot at their mothers' breasts, and all the bodies mutilated in the most horrible manner. . . . Col. J. M. Chivington all the time enciting his troops to their diabolical outrages. . . ."

Since this report was only intended to present results of a preliminary inquiry to determine the desirability of any future action, the lack of adequate supporting evidence would not ordinarily be a matter of grave consequence. However, this unsworn unsubstantiated document, which by its terms was based on hearsay, and which was largely the figment of Wynkoop's vindictive imagination, was accepted, with its attached affidavits, as evidence in each of the three hearings on the Sand Creek affair. It forms the part of the record at each hearing which appears the most defamatory, and the only part which, if true, would connect Colonel Chivington personally with any misconduct which may have occurred at the battle.

At the hearing before the Joint Committee on the Conduct of the War,[16] testimony was given by several parties which was largely hearsay or without any real bearing on the matters at issue. In addition numerous affidavits and other documents,

---

[16]*Senate Document 142, Vol. 3,* 38th Cong., 2d sess.

which were primarily of a hearsay or immaterial nature, were received in evidence. The principal witnesses were S. G. Colley, John S. Smith, Major Anthony, Governor Evans and Colonel Chivington, whose testimony was in the form of a deposition. Except for hearsay witnesses, only John Smith gave any substantial evidence adverse to the Fighting Parson and his men. Generally, he repeated the matter set forth in his affidavit attached to Wynkoop's report. In spite of the reasons that Smith had for coloring his testimony to vent his anger on Colonel Chivington, and the weight of responsible evidence on the other side of the issues which was received at the hearing, the committee accepted Smith's story as the true version. Under these circumstances, Colonel Chivington was castigated in the most intemperate terms in the committee's report on the incident entitled "Massacre of Cheyenne Indians."

This action of the committee, in basing its findings on the testimony of one unreliable witness and certain hearsay documents, is truly astounding. Some of the supporters of these findings have contended that the report could be relied on as fair since it was signed by the committee chairman, "Honest Ben" Wade. As a matter of fact, it appeared from his own statement, made on the floor of the Senate on April 24, 1866, that Senator Wade did not write the report, and had little or nothing to do with the investigation.[17]

The admission occurred at a session when Governor Evans was present in the Senate chamber awaiting action on a bill to admit Colorado into the Union. In case of favorable action, he would have been seated as one of the senators from the new state. In the course of the debate he was attacked on the floor by Senator Sumner of Massachusetts, who quoted from the report

---

[17]Hall, *History of Colorado*, Vol. I, p. 344.

of the Joint Committee on the Conduct of the War. The senator read the passage from the report which characterized the governor as a prevaricator for failing to testify in conformity with what appeared to be the committee's preconceived ideas of the facts in question. Senator Lane of Indiana rose to the defense of Evans, clearly showing by the records of the Secretary of War and the Indian Bureau, portions of which he held in his hand, that the Cheyennes were at war with the whites at the time in question. During the debate it developed that, first three, and later only one of the nine members of the committee were actually present at the hearings on Sand Creek. Senator Wade then admitted that, although his name was on the report, he had not personally attended any of the hearings.[18]

An example of the type of unreliable evidence received by the committee is furnished by the testimony of A. C. Hunt, a United States Marshal from Denver. The witness stated that various returning soldiers, only one of whom he could name, had described the battle to him as an indiscriminate massacre, and gave his opinion that Colonel Chivington attacked friendly Indians to gain a promotion. Why it was considered worth while for him to make the long and arduous journey through country infested with hostile Indians to present this sort of testimony would appear to present a mystery. Surely, one of his soldier informants would have been a preferable witness. Hunt's motives are not so difficult to find. He was the leader of the small, but constantly active and irritating Anti-State faction[19] which was using the Sand Creek affair to defeat those advocating statehood. He finally received his reward for this sort of activity when President Johnson appointed him as Governor of Colorado in May, 1867,

---

[18]Dormois, John T., "More About 'Friendly' (?) Indians" *The Masonic News-Digest* (Kansas City, Kansas), Sept. 13, 1957.

[19]Hall, *History of Colorado*, Vol. I, p. 369.

an office which he held until he was relieved by Edward H. Mc-
Cook, an appointee of President Grant, in June, 1869.[20]

The record of the Joint Special Committee to Inquire into the
Condition of the Indian Tribes,[21] which held its hearings at a
later date, contains the testimony of some of the witnesses who
appeared before the other congressional committee, together
with a number of affidavits and documents similar to those in the
first proceeding. The tenor of the evidence was about the same,
and any inferences adverse to Colonel Chivington and his soldiers rest primarily on the testimony of John Smith.

Based on Wynkoop's report and the instructions of the War
Department, General Curtis ordered the appointment of a military commission to investigate the Sand Creek campaign. This
commission held hearings at Denver and Fort Lyon, meeting on
seventy-six separate days between February 9 and May 30, 1865.
This inquiry, which was headed by Lieutenant Colonel Samuel
F. Tappan, was initiated by Special Order No. 23, Headquarters
Military District of Colorado, "to investigate the conduct of the
late Colonel first regiment Colorado Cavalry in his recent campaign against the Indians . . ."[22]

The other two hearings were prejudiced and one-sided, and
this one was all of that. In addition, it was managed by Lieutenant Colonel Tappan, Colonel Chivington's implacable personal enemy, who never forgave him for being promoted in
Tappan's place. All of the members of the commission were
officers of Tappan's own Veteran Battalion First Colorado Cavalry, and nearly all of the military witnesses called by the commission were members of this battalion or of Major Wynkoop's
command. All of the nineteen witnesses called by the commis-

---

[20]Bancroft, *Nevada, Colorado and Wyoming*, p. 436.
[21]*Senate Report 156*, 39th Cong. 2d sess.
[22]*Senate Executive Document 26*, 39th Cong., 2d sess.

sion testified to asserted facts reflecting adversely on the conduct of the colonel and his men, or to circumstances of an extraneous nature. Thereafter, Chivington was allowed to present a "defense" as though he were actually on trial, and he produced sixteen witnesses to testify in his behalf, fifteen in person and one by deposition. Several documents were also received in evidence, including Wynkoop's report of preliminary investigation.

The hearing was secret, and it was conducted in an atmosphere of extreme hostility to the Fighting Parson and his citizen soldiers. The proceedings started with Colonel Chivington's written objection to Tappan as prejudiced, on the grounds that he had "repeatedly stated that the 'Sand Creek Affair' was a disgrace to every officer connected with it," and that he had said that he "would make it appear so in the end." Tappan's written reply set forth that he had merely said that it "appeared" that the Sand Creek affair was a disgrace to every officer connected with it, and that it would be shown so to be in the end. The commission overruled the protest.

Considering the evidence produced at all three hearings, it clearly appears that the attack was justified by the proven hostile character of the Indians at Sand Creek, and that there was no evidence to indicate that Colonel Chivington issued any orders for an indiscriminate slaughter. It is also apparent that, although there was considerable scalping, other mutilations of Indians' bodies were not extensive, and that Colonel Chivington neither had advance knowledge of nor authorized any mutilations. Finally, the records show that the affair was a bona fide engagement lasting most of the day, and was not in any sense a "massacre."[23]

---

[23]Grinnell says (*The Fighting Cheyennes,* p. 165) that, from the testimony given before the Joint Special committee of Congress *(Sen. Rept. 156),* it seems clear that Wynkoop did promise the chiefs protection, and that relying on this

To a large degree, such scalping and other mutilation as may have occurred at the battle was the result of a belief on the part of many frontiersmen that, as a matter of policy, Indians should be fought just as they fought. The tribesmen of the western plains had no fear of death, but scalping and mutilation filled them with terror. It was their religious belief that the spirit of a dead warrior would suffer in the next world from the same in-

---

promise and the governor's circular, "they moved in to Sand Creek, believing that peace had been made or soon would be made." Although Agent Colley's testimony at this hearing indicated that the Indians who came in to Fort Lyon and were fed for a time by Wynkoop and Anthony included Black Kettle's Cheyennes, his earlier testimony before the Joint Committee on the Conduct of the War (*Sen. Doc. 142, V. 3*, p. 31) is directly to the contrary. Thus, only John Smith is left as testifying unequivocally that any of the Cheyennes ever tried to make even a token surrender, or were promised protection; and his testimony is disputed by the sworn evidence of four other witnesses at the various hearings, as referred to in Note 8 of Chapter XII. Grinnell bases his description of the Sand Creek attack (*The Fighting Cheyennes*, pp. 170-180) largely on the un-sworn story of the affair related to him by George Bent. This was the account of a murdering renegade half breed (See *Bent's Fort*, Doubleday & Co., Inc., Garden City, 1954, pp. 350, 355, 363, where David Lavender describes the active part which George Bent and his brother Charles took in the savage attacks of the Cheyennes on the whites, both before and after Sand Creek). However, Grinnell seems to have preferred this account to the sworn testimony of white officers and soldiers and official reports prepared before the controversy began. Many other persons have considered that the Sand Creek incident was proven to have been an indiscriminate slaughter of peaceful Indians ordered by Col. Chivington, based primarily on the report of the Committee on the Conduct of the War entitled "Massacre of Cheyenne Indians" (*Sen. Doc. 142, V. 3*). Others have accepted at full value the unsubstantiated statements in Wynkoop's report of preliminary investigation, which were received as "evidence" at all three hearings. It must be obvious, however, that the mere publication of this matter in the records of Congress does not impart any validity to the statements made therein. As was pointed out earlier in this account, the report of the Committee on the Conduct of the War is based almost entirely on the testimony of John Smith, and the other witnesses with knowledge of the facts are ignored. In fact, there was no evidence whatever received by the committee to support some of the charges in its report. Wynkoop's report is not based on any claimed knowledge of the facts, and has no value as evidence. A careful reading of the records of the hearings, discarding all irrelevant and hearsay material, will convince any fair-minded person that the charges against Col. Chivington and his men rest on very unsubstantial grounds.

juries as might be inflicted on his body here. For this reason they carried off the bodies of their own dead, where possible, and mutilated those of their slain enemies. Therefore, they had a much healthier respect for and fear of those white men who fought them in the Indian manner than for those who scrupulously followed the rules of civilized warfare.[24] The other reason for scalping and mutilation was vengeance. There is some justice in paying a man back in his own coin, and the people of Colorado had old accounts to settle involving torture, murder and rape. There is no evidence that Colonel Chivington condoned any acts of mutilation on these grounds, but it is understandable for some of his men to have been influenced by such considerations.

Although it has often been stated that Colonel Chivington was court-martialed, the fact is that the three indecisive hearings were not followed by any further official action. Nevertheless, for nearly twenty years after the close of the war, Colonel Chivington was the object of vicious attacks in the public press and elsewhere, based on the adverse portions of the records of the hearings. Through all of this denunciation, he never wavered nor trembled. Others who were connected with the affair, in some cases, dodged, apologized or crawled, but not Chivington. He did not lay the blame, if any, on superior officers, as he might have; nor did he complain of misinformation from inferior officers, which he also might have. He merely stood under the rain of abuse and answered, "I stand by Sand Creek."[25]

---

[24]Dunn, *Massacres of the Mountains*, p. 426.
[25]Dunn, *Massacres of the Mountains*, pp. 445-446.

XV

Pacification of the Cheyennes

No account of the Sand Creek campaign can be considered complete unless it includes a description of concurrent military operations and briefly follows the fortunes of the Cheyennes to the ultimate conclusion of their hostilities. In order to assist in the war against the federated plains tribes, General Carleton, commanding the Military Department of New Mexico, sent Colonel Christopher ("Kit") Carson into the panhandle of Texas to attack the Comanches and Kiowas.[1] Carson's expedition was composed of three hundred and thirty-five volunteers, including about one hundred infantry and the remainder cavalry, with seventy-five Ute and Apache scouts.[2] He was furnished with two mountain howitzers, a supply train of twenty-seven wagons, and rations for forty-five

---

[1]*Sen. Rept. 156*, pp. 202-203 (Carlton to Carson—Oct. 23, 1864).
[2]*Sen. Rept. 156*, p. 263.

days. His orders were to find and engage the Indians, and he was given a free hand in his operations.

The command proceeded down the valley of the Canadian River in the direction of the old ruins known as Adobe Walls, where the old mountain man intended to establish his head-quarters. From this base, he planned to ride out on the plains with cavalry and a pack train, which would give him sufficient mobility to overtake the elusive savages. It turned out that this maneuver was unnecessary. The "cussed Injuns" were waiting for him at Adobe Walls.

Early in the afternoon of November 23, 1864, Carson was at Mule Springs, where his scouts reported a large body of Indians fifteen miles away, near Adobe Walls. Marching there, he kept an alert throughout the night. At dawn on the 24th he ordered an attack against an Indian encampment on the opposite side of the river, which was carried out by the scouts and cavalry, with artillery in support. He captured the village, but had no time to burn it, since he was busily engaged in driving the hostiles away from his front.

At nine o'clock the old frontiersman called time out for breakfast, and the men unsaddled and tethered their horses while they ate. After breakfast it was his intention to march down the river and destroy the other camps visible in the dis-tance, as well as the one he had captured. However, looking through his glass, he discovered a large force of Indians advanc-ing from one of the down-river villages, which appeared to be composed of about three hundred and fifty lodges. The colonel at once ordered his men to saddle, mount and form in line of battle, and soon he was desperately engaged with at least one thousand well mounted warriors.

The fight went on all afternoon, with Carson and his men opposed by three thousand Comanches, Kiowas and some Arapahoes. Near sundown, the soldiers managed to recapture the village they had taken in the morning; and the camp was looted and burned. In the lodges they found white women's clothing and captured army equipment to confirm the hostile character of its occupants. Kit then started a long retreat in the darkness, marching away from the burning camp. After twenty-four hours of marching and fighting, the exhausted column met its delayed wagon train with the precious supplies, which were so badly needed to get them back to the nearest settlements, two hundred miles away. Carson's report, written by a subordinate, described the battle of Adobe Walls as a glorious victory, but it was in fact a bad defeat, which just missed being a disaster.[3]

The military careers of Kit Carson and John M. Chivington offer some interesting parallels and contrasts. Both men served as colonels of volunteer regiments, and both fought the Texans and the Indians. In the only other major operation under his command, Carson attacked the Navajos at Canyon De Chelly, in January 1864, in order to put a stop to their raids against the ranchers' herds. He destroyed their villages and fields, killed or captured all of their sheep and cut down their peach trees, which numbered from two to three thousand.[4] This operation resulted in the transportation of the entire tribe, some seven thousand in number, who were marched by Carson to the Bosque Redondo near Fort Sumner, three hundred miles to the east. Here they were held in captivity, and at times near starvation, for four years—a pretty drastic punishment for their more or less minor depredations.

---

[3]This account taken from Vestal, Stanley, *Kit Carson*. Boston and New York: Houghton Mifflin Co., 1928, pp. 281-292. See *Sen. Rept. 156*, pp. 213-214, where Gen. Carleton calls it a "brilliant affair."

[4]*Sen. Rept. 156*, p. 97 (testimony of Col. Carson).

Thus, with one ruthless victory to his credit, against the comparatively peaceful Navajos, and no demonstration of outstanding military leadership, Kit Carson was promoted to brigadier general, in spite of the fact that he could neither read nor write. Further, he has been universally revered as a great western hero. Chivington, on the other hand, after winning one well directed campaign against the Confederates and one against the wild savages of the plains, has received, as his reward, a reputation by many of our historians as a scoundrel who plotted the murder of women and children for his own personal advantage.

Returning to the story of the Cheyennes, Black Kettle and his warriors, after their defeat at Sand Creek, joined the main body on the Smoky Hill River, and all of the tribe fled northward. Pausing briefly at Julesburg to loot and burn the settlement and several wagon trains camped nearby, they crossed the Platte and continued their journey without interference.[5] Operating from points of refuge in the north, and thirsting for vengeance for their defeat by the Colorado Volunteers, the Cheyennes and their allies continued their war against the whites during the winter of 1864-65. Abandoning their usual practice of resting during the winter season, the savages launched large scale attacks on the settlements and routes of travel.[6] Several companies of Colorado militia were raised and placed in service guarding the Overland Trail between the Kansas line near Julesburg and Denver. However, the Indians avoided this area, apparently desiring no further contact with Colorado troops.

Late in the spring, the end of the war in the east permitted the transfer of large forces for the subjugation of the hostile tribes. Accordingly, the militia was released and the regular

---

[5]Chivington, "The Pet Lambs," *Denver Republican,* May 18, 1890, p. 18.
[6]*Rebellion Records,* Series I, Vol. XLVIII, pt. 1, pp. 40-44.

troops took over. After a summer campaign, these forces succeeded in temporarily subduing the Indians, and a peace treaty
was concluded with them in October, 1865.[7] The savages delivered up some of their captive women and children and agreed
to release the rest in return for an annual payment varying from
ten to twenty dollars for each Indian. Although the Cheyennes
and Arapahoes, who were represented at the council by Black
Kettle and Little Raven, respectively, gave up any claim to lands
in Kansas, there was never any reservation assigned to them
under this treaty.[8] Dissatisfied with this condition, and feeling
that they had given up all rights except to make war, they were
soon again engaged in this pursuit. During the course of the
ensuing campaign, General W. S. Hancock, in the summer of
1867, assaulted and destroyed a Cheyenne village of three hundred lodges. Like Chivington, he was severely attacked for this
action by eastern sentimentalists, the Indian Bureau and Colonel
Wynkoop, who had been promoted and appointed agent for the
Cheyennes and Arapahoes. The general claimed the Indians
attacked were hostile and Wynkoop, as usual, that they were
friendly.[9]

The Report of the Joint Special Congressional Committee to
Inquire into the Condition of the Indian Tribes endeavored to
lay most of the blame for Indian wars on the military. Pursuant
to this report, President Johnson, on July 20, 1866, approved an
act creating a "Peace Commission" to negotiate new treaties
with the plains tribes.[10] The original commission was composed
of N. G. Taylor, Commissioner of Indian Affairs; J. B. Hender-

---

[7]Hall, *History of Colorado*, Vol. I, p. 361.

[8]Rister, *Border Captives*, pp. 129-130.

[9]*Report, Secretary of the Interior (1867-68)*, p. 542.

[10]Sherman, W. T., *Personal Memoirs*, New York, 1891, Vol. II, p. 434.

son, Chairman of the Senate Committee on Indian Affairs; J. B. Sanborn and S. F. Tappan. The president later appointed Generals W. S. Harney, A. H. Terry and C. C. Augur to represent the War Department. He also requested General W. T. Sherman to act with the commission, since he was in command of the Division of the Missouri. It was the announced purpose of the commission to conclude arrangements with the Indians which would stop their wars, provide for the security of the western settlements and facilitate the construction of railroads. It was proposed to accomplish these ends by placing all of the tribes on two large reservations, one in the Sioux country and the other in the Indian Territory which presently forms the State of Oklahoma.[11] It was obvious that this plan had many obstacles to its success.

The records of the conferences with the savages and of the agreements attempted by the commission show clearly that the civilian members, who exercised the primary authority, were unqualified for their assignment. Taylor, in particular, has been described as a White House courtier with a sanctimonious air, who gave long, florid speeches to the Indians, while all of his utterances were accepted as gospel by the visionary and impractical Tappan.[12]

In October 1867 these commissioners met the Indians on Medicine Lodge Creek, seventy-five miles south of Fort Larned. Here they negotiated the last treaty with the four major southern plains tribes, the Arapahoes, Cheyennes, Comanches and Kiowas. The commissioners apparently thought they dealt firmly with the savages. The red men were required to stop their border warfare, to give up their extensive hunting grounds and

---

[11]Hafen and Rister, *Western America.* Second edition, p. 481.
[12]Rister, *Border Captives,* pp. 137-138.

accept smaller reservations, and to learn to farm with aid to be
furnished by the government. They would be allowed to hunt
in their old areas for three years, following which they would
have to retire permanently to their new reservations in Indian
Territory. A location of approximately five thousand five hundred square miles was assigned to the Comanches, Kiowas and
Katakas, and an area slightly larger and to the north was set
aside for the Cheyennes and Arapahoes.[13]

The chiefs of some of the bands of the affected tribes did not
attend the council, and it is doubtful if those who signed the
treaty thoroughly understood its import. As was usually the case
in treaty councils, the main attention of the savages was centered
on the fine presents brought by the white men. In view of their
experience with other treaties which had not been observed by
either side, they had no thought that attempts would be made to
enforce this one. To them the situation appeared as usual. As
soon as the presents were distributed and the council concluded,
the white men would leave and the Indians could resume their
warpath as they had often done in the past. Further, the commission, in its desire to secure its main objectives, failed to require
the release of the many white prisoners being held in misery,
and made no provision for protecting the settlers. Since the
Medicine Lodge treaty prohibited white men from trespassing
on the new Indian lands, the savages were enabled to use these
areas as safe bases for their border raids.[14]

Upon learning of the issue of arms and ammunition to the
Indians in the spring of 1868, the military authorities ordered
the practice discontinued. Although the tribesmen preferred
bows and arrows for hunting buffalo, the Indian agents and

---

[13]Rister, *Border Captives*, pp. 138-139.
[14]Rister, *Border Captives*, p. 142.

peace advocates raised the objection that the savages could not hunt without the issue and were, therefore, being starved by the Army. The result was adverse publicity and political pressure which caused the order to be revoked. On August 1 the Arapahoes received a substantial issue of arms and ammunition; and, on August 10, Colonel Wynkoop reported: "I yesterday made the whole issue of annuity goods, arms and ammunition to the Cheyenne chiefs and people of their nation; they were delighted at receiving the goods, particularly the arms and ammunition, . . . They have now left for their hunting grounds, and I am perfectly satisfied that there will be no trouble with them this season." Thirty days later he was explaining that they had taken the war trail because of the delay in issuing "their arms and ammunition."[15]

As a matter of fact, the chiefs who had not signed the Medicine Lodge Treaty, and most of the young men of all four southern plains tribes, had declared the treaty to be unsatisfactory to them very soon after it was made. Many groups of these tribes had been raiding for some time before the wholesale outbreak of the Cheyennes, which began on the very day they were issued arms and ammunition. The opening of their large scale attacks is described in the following journal entry of General Sheridan:

August 10. A band of 200 Cheyennes, 4 Arapaho and 20 Sioux, . . . in the Saline Valley, Kansas, robbed several houses and ravished women until insensible. They then went to settlements on Solomon, about 12th August, and robbed homes, run off stock, ravished women and murdered 13 men; 2 of the women outraged were also shot and badly wounded; a small party then crossed the Republican and killed 2 men there.

Under the leadership of Black Kettle and Roman Nose, the Cheyennes and Arapahoes swept through western Kansas with a ferocious series of attacks as devastating as the cyclones of the

---

[15]Dunn, *Massacres of the Mountains,* p. 439.

area. Workmen on the Kansas Pacific Railroad were forced to lay aside their tools and defend themselves with rifles. The Indians raided isolated farms, slaughtered men, women and children and drove off stock. From June to December one hundred and fifty-four settlers and travelers were killed by the savages, thirty to forty women and children were captured, twenty-four farm houses burned and several stage coaches and wagon trains attacked.[16]

During the summer of 1868 Sheridan was unable to do any more than maintain a defensive attitude and send minor expeditions into the Indian country. In one of these forays Colonel George A. ("Sandy") Forsythe, with a party of fifty specially enlisted scouts, was surrounded on an island in the Arikaree fork of the Republican. Here he was attacked for several days by wave after wave of mounted Indians, with a total estimated strength of one thousand warriors. After the death of their leader, Roman Nose, the savages abandoned the attack, and the surviving white men managed to withdraw.[17]

General Sherman wrote with bitterness that the Indians had resumed their old practice of attacking the settlements and lines of communication in the summer when their ponies could forage, and resting in remote villages with their plunder in the winter. On this basis he convinced a majority of the "Peace Commission" that the savages should be punished, and, on October 15, 1868, he issued orders for a campaign against them.

Samuel F. Tappan vigorously opposed this action; and, with the help of Indian Agents J. H. Leavenworth and E. W. Wynkoop, he made an unsuccessful effort to arouse public opinion

---

[16]Johnson, Charles L., *Famous Indian Chiefs*. Boston: The Page Co., 1938, p. 381.

[17]For a detailed account of this famous incident see Whitney, Chauncey B., *Diary*, Kansas State Historical Collections (Topeka, 1911-12), Vol. XII, p. 296.

against Sherman and Sheridan for their decision to attack the hostiles. Tappan accused the army commanders of an intention to reenact the Sand Creek affair. Sherman replied, in a letter full of indignation, that Tappan was actuated by "mono-mania," and declared that he did not intend to have his actions determined by "Indian Apologists."[18] Further, he said that the renewed war by the Indians was inexcusable, since they had been given food and clothing and promised security in return for their agreement to keep the peace.

In November 1868 Sheridan started southward with three columns of troops in a winter campaign of reprisal.[19] He had no difficulty in separating the peaceful from the hostile Indians so far as the Cheyennes were concerned. There were no "good" Indians to be found on their reservation, which was completely vacant. Following their summer of war and raiding in Kansas, the "bad" Indians had gone into winter quarters far to the south. The entire nation of southern Cheyennes was encamped on the Washita on lands where they did not even have the right to hunt under the terms of their treaty. Together with the hostile Kiowas, Arapahoes, Comanches and Apaches, their camps extended for twelve miles along the river.[20]

Sheridan halted his main column at a base known as "Camp Supply," and sent Colonel Custer and his Seventh Cavalry to follow the trail of marauding Indians, which the scouts had found in the deep snow leading from the despoiled Kansas settlements.[21] At the end of the trail he found Black Kettle's camp of sixty lodges. At dawn on November 27 he surrounded and

---

[18]Rister, *Border Captives*, pp. 151-153; Hafen and Rister, *Western America*, p. 483.

[19]*Annual Report of the Secretary of War, 1869* (Abridgement), p. 42.

[20]Dunn, *Massacres of the Mountains*, p. 440.

[21]Sheridan, P. H., *Personal Memoirs*, New York, 1888, V. II, pp. 312-313.

attacked the village, captured and burned the camp, killed one hundred and three Indians, including Black Kettle and a few women and children, and captured and destroyed eight hundred and seventy-five horses and all supplies.[22]

A search of the camp before its destruction disclosed a considerable amount of plunder from Kansas settlements. Custer was forced to retreat rapidly to avoid defeat by a large body of Indians, which had gathered from other bands along the Washita. When he returned with Sheridan and the main column, he found the bodies of a captive white woman and two white children, who had been killed by the Cheyennes to prevent their rescue. Earlier, during the attack, some of the soldiers had observed a squaw trying to escape with one of these children, a ten-year-old boy. When it appeared that she could not get away, the soldiers saw her take a knife and rip the boy's abdomen open; and, as he fell dead, they killed his murderess with a volley of rifle fire.[23] Thus, once again there was abundant evidence of the hostile character of Black Kettle and his band.

It was indeed another Sand Creek, as Tappan had feared; and, like Chivington, Custer was viciously attacked for his assault on the identical band of "friendly" Indians. However, Custer was a regular officer, and the military came to his defense, with the result that his detractors were soon silenced.[24] It is indeed regrettable that a volunteer officer did not receive the same support from his immediate commanders when unjustifiably attacked for the performance of his simple military duty.

As a result of conferences with the Indians in January 1869 Custer and Sheridan obtained an agreement from most of the

---

[22]Sheridan, *Personal Memoirs*, Vol. II, p. 316.

[23]Rister, *Border Captives*, pp. 157-158.

[24]Howbert, *Memories of the Pike's Peak Region*, p. 162; Dunn, *Massacres of the Mountains*, p. 443.

hostile bands to accept the Medicine Lodge Treaty and reservations. A short time later Custer went out with the cavalry and brought in other bands to end the campaign. Except for small-scale summer raids the Cheyennes and Arapahoes remained fairly peaceable for the next five years. However, the Comanches and Kiowas, who had not suffered so heavily in the winter campaign of 1868-69, continued raiding on a large scale. Finally, in 1874, all four tribes began unlimited war on the whites, largely in anger at the slaughter of the buffalo by commercial hunters.

In a hard-fought campaign the Indians were relentlessly pursued from one refuge to another, and fourteen pitched battles took place between the hostiles and the troops. Finally, the war was concluded with the arrest and imprisonment of the principal war chiefs. This was the end of hostilities by the Southern Cheyennes, except for Dull Knife's outbreak in 1879 when he fought his way north in an effort to join the Sioux. The campaign of 1874 vindicated Sheridan's policy of "punishment follows crime" as a means of pacifying the hostile tribes, although the destruction of the buffalo and the settlement of the country aided in putting an end to the wars with the plains Indians.[25] Nevertheless, there was no real civilizing of these tribesmen until a generation had been educated in the agency schools.

It was of course inevitable that the rapid settlement of the western lands would be accompanied by some warfare between the whites and the Indians. However, the government's lack of uniform policy, and its alternating between extreme severity and foolish sentimentality in dealing with the savages, only accentuated and prolonged the conflict. Chivington's aim was to punish the Indians and to thus deter them from continuing their

---

[25]Rister, *Border Captives,* p. 194.

fiendish outrages against the settlers, regardless of what their grievances may have been. In this he was following the same course later adopted by Sheridan, but he was the victim of the government's wavering policy, since the sentimentalists were in control at the time.

XVI

The Parson's Fight Ends

A FTER THE close of the long series of hearings held by the
military commission on May 30, 1865, Colonel Chivington was finally enabled to return attention to his
private affairs. From August 26, 1861 until January 6, 1865, he
had been in the military service.[1] The hearings had begun soon
after his release from active duty, and for nearly four months
he had appeared almost daily, conducting a desperate fight to
defend himself and his men. With only Major Downing as his
aide for advice and assistance, he acted as his own advocate in
a proceeding which was thoroughly controlled by his personal
enemies. It must have been a nerve-wracking experience for a
man of the Fighting Parson's temperament.

At the time of Chivington's entry into the military service his
status as an active minister of the church was temporarily sus-
pended. As an army officer other than a chaplain, he was not

---

[1]*Record of Service of John M. Chivington, War Dept., Record & Pension
Division.* National Archives, Record Group No. 15B, WC 416-181.

serving as a pastor. Therefore, the Kansas Conference of the Methodist Episcopal Church, which included Colorado, "located" him, which, in the terminology of the church, meant placing him on an inactive status under which he was not subject to appointment. Following the Sand Creek hearings he did not apply for reassignment to the church's roll of active ministers. His heart was filled with bitterness from the unjustified and vicious attacks made upon him and his men as a result of their performance of duty. Accordingly, he felt himself incapable of preaching forbearance and brotherly love to others. Further, he had no desire to plunge the church into the controversy which was raging between the different factions relative to the Sand Creek engagement.

Although he was never again assigned as the pastor of any local congregation, he was apparently again designated as an active minister of the church a few years later. In 1868 he was appointed an agent of the Nebraska Conference Church Extension Society and assigned to the quarterly conference of Nebraska City, where he served two years and was again "located" in 1870.[2]

Starting out as a civilian in the spring of 1865 Chivington used his slender savings to enter the freighting business, which he carried on in Nebraska for two years. However, it was a risky venture, and losses were frequent with the continued Indian hostilities. Further, his heart was no longer in his work, since he had lost the two people with the highest place in his affections. His son Thomas was drowned while attempting a crossing of the North Platte River with a load of government freight on June 26, 1866.[3] With the death of his wife, Martha, in August

---

[2]*Minutes of the Annual Conferences of the Methodist Episcopal Church* for years 1868 and 1870, pp. 98 and 84, respectively.

[3]Speer John, *Rept. of Interview with Mrs. J. M. Chivington.*

1867, he felt there was nothing to hold him in Nebraska or Colorado. His daughters were living in widely separated locations, with homes and families of their own; and, although he had many friends, he also had a number of bitter enemies.

Under these circumstances the Fighting Parson sold out his freighting business and moved to San Diego, California. After only a short time in California, he moved again, eventually returning to his old home in Warren County, Ohio. In 1873 he married the forty-year-old widow of a soldier, Mrs. Isabella Arnzen. For a few years he operated a small farm, following which he moved to Blanchester in Clinton County, Ohio, where he purchased the *Press* and edited it for several years. In 1883 he was nominated by the Republicans for member of the State Legislature.

The election campaign soon developed into a bitter contest in which the false and exaggerated stories concerning the Sand Creek campaign were used by the opposition to the fullest extent. These political tactics were especially effective, since the election was to be held in Clinton County, where there were a large number of Quakers. Members of this sect were not only opposed to war in all forms, but also considered themselves as the special guardians of the Indians. Although it was considered by many political experts that he would have won the election by a majority of five hundred or more, Chivington decided to withdraw from the bitter uphill fight.[4]

At about the time he was considering abandonment of the political race the Fighting Parson received an invitation to speak at a meeting of pioneers in Denver celebrating the twenty-fifth anniversary of the settlement of Colorado. The opportunity to leave Ohio in the middle of the campaign and address a gather-

---

[4]Dunn, *Massacres of the Mountains,* p. 443.

ing more sympathetic to him may have influenced his decision on the election. In any event he accepted the invitation from Colorado. He was the principal speaker of the meeting of Colorado Pioneers held at Jewell Park in Denver on September 13, 1883. Many distinguished leaders of an early day were present and given an enthusiastic welcome by the large crowd, but the most demonstrative reception was reserved for Colonel Chivington.

The chairman presented him with the following words: "We all remember the Indian wars of 1864 and '65, and with what joy we received the news that some of them at least had met the reward due their treachery and cruelty. The man who can tell you all about those wars, who can tell you all you want to know of the Indians, and who can give you the true story of Sand Creek is here. I have the honor, ladies and gentlemen, to introduce Colonel Chivington, one of Colorado's 'Pet Lambs.' "[5]

The enthusiastic cheers which accompanied the beginning of the colonel's speech were soon replaced with breathless attention. As he told his story in a simple and straightforward manner, it was apparent from the attitude of the crowd and nods of approval from all sides that they were convinced of the truth of his account. He made no effort to answer the many charges made against him. His report was presented without any attempt at argument until the end of his speech, when he stated, in part: "But were not these Indians peaceable? Oh, yes, peaceable! Well, a few hundred of them have been peaceable for almost nineteen years, and none of them has been so troublesome as they were before Sand Creek. What are the facts? How about the treaty that Governor John Evans did not make with them in the summer of 1864? He, with . . . the usual corps of attachés,

---

[5]Dunn, *Massacres of the Mountains,* p. 444.

under escort, went out on the Kiowa to treat. When he got there they had gone a day's march further out on the plains and would meet him there, and so on day after day they moved out as he approached, until wearied and suspicious of treachery, he returned without succeeding in his mission of peace. He told them by message that he had presents for them, but it was not peace and presents they wanted, but war and plunder. . . . What of the trains captured from Walnut Creek to Sand Creek on the Arkansas route and from the Little Blue to the Kiowa on the Platte route? Of supplies and wagons burned and carried off and of men killed? . . . Aye, what of the scalps of white men, women and children, several of which they had not had time to dry and tan since taking. These, all these, and more were taken from the belts of dead warriors on the battlefield of Sand Creek, and from their tepees which fell into our hands on the 29th of November, 1864. What of the Indian blanket that was captured fringed with white women's scalps? What says the sleeping dust of the two hundred and eight men, women and children, ranchers, emigrants, herders and soldiers, who lost their lives at the hands of these Indians? Peaceable! Now we are peaceably disposed, but decline giving such testimonials of our peaceful proclivities, and I say here, as I said in my home town in the Quaker County of Clinton, Ohio, in a speech one night last week, 'I stand by Sand Creek.' "[6]

On the following day, the *Rocky Mountain News* described the reaction of the crowd to the colonel's speech in the following words: "Colonel Chivington's speech was received with an applause from every pioneer, which indicated that they, to a man, heartily approved the course of the colonel twenty years ago, in the famous affair in which many of them took part, and the man

---

[6]Chivington, "Sand Creek," *Denver Republican*, Oct. 5, 1894.

who applied the scalpel to the ulcer which bid fair to destroy the life of the new colony, in those critical times, was beyond a doubt the hero of the hour." From this reception and other observations made on his trip to Denver, the Fighting Parson was made aware that conditions had changed since 1867. The few, but highly vocal, enemies of the colonel had disappeared or been silenced, and Colorado too stood by Sand Creek. With this thought in mind and the memory of the recent bitter political campaign, he once again moved with his wife to Denver. Here he spent the remainder of his days, honored by his fellow citizens and unaffected by the condemnation of the Sand Creek campaign on the part of eastern sentimentalists.

During his later years the Fighting Parson spent a considerable portion of his time writing. He was on the editorial staff of the *Christian Advocate* of St. Louis for several years, and did editorial work for other papers. He also held several minor public offices in Denver. At one time, while he was holding a position as deputy sheriff, he was given the assignment of capturing the desperado Newt Vorse, who was wanted for the murder of one or more persons. Vorse had barricaded himself in a cabin located in an open area, and threatened to shoot anyone who approached. Chivington managed to reach a point within hailing distance, and called, "Come out with your hands up, Vorse, or I will throw this charge of dynamite and blow you and your cabin to atoms." This ended the siege. Knowing that Chivington would keep his word, the outlaw came out and surrendered.[7]

Strong and vigorous throughout his entire life, the Fighting Parson was finally laid low by cancer. Even with his *gigantic* frame and fighting heart, he could not resist this grim killer,

---

[7] Speer, John, *Rept. of Interview with Mrs. Chivington.*

which claimed his life on October 4, 1894. For several months he had suffered. Finally, unable to take nourishment of any kind, he lay for two weeks in a semiconscious condition, fighting for his life, until his iron constitution gave way.

During Chivington's last illness, he was visited many times by his old friend, the Reverend Isaac Beardsley, who kept him informed on matters relating to the Methodist Church. While the two men were conversing only two hours before the end, the Reverend Beardsley asked, "Colonel, how is it? Is Jesus precious to you?" With a smile, he answered: "His presence dwells within. It's all around me. It fills the room."[8] True to his religious faith, he willingly passed to his Maker, secure in the belief that there was a place prepared for him.

Colonel Chivington's funeral was conducted on October 7 under the direction of the Masonic Grand Lodge of Colorado. It was estimated that six hundred Masons were in the procession following the hearse, which was drawn by four black horses. The services were held in the Trinity Methodist Church, which had been the colonel's charge. There was a vast assemblage in attendance, including people from all walks of life. The lower floor of the building was almost wholly reserved. Masons were seated in the center, several hundred members of the Grand Army of the Republic on the right, and the Colorado Pioneers' Association and Pioneer Ladies' Society on the left. It was the largest gathering of pioneers in many years, representing all sections of the state. Scattered throughout the church were a very few gray-haired men wearing a yellow badge. They were the survivors of the First Colorado Cavalry who were present to pay their last respects to their dead commander.

---

[8]Beardsley, *Echoes From Peak and Plain,* pp. 252-253.

The Reverend Robert McIntyre, pastor of the church and one of Colonel Chivington's closest friends, presided at the services. Sitting with him on the platform were former Governor John Evans and representatives of the Masonic Grand Lodge, the Grand Army of the Republic and the Colorado Pioneer Society. Included in the pall-bearers, who were all Masons, veterans or pioneers, were the Fighting Parson's former comrades-in-arms Majors Jacob Downing and Scott J. Anthony. In his funeral discourse Dr. McIntyre said that Colonel Chivington had fought the good fight in a good cause. "When Colorado lifts aloft the scroll of honor," he said, "the name of Colonel John M. Chivington will be emblazoned near the top."[9]

---

[9]This account of Col. Chivington's funeral is taken from "Death of Bro. J. M. Chivington, First M. W. Grand Master of Masons in Colorado," *The Square and Compass* (Denver), Oct., 1894.

Bibliography

Bancroft, Hubert Howe, *The Works of,* Vol. XXV, *History of Nevada, Colorado, and Wyoming.* San Francisco: The History Co., 1890. (Cited as *Nevada, Colorado and Wyoming.*)

Banta, R. E., *The Ohio.* New York: Rinehart & Co., 1949.

Beardsley, Isaac H., *Echoes From Peak and Plain.* Cincinnati: Curts & Jennings, New York: Eaton & Mains, 1898.

Breakenridge, William H., *Helldorado.* Cambridge: Houghton Mifflin Co., 1928.

Casey, Lee Taylor, "Col. John M. Chivington—Soldier," *Rocky Mountain News,* March 3, 1929.

Chivington, John M., "Sand Creek" (an address delivered to a pioneer reunion in Denver Sept. 13, 1883), as published in the *Denver Republican,* Oct. 5, 1894, in connection with story of Col. Chivington's death on Oct. 4, 1894.

———— *The First Colorado Regiment.* Manuscript on file in Bancroft Library, Univ. of Calif., Berkeley, Calif. Excerpts quoted with permission of Bancroft Library.

———— "The Pet Lambs," *Sunday Denver Republican,* Apr. 20 through May 18, 1890.

———— *The Prospective (Retrospective).* Manuscript on file in Bancroft Library, Univ. of Calif., Berkeley, Calif. Excerpts quoted with permission of Bancroft Library.

Chlanda, Winifred Ottaway, *Notes on Ottaway Family History.* Unpublished manuscript.

Cleland, Robert G., *A History of California, The American Period.* New York: The Macmillan Co., 1930.

Dick, Everett, *The Story of the Frontier.* New York: Tudor Publishing Co., 1941.

Dormois, John T., *Address to Kansas City Posse of Westerners.* March 11, 1958.

———— "The Chivingtons," *The Masonic News-Digest* (Kansas City, Kansas), June 28, 1957.

———— "More About 'Friendly' (?) Indians," *The Masonic News-Digest,* Sept. 13, 1957.

———— Coleman, Francis M. and Farley, Alan W., *Centennial Wyandotte Lodge No. 3, A. F. & A. M.,* a pamphlet published in Kansas City, Kansas, 1954.

Dunn, J. P., Jr., *Massacres of the Mountains.* New York: Harper & Bros., 1886.

Ganoe, William A. (Major, Inf., U.S.A.). *History of the United States Army.* New York: D. Appleton & Co., 1945.

Gardiner, Dorothy, *West of the River.* New York: Thomas Y. Crowell Co., 1941.

Grinnell, George Bird, *The Fighting Cheyennes.* Norman: Univ. of Oklahoma Press, 1956.

Hafen, LeRoy R., *Colorado.* Denver: The Peerless Publishing Co., 1933.

———— and Rister, Carl Coke, *Western America.* Second edition. New York: Prentice-Hall, Inc., 1953.

Hall, Frank, *History of the State of Colorado.* Chicago: The Blakely Printing Co., 1889, Vol. I.

Hall, Martin H., "Colorado Volunteers Save New Mexico for the Union," *Mid-America,* Vol. 38: New Series, Vol. 27: No. 4.

———— "An Introduction to Colonel John M. Chivington's Manuscript 'The First Colorado Regiment,' " *New Mexico Historical Review,* Vol. XXXIII (April, 1958), pp. 144-154.

Hatcher, Harlan, *The Great Lakes.* New York: Oxford University Press, 1944.

Henry, Robert S., *The Story of the Confederacy.* Revised edition. New York: Grossett & Dunlap, 1936.

Hill, Alice Polk, *Tales of the Colorado Pioneers.* Denver: Pierson & Gardner, 1884.

Hollister, Ovando J., *History of the First Regiment of Colorado Volunteers.* (Denver, 1863). Reprinted as *Boldly They Rode.* Lakewood: The Golden Press, 1949. (cited as *History of the First*).

Horgan, Paul, *The Great River, The Rio Grande in North American History.* New York and Toronto: Rinehart & Co., Inc., 1954, Vol. 2.

Howbert, Irving, *Memories of a Lifetime in the Pike's Peak Region.* New York: G. P. Putnam's Sons, 1925. (cited as *Memories of the Pike's Peak Region*).

Inman, Henry (Col. U.S.A.), *The Old Santa Fe Trail.* New York: The Macmillan Co., 1897.

Johnson, Charles H. L, *Famous Indian Chiefs.* Boston: The Page Co., 1938.

Kerby, Robert L., *The Confederate Invasion of Arizona and New Mexico*. Los Angeles: Westernlore Press. 1958.

Kaufman. Patricia Kinney, *Chivington Family History*, in letter of Apr. 23, 1958.

Lavender, David, *Bent's Fort*. Garden City: Doubleday & Co., 1954.

Lowie, Robert H., *Indians of the Plains*. New York: McGraw-Hill Book Co., Inc., 1954.

Lyman, Clarence A., *The Truth About Colonel John M. Chivington*. Unpublished manuscript (written in 1956).

McMechen, Edgar C., *Life of Governor Evans*. Denver: Wahlgreen Publishing Co., 1924.

Mumey, Nolie, "John Milton Chivington—The Misunderstood Man," *Roundup* (published by Denver Posse of Westerners), Nov., 1956.

Nankivell, John H., *History of the Military Organizations of the State of Colorado 1860-1935*. Denver: W. H. Kistler Stationery Co., 1935.

Perrigo, Lynn I., "Major Hal Sayr's Diary of the Sand Creek Campaign," *The Colorado Magazine,* Vol. XV, No. 2, March, 1938 (cited as "Sayr's Diary of the Sand Creek Campaign").

Rister, Carl Coke, *Border Captives*. Norman: Univ. of Oklahoma Press, 1940.

Sandoz, Mari, *Cheyenne Autumn*. New York: McGraw-Hill Book Co., Inc., 1953.

Seymour, Flora Warren, *Indian Agents of the Old Frontier*. New York: D. Appleton-Century Co., 1941.

Shaw, Luella, *True History of Some of the Pioneers of Colorado*. Hotchkiss (Colo.): W. S. Coburn, John Patterson & A. K. Shaw, 1909.

Sheridan, P. H., *Personal Memoirs*. New York: Charles L. Webster and Co., 1888, Vol. II.

Sherman, W. T., *Personal Memoirs*. New York: Charles L. Webster and Co., 1891, Vol. II.

Snyder, Nellie Pollock, *Recollections of the Pioneer Life of Sarah Chivington Pollock, The First White Woman to Gaze upon the San Juan Basin*. Unpublished manuscript dated July, 1932 at Moab, Utah.

Speer, John, *Report to Fred Martin of Interview with Mrs. John M. Chivington,* dated March 11, 1902. Manuscript on file in Library Kansas State Historical Society, Topeka, Kansas.

Stewart, Edgar I., *Custer's Luck*. Norman: Univ. of Oklahoma Press, 1955.

Stirling, Mathew W., *Indians of the Americas*. Washington: National Geographic Society, 1955.

Swanton, John R., *Indian Tribes of North America*. Washington: U. S. Govt. Printing Office, 1953.

Tappan, Samuel F., *Autobiography* (in form of letter dated March 12, 1895). Manuscript in Archives of Kansas State Historical Society, Topeka, Kansas.

Tibbles. Thomas Henry, *Diary* covering his life with the Indians in 1858. Original document published in *Saturday Evening Post*, Aug. 31, 1957 under title "Buckskin and Blanket Days."

Vestal, Stanley, *Kit Carson*. Boston and New York: Houghton Mifflin Co.,1928.

———— *The Missouri*. New York: Farrar & Rinehart, Inc., 1945.

———— *Warpath and Council Fire*. New York: Random House, Inc., 1948.

Ward, Josiah M., "Chivington at the Battle of Sand Creek," *Denver Post*, Jan. 30 and Feb. 6, 1921.

Wharton, Clarence R., *History of Texas*. Dallas: Turner Co., 1935.

Whitford, William C., *Colorado Volunteers in the Civil War*. Denver: The State Historical and Natural History Society, 1906.

Whitney, Chauncy B., *Diary*. Kansas State Historical Collections (Topeka, 1911-12), Vol. XII, p. 296.

Williams, Albert N., *Rocky Mountain Country*. New York: Duell, Sloan & Pearce. 1950.

Annual Report of the Secretary of War, 1869 (Abridgment), p. 42.

Battles and Leaders of the Civil War. (four volumes). New York: Thomas Yoseloff, Inc., 1956 Edition, Vol. 2.

Congressional Globe, Part 1, 38th Cong., 2d sess., Jan. 9, 1865.

History of Warren County, Ohio. Chicago: W. H. Beers & Co., 1882.

Minutes of the Annual Conference of the Methodist Episcopal Church for years 1868 and 1870, pp. 98 and 84, respectively.

Ottaway Family Bible.

Probate Records of Warren County, Ohio. Marriage license—Isaac Chivington and Jane Runyan, p. 57, Book 1; Administration of Estate of Isaac Chivington, Docket of Estates—No. o—pp. 308, 316; Deed, Isaac and Jane Chivington to Benjamin Whitacre, Vol. 12 of Deed Books, p. 109.

Record of Service of John M. Chivington, War Department, Record and Pension Division, No. 1059948. National Archives, Record Group No. 15B, WC 416-181.

Report, Secretary of the Interior (1867-68), pp. 530, 542.

Rocky Mountain News, Apr. 14, 15; May 4; July 23; Aug. 1, 9, 11, 13, 15, 23, 25; Sept. 10, 24, 29; Dec. 12, 13, 17, 22, 30, 1864 and Sept. 14, 1883.

Senate Document 142, Vol. 3, 38th Cong., 2d sess., Report of Joint Committee on the Conduct of the War (section entitled "Massacre of Cheyennes Indians"). Washington: U. S. Govt. Print. Off., 1865.

Senate Executive Document 26, 39th Cong., 2d sess., Report of Secretary of War (transmitting copy of proceedings of military commission). Washington: U. S. Govt. Print. Off., 1867.

Senate Report 156, 39th Cong., 2d sess., Report of Joint Special Committee to Inquire into Condition of Indian Tribes (with appendix). Washington: U. S. Govt. Print. Off., 1867, pp. 26-98, 213-214 (of appendix).

The Square and Compass (Denver), "Death of Bro. J. M. Chivington, First M. W. Grand Master of Masons in Colorado," October, 1894.

War of the Rebellion: Official Records of the Union and Confederate Armies, Series I. (cited as *Rebellion Records.*) Washington: U. S. Govt. Print. Off., 1893, Vol. IX, pp. 487-493, 505-506, 509, 510, 530, 531, 532, 534, 538, 542, 543, 630, 646, 649; Vol. XXXIV, Part 1, pp. 880-885; Vol. XLI, Part 1, pp. 830, 948-972; Vol. XLI, Part 2, pp. 661, 672, 673, 695, 809, 810, 845; Vol. XLVIII, pp. 40-44, 511.

Legal Analysis of the Sand Creek Hearings

By REGINALD S. CRAIG, *of the California Bar*

The official reports of the investigations of the Sand Creek campaign made by two joint congressional committees label the incident as a massacre, and the Judge Advocate General adopts the same view in his official report on the military investigation.[1] All three of these reports strongly condemn Colonel John M. Chivington and his officers and men for their conduct on that occasion. This article will consider the legal sufficiency of the evidence to sustain this position.

The basic uncontradicted facts of this affair are simple. Colonel John M. Chivington, with elements of the First and Third Colorado Cavalry, attacked Black Kettle's band of Cheyennes, which was encamped on Sand Creek, about forty miles northeast of Fort Lyon in southeastern Colorado, on November 29, 1864. Between one hundred and fifty and four hundred and fifty Indians were killed, with a loss of seven soldiers dead, forty-seven wounded and one missing. Colonel Chivington and his friends, including the major portion of the officers and men of his command, considered the affair as a battle. Others labeled it a massacre.

The specific charges considered at the investigations may be briefly summarized as follows:

1. The Indians attacked were either friendly or had surrendered to the military and were under the protection of the authorities at Fort Lyon.

---

[1] *Records of Judge Advocate General.* National Archives, RG 153.

2. When attacked, these Indians were practically defenseless, and were slaughtered in an indiscriminate massacre, without regard to age or sex.

3. Colonel Chivington issued orders to his troops which resulted in this slaughter.

4. The bodies of many of the Indians were mutilated by the soldiers in a most inhuman manner, with the knowledge and approval of Colonel Chivington.

The report of the Joint Committee on the Conduct of the War includes, in a section entitled "Massacre of Cheyenne Indians," a transcript of the evidence taken to investigate the Sand Creek incident.[2] According to this transcript, this congressional committee heard the testimony of nine witnesses, eight in person and one by deposition; and received in evidence three documents, or groups of documents, which had some bearing on the charges involved, as well as numerous copies of reports, correspondence and other documents which had very little bearing on the investigation. The witnesses, D. D. Colley, A. C. Hunt and Jesse H. Leavenworth, did not testify to any facts within their own knowledge which had any bearing on the charges; and, accordingly, their testimony was hearsay and valueless.[3] The matters testified to by Captain S. M. Robbins had no bearing on the charges. Exclusive of the documentary evidence, this leaves for consideration only the personal testimony of John S. Smith, a government employed interpreter and Indian trader; Major Scott J. Anthony, the Post Commander at Fort Lyon, who had taken part in the attack with some of his men; Major S. G. Colley, Indian Agent at Fort Lyon; and Governor Evans, together with the deposition of Colonel Chivington.

---

[2]*Senate Document 142, Vol. 3,* 38th Cong., 2d sess. Washington: U. S. Govt. Print. Off., 1865.

[3]"Subject to certain exceptions, the courts will not receive testimony of a witness as to what some other person told him as evidence of the fact asserted." 31 Corpus Juris Secundum, p. 919.

Among the documents included in the record of the proceedings are the official reports of the Sand Creek engagement,
which, although unsworn, are entitled to full consideration
under the rules of evidence, since they were made at or near
the time of the occurrence by officers having personal knowledge
of the facts, and they are included in the official records of the
War Department.[4] On the other hand, the unsworn report of
Major E. W. Wynkoop, made after his assumption of command at Fort Lyon after the Sand Creek attack, is not entitled
to any consideration, since it is based entirely on hearsay and
does not recite one fact of his own knowledge.[5] The affidavits
attached to Major Wynkoop's report are also valueless as evidence, since they are largely hearsay, are in general rather than
specific terms and are not in the proper question and answer, or
deposition, form normally required for admission in a court of
law.[6] Thus it appears that we have the personal testimony of
four witnesses, the deposition of one witness and one group of
official reports to consider relative to the truth or falsity of the
charges.

The contention that the Indians encamped on Sand Creek
were friendly was based primarily on a claim that Black Kettle
and his band had surrendered to Major Wynkoop and turned
their arms over to him when he was in command at Fort Lyon;

---

[4]"As a general rule, where some enactment or rule of law requires or author-
izes a public official to make a certificate or written statement as to some matter
of fact pertaining to and as a part of his official duty, such writing is competent
evidence of the matter of fact therein recited." 32 C.J.S., p. 478.

[5]"Insofar as documents set forth the mere opinions or conclusions of public
officials they are inadmissible as official records or documents." 32 C.J.S., p.
490. A report of a public official based on hearsay is inadmissible. Harrigan vs.
Chaperon, 118 Cal. App. 2d 167.

[6]"Ex parte affidavits are commonly regarded as weak evidence, to be received
with caution, and not to be used where better evidence is obtainable." 32 C.J.S.,
p. 1075. On the other hand, depositions are a higher type of proof; and some
decisions accord them the same weight as oral testimony. 32 C.J.S., pp. 1075-
1076.

and, in return, had been promised the protection of the military. It was also claimed that, when Major Anthony relieved Major Wynkoop at Fort Lyon, he approved this arrangement and continued to feed those Indians for a while, after which he told them he could no longer provide them with food, and sent them out on Sand Creek to hunt buffalo, in the meantime continuing their status as quasi prisoners of war. On this point Major Anthony testified that, upon reaching Fort Lyon, he found six hundred and fifty *Arapahoes,* and not the band of Cheyennes which was attacked at Sand Creek; that he fed these Indians for a while and then sent them out to hunt; and that they had previously surrendered some arms and stolen stock. Although Major Colley testified that Black Kettle and his band were friendly, he also stated that the Indians encamped near Fort Lyon when Major Anthony arrived were *Arapahoes* who had been fed by Major Wynkoop. Thus, his testimony supports that of Major Anthony. Governor Evans described his unavailing efforts, as Ex-officio Superintendent of Indian Affairs for the Territory of Colorado, to induce the Indians to stop their raids. Also, he conclusively showed that the Cheyennes and Arapahoes had been viciously hostile during the entire summer and fall preceding the Sand Creek engagement, and that this was admitted by Black Kettle and the other chiefs at the council held in Denver in the early fall.

John S. Smith, the interpreter, furnished the only clear evidence that the Sand Creek Indians were friendly when he testified that they had been induced to stay near Fort Lyon, and had been promised protection by the commanding officer of that post. However, there was no evidence from Major Wynkoop relative to this alleged understanding. Since the testimony of one witness that the Indians attacked were friendly is opposed by that of two witnesses that they were hostile, with one other witness supporting both positions in part, it appears that the band was indeed hostile and that the attack was justified. General Frank Hall, in his work on Colorado history,[7] makes this same analysis and comes to the same conclusion.

On the matter of the alleged indiscriminate massacre, Major Anthony's testimony indicates the charge to be false. He did state that he saw one little boy shot; but, on the other hand, he testified that, while the women and children were escaping to a place of safety, the men stood under the creek banks and fought the troops all day. Colonel Chivington, in his deposition, testified that officers who passed over the field by his orders reported that they saw but few women and children dead, no more than would be certain to fall in an attack on a camp where they were. He also testified that he himself saw but one woman who had been killed, one who had hanged herself and no dead children. In the official reports of the engagement, the fighting is described as very fierce and lasting for several hours. Only John Smith testified that the affair was an indiscriminate slaughter. Accordingly, it must be considered that the weight of reliable evidence at the committee hearing establishes the fact that the incident was an engagement and not a massacre.

Although a finding of untrue on the second charge would render it unnecessary to consider the third charge, it seems desirable to investigate the orders or exhortations which Colonel Chivington may have given his men, since the evidence shows that there were probably some excesses committed. The only evidence of John Smith on this matter relates to a statement alleged to have been made by Major Anthony concerning another statement claimed to have been made by Colonel Chivington. This must be rejected as hearsay. Major Anthony testified concerning a conversation with Colonel Chivington relative to the possible danger to the life of Jack Smith, the half-Cheyenne son of Interpreter John Smith who had been found in the camp. In this testimony, Anthony quoted the colonel as stating that he

---

[7]Hall, Frank, *History of the State of Colorado*. Chicago: The Blakely Printing Co., 1889, Vol. I, p. 344.

had told his men not to take any prisoners. Colonel Chivington, in his deposition, stated with reference to wounded Indians, "If there were any wounded, I do not think they could have been made prisoners without endangering the lives of the soldiers; Indians usually fight as long as they have strength to resist." From this scanty evidence, it can only be concluded that no orders were issued which could be construed as the signal for a general massacre of all Indians in the camp. However, it appears that Colonel Chivington may have issued orders not to make prisoners of the warriors to protect the troops. It also appears that these orders did not prevent noncombatants from escaping, nor even surrendering in view of the statement in the colonel's deposition that eight Indians fell into the hands of the troops alive and, with one exception, were sent to Fort Lyon and properly cared for.

On the question of the alleged extensive mutilation of the bodies of the Indians, we have only the affirmative testimony of John Smith. This is opposed by evidence from Major Anthony that he observed some instances of mutilation and scalping, but not to the degree that he had since heard stated, and that the officers did not seem to have control over their men. In view of the obvious hostility and bias of the witness John Smith, due probably to the death of his half-Cheyenne son at the hands of some of the soldiers and the financial loss in trading operations which he sustained as a result of the battle, his evidence must be viewed with suspicion. Accordingly, it appears that there were some cases of scalping and mutilation due, in part, to the failure of the officers to exercise adequate control over the main body of relatively inexperienced troops, coupled with the natural resentment of those soldiers whose families had suffered at the hands of the savages. There is no evidence whatever that such actions were encouraged by Colonel Chivington, nor that they were undertaken with his previous knowledge or consent.

The types of questions asked many of the witnesses and the testimony received indicates that the committee was highly prejudiced. Most of the witnesses hostile to the Colorado colonel, including some who admitted that they knew nothing concerning the matters in issue, were asked their opinions as to the reason that Colonel Chivington made an attack upon unsuspecting "friendly" Indians; and, in each case, the reply was that he wanted to run for Congress or to be promoted.

The report of the Joint Special Committee to Inquire into the Condition of the Indian Tribes[8] contains in an appendix, as part of one of the subcommittee reports, a transcript of the evidence taken by the subcommittee relative to the Sand Creek attack. This record sets forth the testimony of Samuel G. Colley, Jesse H. Leavenworth, John S. Smith and Governor Evans, who all presented evidence to substantially the same effect as that which they had given at the other congressional hearing. The record also includes copies of most of the affidavits, orders and reports received by the other congressional committee and many similar documents. Except for some of the official reports which have no bearing on the points at issue, none of these documents would be admissible as legal evidence, since they are largely hearsay and not in proper question and answer form. Therefore, the evidence relative to the Sand Creek incident taken by the subcommittee for the Joint Special Committee is not substantially at variance with that received by the Joint Committee on the Conduct of the War.

The records of the 39th Congress contain a transcript of the evidence taken in Denver and at Fort Lyon by a military commission, which was convened by Special Orders No. 23, Headquarters District of Colorado, dated February 1, 1865, "to investigate into the conduct of the late Colonel J. M. Chivington, 1st Regiment Colorado Cavalry, in his recent campaign against

---

[8]*Senate Report 156,* 39th Cong., 2d sess. Washington: U. S. Govt. Print. Off., 1867, pp. 26-98 (of appendix).

the Indians."[9] In its investigation, this commission heard the
testimony of thirty-four witnesses in person and two by deposition, and accepted in evidence five documents or groups of documents. Twelve witnesses testified relative to loss of government
property, alleged improper accounting for such property, or
other matters not bearing on the four charges of improper conduct against Colonel Chivington and his men. Similarly, three
groups of documents and one of the depositions have no bearing
on these points. Major Wynkoop's report on the Sand Creek incident with attached affidavits, which were also included in the
proceedings of the two congressional committees, must be considered valueless, as largely hearsay and the type of documents
not admissible in a court of law. This leaves for consideration
the testimony of thirteen witnesses called by the commission,
who were hostile to Colonel Chivington, ten witnesses friendly
to the colonel, who were called by him, nine appearing in person and one by deposition, and one set of documents, official
orders and reports of the expedition.

On the first point, four witnesses testified to facts which indicated that the Indians at Sand Creek were friendly, and eight
to matters indicating that they were hostile. Further, on this
point the testimony of two other witnesses, who were hostile to
the colonel, is ambiguous but provides considerable support for
the position that the Indians were hostile. Captain S. S. Soule,
one of these witnesses, testified that, before the attack, he tried
to send word to Colonel Chivington that the red men encamped
on Sand Creek were friendly and under military protection.
However, he also gave evidence that the Indians who surrendered at Fort Lyon were *Arapahoes,* and not Black Kettle's
band of Cheyennes, which formed the main body of the savages
attacked at Sand Creek. Another of these witnesses, Lieutenant

---

[9]*Senate Executive Document 26,* 39th Cong., 2d sess., Report of Secretary of
War (transmitting copy of proceedings of military commission), Washington:
U. S. Govt. Print. Off., 1867.

Joseph A. Cramer, after testifying that the Indians involved were entitled to protection, admitted on cross examination that very few of the Indians attacked at Sand Creek were at any time encamped at Fort Lyon, where it had been alleged that they surrendered. According to the evidence given by Dr. Caleb S. Birdsall, First Assistant Surgeon of the Third Colorado Cavalry, and two other witnesses, scalps of white men, women and children, some only a few days old, were found in the Cheyenne camp at Sand Creek. Further, the testimony of the witnesses on the affirmative side of this point is with reference to matters which are either hearsay or bear but slightly on the matter in question. Under these circumstances, the testimony of the eight witnesses on the other side of the issue, together with the statements in the official orders and reports of the expedition, must be accepted as proving beyond a reasonable doubt that the Indians at Sand Creek were clearly hostile and not entitled to the protection of the military.

On the second point as to whether or not the Indians in question were defenseless, and were slaughtered without regard for age or sex, five witnesses testified in the affirmative, while two witnesses and the official reports of the expedition support the negative. Captain Soule testified that women and children were shot while attempting to escape, and that some Indians held up their hands to indicate peaceable intentions. However, he also stated that the fighting was still going on when he left the field between two and three in the afternoon, under orders for another assignment; and that he knew some Indians escaped. Lieutenant Cramer testified that several Indians were killed while running toward the troops with their hands up, and that two-thirds of the dead were women and children. The guide, James P. Beckwith, testified that two-thirds of the dead were women and children, and that White Antelope advanced toward the troops with his hands up. According to Lieutenant James D. Cannon about two-thirds of those killed were women and children, and Private N. D. Snyder stated that, when he visited the field with a patrol some time after the attack, about one-half of the bodies found were those of women and children. Lieutenant Stephen Decatur testified that he went over the field and counted the bodies on the orders of Lieutenant Colonel Bowen, that he found four hundred and fifty dead savages, that those killed included very few women and that the women's bodies were found in rifle pits. He further stated that, although he had taken part in four battles, he had never seen harder fighting on both sides. Private Alexander Safely testified that the Indians began the firing, and that White Antelope advanced toward the troops firing a revolver. From the testimony of several other witnesses and the official reports of the expedition, it seems clear that the fighting continued from sunrise to late afternoon, and that the attack was from the south and east, leaving escape routes to the north and west. A bona fide engagement that lasted all day, with avenues of escape open for noncombatants and even for withdrawing combatants, can hardly be considered a massacre, nor regarded to be planned as one, since the village could have been surrounded in view of the surprise nature of the attack. Accordingly, the evidence does not establish that there was any general indiscriminate slaughter of defenseless Indians.

There is no direct positive evidence on the question of whether or not Colonel Chivington issued orders which led to the killing of women and children. James Beckwith testified to a long enciting address by the colonel, exhorting the soldiers to remember their mothers, father, brothers and sisters who had been killed on the Platte. Captain Gill quotes the expedition commander as saying, "Now boys, I shan't say who you shall kill, but remember our murdered women and children." Lieutenant Cannon, who was obviously extremely hostile to Colonel Chivington based on his statements in an affidavit attached to Wynkoop's report, testified that the colonel addressed the command before the attack, saying, "Men remember the murdered women and children on the Platte," that the troops were then ordered to charge, and that *there were no other orders given.* Colonel George L. Shoup, in his deposition, testified that Colonel Chivington made no remarks to the troops in his hearing, but that the expedition commander told him, "we must not allow John Smith and family to be harmed," and that he did not intend to take any prisoners. From this scanty evidence, it is obvious that the charge that Colonel Chivington issued orders leading to a massacre, or the killing of women and children, is certainly not established.

On the fourth point regarding outrages to the Indians' bodies, three witnesses testified positively to extensive mutilation, namely, Captain Soule, Lieutenant Cannon and Private Louderbach. The first two were obviously extremely hostile to Colonel Chivington. Captain Soule was vague with reference to details, and most of his testimony refers to the taking of scalps by soldiers, including a few children's scalps, although he could not say how many of such cases he observed. Lieutenant Cannon was even more vague on this subject, and some of his testimony is purely hearsay. Private Snyder testified that he saw no mutilations taking place at the time of the battle, but that, when he returned later with a patrol, some mutliated bodies were found. Beckwith stated that there was some scalping, but no other mutilation except on the body of White Antelope. Captain Gill saw one soldier scalp an Indian; and three enlisted men testified with reference to scalping, including one who referred to "some" scalping. Lieutenant Decatur stated that he saw no scalping or other mutilating. Based on this meagre evidence, and in view of the moderation in the testimony of Beckwith, who was obviously extremely antagonistic to Colonel Chivington, it appears that any mutilation other than scalping was confined to a very few instances. There is no competent evidence relative to any knowledge or approval of Colonel Chivington of scalping or any other mutilation which may have occurred.

The record shows that the hearing was conducted in a manner extremely hostile to the Colorado colonel and the citizen soldiers who constituted his command at Sand Creek. The order setting forth the duties of the commission specified that, "This commission is not intended for the trial of any person, but simply to investigate and accumulate facts called for by the government, to fix the responsibility if any, and to insure justice to all parties."[10] In spite of these clear instructions to secure the facts without regard to their nature, the commission failed to secure any witnesses favorable to Colonel Chivington; and all of the nineteen witnesses which it called testified to matters reflecting adversely on the conduct of the colonel and his men, or to matters of largely an extraneous nature. The colonel was then allowed to present a "defense" as though he were actually on trial; and he produced sixteen witnesses to testify on his behalf, fifteen in person and one by deposition.

The testimony of Captain Cree related to a conversation with Lieutenant Cramer in which the lieutenant said that Colonel Chivington was working to become a brigadier general, and that the lieutenant and his associates would make a massacre out of the Sand Creek affair and crush him. This evidence, which would be legally competent to prove a state of mind,[11] indicates a hostile and prejudiced attitude on the part of one of the commission's principal witnesses, as well as a possible conspiracy to falsely blacken the colonel's reputation. The procedure at the hearing was a further indication of the preju-

---

[10]Letter of instructions of Dist. Commander, supplementing Special Order 23, Hq. Dist of Colo., as given in report of Sec. of War cited in Note 9, supra. Although Special Order 23 referred to the board appointed thereunder as a "military commission," it was in fact a court of inquiry, since military commissions are courts organized for the trial of persons not in the land or naval forces (93 C.J.S. p. 119); while courts of inquiry are lower courts instigated for investigatory purposes. 6 C.J.S. p. 438.

[11]This is not hearsay, since its probative force does not depend on the competence and credibility of some person other than the witness. 31 C.J.S. p. 919.

diced attitude of the commission. Practically all of Colonel Chivington's objections were overruled and most of his requests denied. Many of the witnesses testified largely in answer to leading questions from the attorney for the commission, which would be contrary to proper procedure in a court of law.[12]

Much hearsay evidence was received, and a copy of the unsworn, unsubstantiated, hearsay report of the battle made by Major Wynkoop, with the attached affidavits, also largely hearsay, was admitted in evidence over the objection of Colonel Chivington. The crowning injustice was the service of Lieutenant Colonel S. F. Tappan as president of the commission, in view of his well known enmity to Colonel Chivington arising from the fact that Tappan was passed over when Chivington was promoted to Colonel of the First Colorado Regiment.

The conclusions to be drawn from the evidence in each of the hearings are very much the same. In considering the three hearings together, it appears conclusively proven that the Indians who were attacked at Sand Creek were definitely hostile, that fresh scalps of white men, women and children were found in their village, and that the engagement was actually a battle lasting all day, and not a massacre. Further, there is a complete lack of any evidence to show that Colonel Chivington authorized, approved or even knew of any mutilations of Indians' bodies that may have occurred. Left in doubt by the combined reliable evidence of these hearings is the proportion of women and children among the Indian dead, the extent of mutilation of bodies, other than scalping, which undoubtedly took place to some degree, and the exact orders given by the colonel to the troops.

In the last analysis, the solution to the doubtful questions rests on the probable veracity of the principal witnesses testifying on each side, namely, Major Anthony, Colonel Chivington,

---

[12]*McKelvey on Evidence.* St. Paul: West Pub. Co., 1898, p. 325; People vs. Mather, 4 Wend. (N. Y.) 229; Osborn vs. Forshee, 22 Mich. 209.

Colonel Shoup and Lieutenant Decatur for the colonel and his men, as opposed to John Smith the interpreter, James Beckwith the guide, Captain Soule, Lieutenant Cramer and Lieutenant Cannon. Major Anthony and Colonel Chivington were men of standing in the community, in both civilian and military circles. Colonel Chivington was a minister of the Gospel in civilian life, and, prior to entering the service, he was Presiding Elder of the Rocky Mountain Conference of the Methodist Episcopal Church. Colonel Shoup was also highly regarded by his fellow citizens, and, somewhat later, he served for a number of years as United States Senator from the State of Idaho. John Smith and James Beckwith were closely associated with the Indians and probably prejudiced in their favor. The testimony of Captain Soule and Lieutenant Cramer may have been affected by their loyalty to their former commander, Major Wynkoop, who was obviously extremely hostile to Colonel Chivington.

The most defamatory part of the record of the hearings is formed by the report of investigation made by Major Wynkoop. In this report the major stated that "the most fearful atrocities were committed that ever was heard of," that "women and children were killed and scalped, . . . and all bodies mutilated in the most horrible manner." He also stated that numerous eye-witnesses had described scenes to him of the "most disgusting and horrible character," including the profaning of the dead bodies of females, with "Col. J. M. Chivington all the time enciting his troops to their diabolical outrages." There is no sworn testimony whatever to verify these unfounded charges. Nevertheless, the official records of both of the congressional committees and the military commission contain, *as a document received in evidence,* the full text of Major Wynkoop's unsworn and unsubstantiated report, which, by its terms, is based on hearsay. Under these circumstances, and particularly since it forms the only part of the record of any of the proceedings which, if true, would indicate misconduct by Colonel Chivington, it seems clear that it is the major item in the record upon which the battle of Sand Creek has been classified by a number of historians as a "massacre." It is also undoubtedly the basis for the report of the Joint Committee on the Conduct of the War, which flayed Colonel Chivington for what the committee considered as his outrageous conduct. Further, the Judge Advocate General of the Army, in a report on the record of the military commission,[13] which may have been influenced by the Wynkoop report, stated that Colonel Chivington could not be tried by court-martial since he had been released from service, and castigated those responsible for the "crimes" committed at Sand Creek.

If the military commission, as the primary investigating body, felt that Colonel Chivington was guilty of the acts charged, it was its duty to recommend prosecution. Having been mustered out of service, he could not be tried by a military court. However, since the acts charged were in violation of the laws of the Territory of Colorado relating to murder, mayhem and robbery, the commission could have recommended that he be referred to the civil courts for prosecution, or the War Department could have instituted such action based on the record.[14] On the other hand, if the evidence did not support the charges, it was the commission's duty to so state in its final report "to insure justice to all parties" as specified in its instructions from the appointing authority.

---

[13]See Note 1, supra.

[14]The Articles of War do not deprive the civil courts of concurrent jurisdiction over crimes against either federal or state laws committed within the geographical limits of the United States by persons subject to military law. 6 C.J.S. pp. 425-426; U. S. vs. Hirsch (D. C. N. Y.), 254 Fed. 109; Coleman vs. Tennessee, 97 U. S. 509. While a person discharged from service may not be subject to court-martial, he can be prosecuted under the general laws for crimes committed during his active service, unless previously put in jeopardy. 6 C.J.S. p. 448; U. S. vs. MacDonald (D. C. N. Y.), 265 Fed. 695. In the Coleman case the court construed the Act of Congress of March 3, 1863 setting forth the rules for court-martial and crimes punishable thereunder, which was in force when the battle of Sand Creek took place.

Having considered the purport of the evidence, it now becomes desirable to briefly discuss the legal significance of the hearings. One phase of this discussion involves the question of possible abuse by congressional committees of the power to investigate and accumulate facts as a basis for contemplated legislation. There has always been a tendency on the part of some of these committees to make inquiries for political purposes, or to uncover questionable acts on the part of various segments of the population. Even though much of this activity is well meaning, legally and as a matter of good governmental procedure, the investigation of wrongdoing should be left to federal or local grand juries.

A judicial attitude, or lack of it, was displayed in a number of congressional actions during the period immediately following the Civil War. This is typified by the action of the Fortieth Congress, not long after the Sand Creek hearings, when the Senate failed by only one vote to impeach President Johnson on the grounds of treason, in spite of the lack of any substantial evidence to support the charges, which had been voted by a large majority in the House of Representatives.

In the Sand Creek case, it appears that the investigatory power of Congress was grossly abused to blacken the reputations of a volunteer officer and his men without any substantial, competent legal evidence to support the charges against them. In any event, the findings of the congressional committees are null and void to the extent that they indicate any persons to be guilty of criminal acts, since the legislative branch has no power to encroach on the functions of the courts.[15] Further, the report of the Committee on the Conduct of the War made no recommendations concerning the necessity for any legislation covering

---

[15]Each branch of the legislature (Congress) has powers to conduct investigations to determine the necessity and expediency of contemplated legislation. However, the legislative body is without power to pass an act or resolution authorizing an investigation by a committee where such investigation is judicial in nature. 16 C.J.S. 510; Kelbourn vs. Thompson, 103 U. S. 168.

the matters at issue, which would form the only legal basis for its investigation. Also, the transcript of the Sand Creek hearing held by the other congressional committee contained very little, if any, material bearing on the legislation which it finally proposed. Accordingly, the whole proceeding of each committee in connection with the Sand Creek incident may well be considered to be without legal significance, as public, judicial investigations beyond the constitutional powers of Congress.[16] Moreover, the report of the Judge Advocate General, based on the record of the military commission, is without legal effect to find any person guilty of criminal offenses, since the military commission was in reality a court of inquiry,[17] and courts of this nature are instituted solely for investigation and are not judicial tribunals.[18]

---

[16]Although a legislature has power to obtain information upon any subject upon which it has power to legislate, it cannot conduct a public and judicial investigation of charges made against an institution or individual under the pretense or cloak of legislation. Greenfield vs. Russel (Supreme Ct. of Ill:, 1920), 127 N.E. 102.

[17]See Note 10, supra.

[18]Army and Navy Courts of Inquiry are not judicial tribunals, being instituted solely for the purpose of inquiry; and their proceedings are in no sense a trial of an issue of an accused person. 6 C.J.S. p. 440; 25 Op. Atty.-Gen. 623.

Extract from Proceedings of Joint Congressional Committee on the Conduct of the War

38th Cong. 2d Sess.

LETTER JAN. 12, 1865
GEN. CURTIS TO GEN. HALLECK, CHIEF OF STAFF

Your dispatch of yesterday, directing me to investigate Colonel Chivington's conduct towards the Indians is received and will be obeyed. Colonel Chivington has been relieved by Colonel Moonlight, and is probably out of the service under provisions of Circular No. 36, War Department. . . . Although the colonel may have transgressed my field orders concerning Indian warfare, (a copy of which is here enclosed) . . . still it is not true . . . that such severity is increasing Indian war. On the contrary it tends to reduce their numbers and bring them to terms. . . . I fear that Colonel Chivington's assault at Sand Creek was upon Indians who had received some encouragement to camp in that vicinity under some erroneous supposition of the commanding officer at Lyon that he could make a sort of "City of Refuge" . . . However wrong that may have been, it should have been respected and any violation of known arrangements of that sort should be severely rebuked. But there is no doubt a portion of the tribe assembled were occupied in making assault on our stages and trains, and the tribes well know that we have to hold the whole community responsible for acts they could restrain if they would properly exert their efforts in that way.

DEPOSITION OF JOHN M. CHIVINGTON

3Q—Did you, as colonel in command of Colorado troops, about the 29th of November, 1864, make an attack on an Indian village or camp at a place known as Sand Creek? If so, state particularly the number of men under your command; how armed and equipped; . . .

3A—On the 29th of November, 1864, the troops under my command attacked a camp of Cheyenne and Arapaho Indians at a place known as Big Bend of Sandy, about forty miles north of Fort Lyon, Colorado Territory. There were in my command at that time about (500) five hundred men of the 3rd regiment Colorado cavalry, under the immediate command of Colonel George L. Shoup, of said 3rd regiment, and about (250) two hundred and fifty men of the 1st Colorado cavalry;... The 3rd regiment was armed with rifled muskets, and Star's and Sharp's carbines. A few of the men of that regiment had revolvers. The men of the 3rd regiment were poorly equipped; the supply of blankets, boots, hats, and caps was deficient. The men of the 1st regiment were well equipped;...

4Q—State as nearly as you can the number of Indians that were in the village or camp at the time the attack was made; how many of them were warriors; how many were old men, how many of them were women, and how many of them were children?

4A—From the best and most reliable information I could obtain, there were in the Indian camp, at the time of the attack, about eleven (11) or twelve (12) hundred Indians; of these about seven hundred were warriors, and the remainder were women and children. I am not aware that there were any old men among them. There was an unusual number of males among them, for the reason that the war chiefs of both nations were assembled there evidently for some special purpose.

5Q—At what time of the day or night was the attack made? Was it a surprise to the Indians? What preparation, if any, had they made for defense or offense?

5A—The attack was made about sunrise. In my opinion the Indians were surprised; they began, as soon as the attack was made, to oppose my troops, however, and were soon fighting desperately. Many of the Indians were armed with rifles and many with revolvers; I think all had bows and arrows. They had excavated trenches under the bank of Sand Creek, which in the vicinity of the Indian camp is high, and in many places precipitous. These trenches were two to three feet deep, and, in connection with the banks, were evidently designed to protect the occupants from the fire of the enemy. They were found at various points extending along the banks of the creek for several miles from the camp;...

7Q—What number of Indians were killed; and what number of the killed were women, and what number were children?

7A—From the best information I could obtain, I judge there were five hundred or six hundred Indians killed; I cannot state positively the number of killed, nor can I state positively the number of women and children killed. Officers who passed over the field, by my orders, after the battle, for the purpose of ascertaining the number of Indians killed, report that they saw but few women or children dead, no more than would certainly fall in an attack upon a camp in which they were. I myself passed over some portions of the field after the fight, and I saw but one woman who had been killed, and one who had hanged herself; I saw no dead children. From all I could learn, I arrived at the conclusion that but few women or children had been slain. I am of the opinion that when the attack was made on the Indian camp the greater number of squaws and children made their escape, while the warriors remained to fight my troops.

8Q—State, as nearly as you can, the number of Indians that were wounded, giving the number of women and the number of children among the wounded.

8A—I do not know that any Indians were wounded that were not killed; if there were any wounded, I do not think they could have been made prisoners without endangering the lives of soldiers; Indians usually fight as long as they have strength to resist. Eight Indians fell into the hands of the troops alive, to my knowledge; these, with one exception, were sent to Fort Lyon and properly cared for. . . .

10Q—What reason had you for making the attack? What reasons, if any, had you to believe that Black Kettle or any other Indian or Indians in the camp entertained feelings of hostility towards the whites? Give in detail the names of all Indians so believed to be hostile, with the dates and places of their hostile acts, so far as you are able to do so.

10A—My reason for making the attack on the Indian camp was that I believed the Indians in the camp were hostile to the whites. That they were of the same tribes with those who had murdered many persons and destroyed much valuable property on the Platte and Arkansas rivers during the previous spring, summer and fall was beyond a doubt. When a tribe of Indians is at war with the whites it is impossible to determine what party or band of the tribe or the name or names of the Indian or Indians belonging to the tribe so at war are guilty of the acts of hostility. The most that can be ascertained is that Indians of the tribe have performed the acts. During the spring, summer and fall of 1864, the Arapaho and Cheyenne Indians, in some instances assisted, or led by the Sioux, Kiowas, Comanches and Apaches, had committed many acts of hostility . . . Their rendezvous was on the headwaters of the Republican, probably 100 miles from where the Indian camp was located. I had every reason to believe that these Indians were either directly or indirectly concerned in the outrages which had been committed upon the whites. I had no means of ascertaining what were the names of the Indians who had committed these outrages other than the declarations of the Indians themselves; and the character of the Indians in the western country for truth and veracity, like their respect for the chastity of women who may become prisoners in their hands, is not of that order which is calculated to inspire confidence in what they may say. . . .

11Q—Had you any, and if so, what reason, to believe that Black Kettle and the Indians with him, at the time of your attack, were at peace with the whites, and desired to remain at peace with them?

11A—I had no reason to believe that Black Kettle and the Indians with him were in good faith at peace with the whites. The day before the attack Maj. Scott J. Anthony, 1st Colorado cavalry, then in command at Fort Lyon, told me that these Indians were hostile; that he had ordered his sentinels to fire on them if they attempted to come to the post, and that the sentinels had fired on them; that he was apprehensive of an attack from these Indians, and had taken every precaution to prevent a surprise. Maj. Samuel G. Colley, United States Agent for these Indians, told me on the same day that he had done everything in his power to make them behave themselves, and that for the last six months he could do nothing with them. These statements were made to me in the presence of the officers of my staff whose statements can be obtained to corroborate the foregoing. . . .

19Q—Make such further statement as you may desire, or which may be necessary to a full understanding of all matters relating to the attack upon the Indians at Sand Creek.

19A—. . . I could not do anything till the 3rd regiment was organized and equipped, when I determined to strike a blow against this savage and determined foe. When I reached Fort Lyon, after passing over from three to five feet of snow, and greatly suffering from the intensity of the cold, the thermometer ranging from 28 to 30 degrees below zero, I questioned Major Anthony in regard to the whereabouts of hostile Indians. He said there was a camp of Cheyennes and Arapahoes about fifty miles distant; . . . that these Indians had threatened to attack the post, &c., and ought to be whipped, all of which was concurred in by Major Colley, . . . which information, with the positive orders from Major General Curtis, commanding the department, to punish these Indians, decided my course, and resulted in the battle of Sand Creek, which has created such a sensation in congress through the lying reports of interested and malicious parties. . . .

TESTIMONY OF SCOTT J. ANTHONY

Q—Were you present at the killing of the Cheyenne Indians, on their reserve, not far from Fort Lyon, on Sand Creek?

A—It was not an Indian reserve. I was present at the time.

Q—State what force was organized, under what orders it acted, under whose command it was, and what was done.

A—. . . The Indians were attacked by us, under command of Colonel Chivington, about sunrise in the morning. . . . Quite a party of Indians took position under the bank, in the bed of the creek, and returned fire upon us. We fought them about seven hours, I should think, there being firing on both sides. The loss on our side was 49 men killed and wounded; on theirs I suppose it was about 125. . . .

Q—You held a conference with the Indians. State what occurred.

A—At the time I took command of the post there was a band of Arapahoe Indians encamped about a mile from the post. . . . I talked with them, and they proposed to do whatever I said; whatever I said for them to do they would do. I told them that I could not feed them; that I could not give them anything to eat; that there were positive orders forbidding that; and that I could not permit them to come within the limits of the post. At the same time they might remain where they were, and I would treat them as prisoners of war if they remained; that they would have to surrender to me all their arms and turn over to me the stolen property they had taken from the government or citizens. These terms they accepted. They turned over to me some 20 head of stock, mules, and horses, and a few arms, but not a quarter of the arms that report stated they had in their possession. The arms they turned over to me were almost useless. I fed them for some ten days. At the end of that time I told them I could not feed them any more; that they had better go out to the buffalo country where they could kill game to subsist upon. I returned their arms to them, and they left the post. . . . A delegation of Cheyennes, numbering, I suppose, 50 or 60 men, came in just before the Arapahoes left the post. I met them outside of the post and talked with them. They said they wanted to make peace; . . . and they had no desire to fight any longer. I told them I had no authority from department headquarters to make peace with them; that I could not permit them to visit the post and come within the lines; . . . In the meantime I was writing to district headquarters constantly, stating to them that there was a band of Indians within forty miles of the post—a small band—while a very large band was about 100 miles from the post. That I was strong enough with the force I had with me to fight the Indians on Sand Creek, but not strong enough to fight the main band.

... But before the reinforcements came from district headquarters, Colonel Chivington came to Fort Lyon with his command, and I joined him and went out on that expedition to Sand Creek. . . .

Q—Did you not feel that you were bound in good faith not to attack those Indians after they had surrendered to you, and after they had taken up a position which you yourself had indicated?

A—I did not consider that they had surrendered to me; I would never consent that they should surrender to me. . . .

Q—The Arapahoes had surrendered to you?

A—I considered them differently from the Cheyennes.

Q—Did you know at the time you made this attack that those Arapahoes were there with the Cheyennes?

A—I did not. . . .

The instructions we constantly received from the headquarters, both of the district and the department, were that we should show as little mercy to the Indians as possible.

MAJOR ANTHONY'S REPORT OF NOV. 6, 1864

Nine Cheyenne Indians today sent in, wishing to see me. They state that 600 of that tribe are now 35 miles north of here, coming towards the post, and 2000 about 75 miles away, waiting for better weather to enable them to come in. I shall not permit them to come in, even as prisoners, for the reason that if I do, I shall have to subsist them upon a prisoner's rations. I shall, however, demand their arms, all stolen stock, and the perpetrators of all depredations. I am of the opinion that they will not accept this proposition, but that they will return to the Smoky Hill. They pretend they want peace, and I think they do now, as they cannot fight during the winter, except where a small band of them can find an unprotected train or frontier settlement. . . .

Extract from Proceedings of Joint Special Committee to Inquire Into Condition of Indian Tribes

39th Cong. 2d Sess.

AFFIDAVIT OF WILLIAM BENT

William Bent sworn: . . . In answer to your inquiry, I must say there have been a good many goods sent by the government to the Indians which were never delivered. . . . I believe there are agents, or agents' relatives, in this country who have made very good speculations. The son of Major Colley, the Indian agent of the Cheyennes and Arapahoes, was an Indian trader for the Cheyennes, Arapahoes, Kiowas, and Comanches. He came to this country the fall after his father was appointed agent. When he first came here he could not have had property of the value to exceed fifteen hundred dollars, which consisted of some thirty or forty head of cows. From what he said to me he must have made twenty-five or thirty thousand dollars in the two or three years he was trading with the Indians. John Smith acted as the Indian trader, and was considered as a partner in the business. It is hard to identify Indian goods, but I am satisfied that a portion of the goods traded with the Indians was annuity goods. From comparison of the goods traded and the annuity goods, I am satisfied they were identically the same goods. The Indians knew they were purchasing their own goods, but did not complain about it. At the time I was trading the same village with Mr. Colley, one of my men went into his lodge and brought back to me a top of a box marked "U. S. Upper Arkansas Agency." . . . Some Cheyennes in whom I have confidence stated to me that they have no confidence in Major Colley, knowing he was swindling them out of their goods. . . .

Testimony of Samuel G. Colley

By Mr. Nesmith: Q—How many Indians were there (at Sand Creek), and did the number embrace both Cheyennes and Arapahoes?

A—About one-half of each tribe was there.

Mr. Doolittle: Q—You think about one-half of the Cheyennes and one-half of the Arapahoes were in the camp?

A—Yes sir.

Q—Of these what proportion were of their warriors?

A—I should think an equal portion of their warriors were with them.

Mr. Ross: Q—Half of the warriors of the two tribes?

A—I should think there were. So far as I know, the young men of the bands who were with them were there. There were warriors, and women and children too.

. . .

By Mr. Nesmith: Q—How did you regard those Indians who were in that encampment?

A—I regarded them as at that time friendly.

Q—Was it your understanding that they made restitution of all stolen property prior to the attack?

A—The Arapahoes said they gave up all their government property. I think they had property belonging to citizens which they did not give up.

Q—Did they give up all their arms?

A—I am not able to say. I think it is doubtful whether they did. We did not think at the time that they did give up all their arms.

Q—How many guns did they give up?

A—But very few. They had not many guns. I thought they had more guns than they brought in and gave up.

Report of Council with Cheyenne and Arapahoe Chiefs
As taken down by United States Indian Agent Simeon Whiteley

Camp Weld, Denver
Wednesday, September 28, 1864

His Excellency Governor Evans asked the Indians what they had to say.

Black Kettle then said: On sight of your circular of June 27, 1864, I took hold of the matter, and have now come to talk to you about it. I told Mr. Bent, who brought it, that I accepted it, but it would take some time to get all my people together . . . I followed Major Wynkoop to

Fort Lyon, and Major Wynkoop proposed that we come up to see you. We have come with our eyes shut, following his handful of men, like coming through the fire. All we ask is that we may have peace with the whites. . . . I want you to give all these chiefs of the soldiers here to understand that we are for peace, and that we have made peace, that we may not be mistaken by them for enemies. I have not come here with a little wolf bark, but have come to talk plain with you. . . .

Governor Evans replied: I am sorry you did not respond to my appeal at once. You have gone into an alliance with the Sioux, who were at war with us. You have done a great deal of damage—have stolen stock, and now have possession of it. However much a few individuals may have tried to keep the peace, as a nation you have gone to war. . . . Hearing last fall that you were dissatisfied, the Great Father at Washington sent me out on the plains to talk with you and make it all right. I sent messengers out to tell you I had presents, and would make you a feast, but you sent word to me that you did not want anything to do with me, and to the Great Father at Washington that you could get along without him. Bull Bear wanted to come in and see me at the head of the Republican, but his people held a council and would not let him come.

Black Kettle: That is true.

.   .   .

Governor Evans: So far as making a treaty now is concerned, we are in no condition to do it. Your young men are on the warpath. My soldiers are preparing for the fight. You, so far, have had the advantage; but the time is near at hand when the plains will swarm with United States soldiers. . . . The time when you can make war best is in the summer time; when I can make war best is in the winter. You, so far, have had the advantage; my time is just coming. I have learned that you understand that the whites are at war among themselves, you think you can drive the whites from this country; but this reliance is false. The Great Father at Washington has men enough to drive all the Indians off the plains, and whip the rebels at the same time. . . . Another reason that I am not now in a condition to make a treaty is that war is begun, and the power to make a treaty of peace has passed from me to the great war chief. . . .

White Antelope: How can we be protected from the soldiers on the plains?

Governor Evans: You must make that arrangement with the military chief.

White Antelope: I fear that these new soldiers who have gone out may kill some of my people while I am here.

Governor Evans: There is great danger of it.

White Antelope: When we sent our letter to Major Wynkoop, it was like going through a strong fire or blast for Major Wynkoop's men to come to our camp; it was the same for us to come to see you. We have our doubts whether the Indians south of the Arkansas, or those north of the Platte, will do as you say. . . .

Governor Evans: Again, whatever peace they make must be with the soldiers, and not with me. Are the Apaches at war with the whites?

White Antelope: Yes, and the Comanches and Kiowas as well; also a tribe of Indians from Texas, whose names we do not know. There are thirteen different bands of Sioux who have crossed the Platte, and are in alliance with the others named.

. . .

Governor Evans: Who committed the murder of the Hungate family on Running Creek?

Neva: The Arapahoes; a party of the northern band, who were passing north. It was Medicine Man, or Roman Nose, and three others. I am satisfied from the time he left a certain camp for the north that it was this party . . .

Governor Evans: Who killed the man and boy at the head of Cherry Creek?

Neva (after consultation): Kiowas and Comanches.

Governor Evans: Who stole soldiers' horses from Jimmy's camp twenty-seven days ago?

Neva: Fourteen Cheyennes and Arapahoes together.

. . .

Governor Evans: We feel that they have, by their stealing and murdering, done us great damage. They come here and say they will tell me all, and that is what I am trying to get.

Neva: The Comanches, Kiowas and Sioux have done much more injury than we have. We will tell what we know, but cannot speak for others.

Governor Evans: I suppose you acknowledge the depredations on the Little Blue, as you have the prisoners taken in your possession.

White Antelope: We (the Cheyennes) took two prisoners west of Fort Kearney, and destroyed the trains.

. . .

Colonel Chivington: I am not a big war chief, but all the soldiers in this country are at my command. My rule of fighting white men or Indians is to fight them until they lay down their arms and submit to military authority. They are nearer Major Wynkoop than anyone else, and they can go to him when they are ready to do that.

The council then adjourned.

AFFIDAVIT OF PRESLEY TALBOT

Presley Talbot sworn: . . . I entered the service as captain in the 3rd regiment Colorado one-hundred-days men; the only battle I was engaged in was at Sand Creek. I was at Fort Lyon the day before the battle; I had a conversation with Major Anthony, who expressed himself glad that we had come, saying he would have attacked the Indians himself if he had had sufficient force. I did not understand from any source that the Indians had been placed there at Sand Creek under the protection of the government. . . . I think we moved from Fort Lyon with about 650 men and four pieces of artillery, passing a distance of about forty-five miles, reaching the Indian village about sunup, surprising the Indians; . . . I received orders to march up the right side of the creek and attack, which I obeyed; the troops on the other side of the creek had commenced firing before; the artillery was also playing on the Indians. My company was permitted to charge the banks and ditches. No orders were given about taking prisoners. I was wounded and taken from the field about half an hour after the battle began, and know nothing of the fight after that time; . . . I occupied a room while wounded adjoining the room of Major Colley, and was shown papers by John Smith against the government for 105 buffalo robes, two white ponies and a wagon-load of goods. This account was made out in favor of John Smith and Colley for $6,000. They claimed they had other demands against the government, and Smith said they would realize $25,000 out of it, and damn Colonel Chivington. They were very bitter in their denunciations of Colonel Chivington and Major Downing. Private Louderback swore to the accounts; he was detailed as a nurse for me, but did writing for Smith and Colley.

AFFIDAVIT OF DR. CALEB S. BIRDSALL

Dr. Caleb Birdsall sworn: . . . I was at the battle of Sand Creek as assistant surgeon of the third Colorado cavalry; it commenced by our men corraling the ponies; Colonel Chivington and Colonel Shoup gave orders to form in line of battle, but it could not be kept; firing commenced, and I was soon afterwards engaged attending to the wounded. On the afternoon of the 29th of November, while in one of the lodges dressing wounded soldiers, a soldier came to the opening of the lodge and called my attention to some white scalps he held in his hand; my impression, after examination, was that two or three of them were quite fresh. I saw in the hands of soldiers silk dresses and other garments belonging to women; I saw some squaws that were dead, but did not go over the ground; I did not see any Indians scalped, but saw the bodies after they were scalped; I saw no other mutilations; I did not see any kind of a flag in the Indian camp. There were none left wounded on the field; I know of none being killed after being taken prisoner; . . .

Extract from Proceedings
of
Military Commission (Sen. Ex. Doc. 26)

39th Cong. 2d Sess.

TESTIMONY OF PRESLEY TALBOT

. . . I was at the battle of Sand Creek; was ordered to go into the fight by Colonel Chivington; ordered to cross Sand Creek to the right side of the bank. There I received so very galling a fire from the Indians under the bank and from the ditches dug out just above the bank that I ordered my company to advance, to prepare to dismount and fight on foot. At the command to fight on foot I was shot, with a ball about fifty to the pound, from the rifle of a chief known by the name of One-Eye . . . Indians twenty-five or thirty in number, (bucks) made charge, were repulsed, some of my men clubbing their guns on account of guns refusing to discharge, and forced Indians to seek shelter under the banks, and in holes dug out for concealment. Firing ceased for not more than five minutes; one Indian, which proved to be Big Head, who as a signal showed buffalo robe to the height of a person, as a means of drawing fire from the soldiers, so that they would empty their guns, and then would give a whoop and rise *en masse* and fire arrows, shoot muskets and squirrel rifles, . . . There was a lull in hostilities for a few minutes. The Indians *en masse*, at least thirty in number, made a charge which was repulsed by eight of Company M; being wounded I was taken from the field. . . .

Had several consultations with Major Colley and John Smith, Indian interpreter; stated they had considerable sympathy for me, being wounded; and would give me all the attention and assistance in their power, but they would do anything to damn Colonel John M. Chivington or Major Downing; that they had lost at least $6000 each by the Sand Creek fight, that they had one hundred and five robes and two white ponies bought at the time of attack, independent of the goods which they had on the battle-ground, which they never had recovered, but would make the general government pay for the same and damn old Chivington eventually. Furthermore John Smith had a bill made out against the government—showed me the same—for government indebtedness to him, sworn and subscribed to by one David Louderback, stating that he would go to Washington City and present the same, and that he had friends who would help him get it. Smith and Colley both told me that they were equally interested in the trade with the Indians. . . .

I heard a portion of a letter read in the adjoining room, in which I lay wounded, in which I recognized the voices of Smith, Colley and Olmsted, the purport of which was denouncing Colonel Chivington and the Sand Creek fight, addressed to the Superintendent of Indian Affairs, Washington City. I also heard Smith boastingly in my presence state that the eastern papers would be filled with letters from that post (Fort Lyon) denouncing the same, and that Colonel Chivington had murdered his boy, and that he would be avenged by using every effort with the department possible. Furthermore, he said with tears in his eyes, that he was a bad boy and deserved punishment, but it was hard for a father to endure it. . . . Colley and Smith stated to me in person that they would go to Washington and represent the Sand Creek battle as nothing more than a massacre; and Smith said he would realize $25,000 from his losses. . . .

APPENDIX F

Extract From Reports on Engagement With Indians on Sand Creek

War of the Rebellion: Official Records
No. 1

Reports of Col. John M. Chivington, First Colorado Cavalry, commanding expedition.

HEADQUARTERS DISTRICT OF COLORADO

In the Field, Cheyenne County, South Bend of Big Sandy,
November 29, 1864.

In the last ten days my command has marched 300 miles, 100 of which the snow was two feet deep. After a march of forty miles last night I, at daylight this morning, attacked Cheyenne village of 130 lodges, from 900 to 1,000 warriors strong; killed Chiefs Black Kettle, White Antelope, Knock Knee, and Little Robe (Little Raven), and between 400 and 500 other Indians, and captured as many ponies and mules. Our loss (was) 9 killed and 38 wounded. All did nobly. Think I will catch some more of them eighty miles, on Smoky Hill. Found white man's scalp, not more than three days old, in one of lodges.

J. M. CHIVINGTON.

Col. Cmdg. First Dist. of Colo. and First Indian Expedition.
Maj. Gen. S. R. Curtis,
    Fort Leavenworth, Department of Kansas.

HEADQUARTERS DISTRICT OF COLORADO,
Denver, Colo. Terr., December 16, 1864.

GENERAL: I have the honor to transmit the following report of operations of the Indian expedition under my command, of which brief notice was given you by my telegram of November 29, 1864:

Having ascertained that the hostile Indians had proceeded south from the Platte and were almost within striking distance of Fort Lyon, I ordered Col. George L. Shoup, Third Regiment Colorado Volunteer Cavalry, 100-days' service, to proceed with the mounted men of his regiment in that direction. On November 20 I left Denver, and at Booneville, Colo. Terr., on the 24th of November, joined and took command in person of the expedition, which had been increased by battalion First Cavalry of Colorado consisting of detachments of Companies C, E and H. I proceeded with the utmost caution down the Arkansas River, and on the morning of the 28th ultimo arrived at Fort Lyon, to the surprise of the garrison of that post. On the same evening I resumed my march, being joined by Maj. Scott J. Anthony, First Cavalry of Colorado, with 125 men of said regiment, consisting of detachments of Companies D, G, and K, with two howitzers. The command then proceeded in a northeasterly direction, traveling all night, and at daylight of 29th November striking Sand Creek, about forty miles from Fort Lyon. Here was discovered an Indian village of 130 lodges, comprised of Black Kettle's band of Cheyennes and eight lodges of Arapahoes with Left Hand. My line of battle was formed with Lieutenant Wilson's battalion, First Regiment, numbering about— men, on the right; Colonel Shoup's (Third) regiment, numbering about 450 men, in the center, and Major Anthony's battalion, numbering 125 men, First Regiment on the left. The attack was immediately made upon the Indian camp by Lieutenant Wilson, who dashed forward, cutting the enemy off from their herd, and driving them out of their camp, which was subsequently destroyed. The Indians, numbering from 900 to 1000, though taken by surprise, speedily rallied and formed a line of battle across the creek, about three-fourths of a mile above the village, stubbornly contesting every inch of ground. The commands of Colonel Shoup and Major Anthony pressed rapidly forward and attacked the enemy sharply, and the engagement became general, we constantly driving the Indians, who fell back from one position to another for five miles, and finally abandoned resistance and dispersed in all directions, and were pursued by my troops until night-fall. It may perhaps be unnecessary for me to state that I captured no prisoners. Between 500 and 600 Indians were left dead upon the ground; about 550 ponies, mules and horses were captured, and all their lodges were destroyed, the contents of which have served to supply the command with an abundance of trophies, comprising the paraphernalia of Indian warfare and life. My loss was 8 killed on the field and forty wounded of which two have since died. Of the conduct of the Third Regiment, 100-days' service, I have to say that they well sustained the reputation of our

Colorado troops for bravery and effectiveness, were well commanded by their gallant young colonel, George L. Shoup, ably assisted by Lieut. Col. L. L. Bowen, Maj. Hal Sayr, and Capt. Theodore G. Cree, commanding the First, Second, and Third battalions of that regiment. Of the conduct of the two battalions of the First Regiment I have but to remark that they sustained their reputation as second to none, and were ably handled by their commanders, Major Anthony, Lieutenant Wilson, and Lieutenant Clark Dunn, upon whom the command devolved after the disabling of Lieutenant Wilson from wounds received. Night coming on the pursuit of the flying Indians was of necessity abandoned and my command encamped within sight of the field.

On the 1st instant, having sent the wounded and dead to Fort Lyon, the first to be cared for, the last to be buried upon our own soil, I resumed the pursuit in direction of Camp Wynkoop, on the Arkansas River, marching all night of 3rd and 4th instant, in hopes of overtaking a large encampment of Arapahoes and Cheyennes under Little Robe (Little Raven), but the enemy had been apprised of my advance, and on the morning of the 5th instant, at 3 o'clock, precipitately broke camp and fled. My stock was exhausted. For 100 miles the snow had been two feet deep, and for the previous fifteen days (excepting November 29 and 30) the marches had been forced and incessant. Under these circumstances and the fact of the time of the Third Regiment being nearly out, I determined for the present to relinquish the pursuit. Of the effect of the punishment sustained by the Indians you will be the judge. Their Chiefs Black Kettle, White Antelope, One Eye and Knock Knee were among the killed, and their bands almost annihilated. I was shown the scalp of a white man found in one of the lodges, which could not have been taken more than two or three days previous. For full particulars and reports of the several commanders, I respectfully refer you to the following copies herewith enclosed: Col. George L. Shoup, Third Regiment, December 7, 1864; Lieut. Col. L. L. Bowen, Third Regiment, November 30, 1864; Maj. Hal Sayr, Third Regiment, December 6, 1864; Capt. Theodore G. Cree, Third Regiment, December 6, 1864; Maj. Scott J. Anthony, First Regiment, December 1, 1864; Lieut. Clark Dunn, First Regiment, November 30, 1864; Lieut. J. J. Kennedy, First Regiment, November 30, 1864.

If all companies of the First Cavalry of Colorado, and the Eleventh Ohio Volunteer Cavalry, stationed at posts and camps near here, were ordered to report to me, I could organize a campaign which, in my judgment, would effectively rid the country between the Platte and Arkansas Rivers of these red rebels. I would respectfully request to be informed, if another campaign should be authorized from here, whether I could employ 100 or 200 friendly Utes (Indians), furnishing them subsistance, arms, and ammunition for the campaign.

I cannot conclude this report without saying that the conduct of Capt. Silas S. Soule, Company D, First Cavalry of Colorado, was at least ill-advised, he saying that he thanked God that he had killed no Indians, and like expressions, proving him more in sympathy with these Indians than with the whites. The evidence is most conclusive that these Indians are the worst that have infested the routes on the Platte and Arkansas Rivers during the last spring and summer. Amongst the stock captured were the horses and mules taken by them from Lieut. Chase, First Cavalry of Colorado, last September; several scalps of white men and women were found in their lodges; also various articles of clothing belonging to white persons. On every hand the evidence was clear that no lick was struck amiss.

I am, with much respect, your obedient servant,

J. M. CHIVINGTON,
Colonel First Cav. of Colorado, comdg. Dist. of Colorado.

Maj. Gen. S. R. Curtis,
Commanding Department of Kansas, Fort Leavenworth.

INDEX

WESTERNLORE GREAT WEST AND INDIAN SERIES

In history dealing with the American West there are few characters more controversial than John M. Chivington. As the hero of the Battle of Glorieta Pass, in which he by brilliant maneuvering, and with a handful of Colorado Volunteers, stopped Sibley's Confederate army cold in its victorious march through New Mexico and Arizona and decisively saved the Great West to the Union, Chivington deserved the highest praise from the nation he so ably served. As the officer who reputedly directed the infamous Sand Creek "massacre" against the Cheyenne Indians shortly thereafter, his name since has lived in infamy. Somewhere in between these two extremes is the real Chivington.

Reginald S. Craig, an attorney and former army officer, became deeply interested in the controversy which has raged over the life and character of Colonel Chivington. Meticulously he assembled all the evidence regarding the Fighting Parson's war with the Confederates and with the Indians. Carefully he went into the private history of this preacher turned army officer, to probe out the truth.

From all the evidence, including the transcripts of the Congressional investigation of Sand Creek, Chivington's own unpublished writings, the personal and family memoirs of a dramatic life, and the careful probing of a scholar, has come an important and timely book. From it a strange and exciting new man emerges, and new perspectives on a much disputed time of history come forth to dispel the mass of conjecture and myth which has obscured much of the facts and truth.

The reader becomes the judge of this man, and in listening to the evidence, is fascinated by a brilliant recital of one of the most dramatic times in America's history.